Country Roads

"Dear Aklilu, Congratulations on your first book. I read it cover to cover. It was an enjoyable experience, reading your book. It is a direct, frank and warm book about transitions and dilemmas written in a very straightforward style. I must say that the book is consistent in its honesty; unsurprisingly as its author is fundamentally honest."

—*Hiruy Amanuel Gebreselassie, Addis Ababa, Ethiopia*

"Selam Aklilu. What a treat it was! I thoroughly enjoyed reading every single page, your stories, your life's journey, especially your reflections at each stage and your profound sense of family and country... Thank you so much for so openly sharing your unique and remarkable journey and the many life lessons you so aptly captured with your signature honesty and humility. Truly inspiring!"

—*Ghion Shewangizaw Eguale, Toronto, Canada*

"Dear Aklilu, Thank you for sending me a signed copy of your fascinating first book. My hats are off for you for pulling it off and you made me proud. However, you kept me away from a bit of my golfing. Because I could not put it down once I started. I finished reading it this morning after being up most of last night."

—*Kefale Gebre Giorgis, Virginia, USA*

"My hat's off to you for this wonderful book "Country Roads" which I absolutely loved and wanted to devour it in a day or so but had to put it away for another day because I didn't want it to end."

—*Semret Asfaha Debessay, Delaware, USA*

"Incredibly enlightening! Offered me such an honest and personal perspective of life in a completely different ecosystem."

—*Leul Daniel Gebre Meskal, California, USA*

Country Roads

A life-journey of fun, exposures, relationships and decisions

Aklilu Kidanu Wolde Giorgis

THE RED SEA PRESS

TRENTON | LONDON | NEW DELHI | CAPE TOWN | NAIROBI | ADDIS ABABA | ASMARA | IBADAN

THE RED SEA PRESS

541 West Ingham Avenue | Suite B
Trenton, New Jersey 08638

Book design: Lemlem Tadesse
Cover design: Ashraful Haque

Cataloging-in-Publication Data may be obtained from the
Library of Congress.

ISBNs: 978-1-56902-632-8 HB
        978-1-56902-633-5 PB

To

my mother, Wo. Asegedetch Wolde Mariam
&
my father, Ato Kidanu Wolde Giorgis

Photograph by my cousin Girma Zewdu, Gore, Illubabor (1960)

'If it works, it works.
If it doesn't, we will see,
And go to where it works.'

W/o Kershi Jimato Aredo
(My wife's paternal grandmother)

'The book is unmistakably nationalistic, country-loving, coun-
try-staying… its my impression that this notion is the blood that
runs through the veins of the book. This strikes a sad note upon
realizing that we (and others like us) are the ones standing at the
other end of longing, outstretched hands that beckon us home.
Our hope (of course) is to not render the welcome an empty
one. We perpetually hope and work for a win-win situation for
all.'

Mizan Kidanu, (Our daughter)

Table of Contents

Foreword

Honestly, I was waiting and hoping against hope that one of the radio talk programs or local newspapers in Addis Ababa would approach me one day and ask me about my life history and my own reflections as they have done so with numerous interesting people before. I guess I wasn't that interesting, important or lucky enough; and it did not happen so far.

So, I dared to write this book because I believe that every person has personal stories to tell and reflections to share. Unfortunately, only a few get the chance to do so, and we have missed far too many of those who did not. So I wrote my memories, stories and reflections mostly as I remembered them, with the help of some notes and documents I had kept over the years, and the discussions I had with friends. But, I would admit that there were times when my memory betrayed me or when I did not keep notes, and I had to re-construct the stories in consultation with my wife of 38 years - to the best approximation of what must have happened.

This book is divided into four chapters.

Chapter 1 begins with personal stories, experiences and learning as I was growing up in Gore, where I started to form an 'identity' which was later supplemented by my stay in Addis Ababa where I completed high school and university education.

Chapter 2 is about my exposure to new cultures and ways of life in far-away lands; the cultural shocks which severely tested my 'identity' and forced me to solidify and/or rethink my positions on a number of contemporary issues.

Chapter3 is about my return to Ethiopia, followed by the counter cultural shock and re-adaptation and, finally, making the full life circle.

Chapter 4 is a series of personal reflections and justifications that fed into a decision making; and some lifelong lessons.

All along, the book is full of stories and examples of how fate, events and individuals changed one's life and, in my case, mostly for the better. These are also stories of how identities were shaped, opinions formed, positions taken, and decisions made through life experience and personal reflections.

This book also honors family members, friends, teachers and colleagues who influenced me one way or another; people who shared their love, inner feelings, ideas and unconditional friendship with me; people who showed me the way forward and, as a result, changed my life for the better. It is my way of saying 'thank you' - with all my heart.

None of the narratives in this book is the result of scientific research at all; hence they should only be seen as personal and informal reflections and views. Also, some of the views that I reflected in this book were my thinking and orientation at the time and may not necessarily indicate how I think now. Most, however, have stayed and will stay with me until I am convinced otherwise. I also mention, with all due respect, names and show photographs when it is a family member or a close friend or colleague who I know would not mind or have minded.

I have asked only a few people, mostly my close family members, to read or review the book and give me comments. This is not because I did not expect to get useful comments, quite the contrary. It was because I was afraid that I would be influenced to modify how or what I wrote outside my own thinking, for whatever it's worth. I know I have lost what could have been important feedback because of that, and I apologize.

I move back and forth in time as I tell my stories and experiences but, with a little bit of attention, it should not be very difficult to follow. I also apologize if some of my views and positions offend those who may not agree with me, but there was no offense meant. Still, in spite of the differences, and I am sure there will be many, I would encourage people to read them in good faith.

Finally, why didn't I write in Amharic, my native language? Two reasons: First, with a first degree in English literature, I was trained in reading and writing in English. Second, I figured I would do a much better job translating an English version into an Amharic version than starting out with an Amharic version. Hence, expect an Amharic translation in the foreseeable future.

I have enjoyed writing this book, and I hope you will enjoy reading it and get something useful out of it too.

Acknowledgements

My sincere gratitude goes to quite a few people who influenced me and changed my life one way or another and got me to the point where I was able to write this book.

The first in this order is my late father Ato Kidanu Wolde Giorgis who actually still lives in me. It was also because my mother, W/o Asegedetch Wolde Mariam, who took such a good care of me that I am as healthy as one could be at age 67! My older brother Miemen, as my daughter Mizan would say about her sister Hasabie, 'is the true representation of me outside me.' These individuals gave me more love and support than I could ever handle or pay back.

Ato Ayalew Admassu, Dr. Richard Caulk and Mrs. Innes Marshal, having seen that I was not strong in the intellect, noted some social skills that they worked on to steer me to where I am now. Dr. Hailu Araya was my advisor at Addis Ababa University who instilled in me the love for literature, particularly the West African literature. Signora Steganini trusted me enough to send me abroad; Professor Andargachew Tesfaye, a sincere and honest man, contributed to my coming back to Addis Ababa University.

My immediate family members, my wife W/o Menbere Alemayehu and our daughters Mizan and Hasabie Kidanu, who not only helped in editing but also in giving me very useful feedback at each stage of writing this book, without necessarily agreeing with me all the time.

The list of people who helped in their own unique ways is too long to mention here, but their names appear throughout the book.

Finally, I want to express my deepest gratitude and respect to my cousin Girma Zewedu who died of Tuberculosis at a very young age. Girma taught me how to ride a bicycle and how to drive a car. He was also a pioneer who took and printed the earlier photos in this book. I thank you all.

Chapter 1.

GROWING UP AND FORMING AN IDENTITY

Growing up in a semi-rural area, early life was marked by childhood and boyhood fun and adventure. With an urban touch later on, it was also a time when I formed an 'identity' reinforced through attachments with my friends, teachers and family members; and a strong bond with my father, in particular.

'Life events happen in many ways; what makes it interesting is you do not know in which.'

Early Life

The beginning

Let me start from what should have been the end of this chapter: an account of when and how I ventured out of the country for the first time in June 1978 at age 28. This was nothing new for people my age in those days except that, in most cases, it was done the hard way[1]. Young and old, men and women braved the incredibly difficult journey, mostly on foot, across the Ethiopian border and, mostly, into the Sudan. Little is known about those who did not make the trips; or who made the trips but failed to get transits to a third country.

Be that as it may, I had finally graduated in English Literature from Addis Ababa University in September 1977 when, like most (or all) university graduates of that era, I was assigned to report at the Ethiopian Standards Agency (ESA) for my government-assigned job. In socialist Ethiopia during the second half of the 1970's and all of the 1980's, with no or very little employment opportunities in whatever remained of a private sector in the country, graduates were assigned jobs by the government – whether they liked or not.

So, not sure what I would be doing at the Agency, but I was informed that my salary was to be 500 Birr a month and, after all kinds of taxes (including some war taxes), I was to be

---

1 Many young people in those days left the country through border crossings on foot enduring untold hardships.

paid a net monthly income of 399 Birr. Most of my friends were also similarly assigned and promptly started working at different public ministries or agencies. For reasons I could not clearly remember now, I delayed reporting to the Agency for a couple of days.

In the meantime, I got a call from Mrs. Innes Marshall, then the Editor of Addis Ababa University Press. She had known me before, and was gracious enough to have gone through my draft bachelor's thesis and given me wonderful feedbacks. Little did I know that this short telephone call would put me in a life-course that I never anticipated.

Mrs. Marshall: *Aklilu, how are you?*
Aklilu: *I am fine Mrs. Marshall, how are you? How is Mr. Marshall?*[2]
Mrs. Marshall: *He is fine. Have you started working yet?*
Aklilu: *I have been assigned, but not started working yet.*
Mrs. Marshall: *Would you be interested in a teaching job at the Italian Cultural Institute in Addis? [aka Italian School]*
Aklilu: *Yes, but what subject?*
Mrs. Marshall: *English, of course, to 9th and 10th grade students.*
Aklilu: *Sure, where do I go?*
Mrs. Marshall: *Go to the Institute and talk to the Directress, her name is Signora Steganini. I will tell her you are coming.*
Aklilu: *Thank you Mrs. Marshall, I will let you know the outcome.*

I immediately visualized myself as a teacher. I had actually enjoyed teaching immensely during my one-year (1974/1975 academic year) Ethiopian University Service (EUS) program[3] at a junior high school in Shire Inda Selassie, a small town in Tigray Region, Northern Ethiopia. The fond memories of those days were still fresh in my mind.

I figured this one could also be another good experience, albeit with different cultural context and much more money. My net salary in Shire Inda Selassie was 180 Birr a month, of which I spent 160 Birr on lodging and food and the remaining

---

2   I had to ask this question; he was my first-year math's teacher after all.
3   Our batch was the last one to go through this program.

twenty on a local drink, *tella,* of course. My relatively old students always tagged along whenever I went for the drink. Just like in Gore, as long as it was a locally brewed drink, there was no conflict with the local norms.

In any case, I called Signora Steganini promptly and introduced myself – as politely as I could. She asked me to come over to her office one weekday afternoon. Her reception was warm, and I immediately liked her middle-age Italian demeanor and her broken English with heavy Italian accent. She wanted to know about my credentials and experience as a teacher. I told her what I knew, stressing my experience in Shire Inda Selassie. And, to my surprise, I was hired. My first ever attempt to find a job on my own was a success!

I was to co-teach English language, with an older Italian teacher, in the ninth and tenth grades. My class size was about twenty-five; and my salary would be 720 Birr a month, and no taxes. I figured that was almost twice what my friends, assigned at various government agencies, were making! Plus, I did not even have to go to school on the days I didn't have classes! I took the job offer and started teaching in earnest in September 1977.

The days and months went fast. In addition to the relatively fat salary, I really enjoyed teaching and my students who were a mix of Italian, half-Italian and Ethiopian teenage boys and girls! Most weren't sure why they were studying English since, upon graduating, they would become *'geometras'* [surveyors] and be engaged in the construction business which, in the Ethiopian context of the time, was dominated by the Italian vernacular anyway.

But, as far as the students were concerned, with a not-so-bad-looking and dashing young man, why not? After all, with the exception of an older male Amharic and a young female French teacher, most of the teachers at the school were middle-aged Italians with strict disciplinary inclinations. I presented a fresh alternative; or so the students calculated. I remembered my own high school years when I liked the subject just because I liked the informality of the teacher. So, nothing knew!

I settled, and the months went by. My informal teaching style, combined with my bell-bottom-afro-hair personality, became so popular that many students from the class of the other Italian English teacher started flocking to my classes. Moreover, some of the relatively older female students secretly flirted with me. On a few occasions I would find a red rose or a card with cupid's drawings on the windshield of my small fiat in the parking lot; there were no names or notes attached, however.

Of course, I did not pursue these since my heart was somewhere else; besides, wouldn't it have been a breach of a teacher's work ethics?. But, I would be lying if I had not admitted that these gestures did boost my manly ego just a little bit. Of course, I told my friends about it with some bravado. Those were the norms of the time, and I would have done a disservice to my friends if I hadn't told them about such things. They expected it!

So, not sure about the directress, but my co-English teacher did not like my informality at all; and he saw a 'rival' in me. He thought I was too loose with the students and setting a dangerous precedence at the school, and I needed to be stopped.

Hence was the start of a chain of events that changed the course of my life in a significant way. It was to be seen if it were a blessing in disguise!

*****

Weekly Friday staff meetings, chaired by the directress Signora Steganini, were a regular at the school. The meetings would start at about 2 pm and last an average of two hours. They were conducted in Italian, of course, and I knew only a few words. Even those, thanks to the Italian movies I had seen as a teenager. But, it wasn't good enough to follow the procession of the meetings.

The only other Ethiopian Amharic teacher, due to the fact that he had worked at the school for many years, spoke Italian and he would seriously follow the discussions in the meetings. So, with no other choice, I would sit next to the young French female teacher who knew no Italian at all. We had one thing in common and had to find ways in which we would 'kill' the meeting time without getting bored to death.

So, as the meetings progressed, I would write a short composition in French, making use of the introductory French I had learnt a couple of years earlier, and would secretly pass it over to her. She would mark my composition, and give it back to me with another title to try a better one. That way we would pass the time with no clue as to what was being discussed in the staff meetings. The directress and the rest of the staff basically ignored us, which was fine with us.

One fateful afternoon in May, however, a few weeks before the school closed for the summer of 1978, we were in a staff meeting as usual. My French teacher colleague was absent, and I was lost. I was there listening to long heated arguments in Italian, and I was bored. So, just before the end of the meeting, which was a bad timing on my part, I raised my hand. Surprised, Signora Steganini, in her broken English with Italian accent that I had come to enjoy over the months, asked me if I had a question or an opinion.

Signora Steganini: *Aklilu, have you a question?*
Aklilu: *Yes, I was just wondering if I could be excused from this meeting or if you would consider conducting the meeting in English.*

Signora Steganini did not even get the chance to respond when my rival Italian co-English teacher burst with an angry voice and, in broken English, 'reminded' me that this was an Italian school and all staff meetings would be held in Italian.

'Then', I calmly responded, *'I should be excused.'* He objected, and he went on to remind me again, this time rather crudely, that we were all employees of the Italian Cultural Institute owned by the Italian government and, hence, the media of education and meetings was Italian - whether I liked it or not.

That would have been enough to calm me down except that he added, *'You are paid to do what you are told to do, which right now is to sit with your mouth shut.'* Wow! To this day, I never liked people who, with little or no other considerations, would tell me that I had to do things because I was paid to do them. In a way, my Italian colleague may have been correct but, for my young-hood ego, I thought he went overboard.

Now, in those days, I had this bad combination of pride and a temper that would escape me once in a while. And this day was one of them. Also, it did not help that I saw this person was getting back at me because I was more popular than him among our students.

Then, I fired back a response that I regret to this date. I 'reminded' my Italian colleague, with everybody in the meeting listening, that we were now in Ethiopia and, if he wanted to conduct his business in Italian, I would suggest that he went back to Italia.[4]

The moment I said it, I knew I should never have said it; it was a big mistake. Not because of losing my job, but because it was plain rude. Even if the school were an Italian property in Ethiopia, at the end of the day, he was my 'guest' in my country, as I was used to thinking about foreigners, beginning right from my boyhood years.

In any case, my 'rival' colleague was not amused by my rude response, of course! He was easily twice as big as me and, with even hotter Italian temperament, charged towards me and a fistfight was looming. The only other time that I ever fought in my life was a very long time ago when a lean fast boy called Hailu Burayu beat me so bad without even landing a single punch myself. I still remember what I looked like after he was done with me, which helped as a deterrent not to fight again. And, I did not want that history to repeat itself here at the Italian School.

So, fortunately for me, someone pushed me out of the meeting room and I was saved a broken nose or a couple of broken ribs, or both. I left the meeting room and went to my

---

4   I am using town names as they are pronounced in Italy.

friends where we usually meet after work hours; after all, it was a Friday afternoon. Even knowing that I had made a mistake, I never intended to apologize. But it also turned out to be the last staff meeting of the academic year for my colleagues, and the final one for me.

The following Monday I, of course, reported to school and continued my teaching as if nothing had happened. One day passed, and another day followed. There was no talk of the disturbance during the previous staff meeting. On my part, I was sure I had lost the job. I thought Signora Steganini, as much as she liked me, would not ask me to come back the following academic year. The prospect of a 399 Birr per month salary and a government job, just like my friends, was more and more becoming a reality.

A few more days passed and, all of a sudden, I was summoned to Signora Steganini's office. On my way to her office, I was ready to calmly accept her decision, but no apology. After all, I was one young and vain Ethiopian male of the 1970's: No apologies!

Signora Steganini: *Aklilu, so sorry what happened last staff meeting.*
Aklilu: *I am sorry too.*
Signora Steganini: *Students like you, no?*
Aklilu: *I guess; I like them too.*
Signora Steganini: *Plan to stay with us next year, no?*
Aklilu: *Yes, if you will have me.*
Signora Steganini: *If so, why don't you learn Italiano! If you learn Italiano between now and September, no problem at staff meetings; no?*
Aklilu: *Actually, I plan to go to visit my relatives in Dire Dawa, especially my aunts in Asebe Teferi, Mieso….*
Signora Steganini: *But, Aklilu, opportunity is good for you! Have you a passport?*
Aklilu: *No, why?*
Signora Steganini: *No? Have you a passport photo?*
Aklilu: *No, why?*
Signora Steganini: *You see what I am saying?*
Aklilu: *No, what?*

Signora Steganini: *When school close in two weeks, I want to send you to Italia to study Italiano. So when you come back in September, have you no problem at staff meetings. But, I ask your promise to comeback. Agree?*
Aklilu: *So, all you want is a passport photo?*
Signora Steganini: *Yes, go bring me a passport size photo.*

I was lost, what is this lady talking about? I knew she liked me; but after what happened at the staff meeting, I did not expect this at all! Me, a young man in my mid-twenties, in Italia? It was inconceivable! I also knew, in those days, no one would leave Ethiopia via Bole airport, especially not a young man like me!

But, the lady was serious. I thought maybe the Italian Embassy which owned the school might have an influence in getting me a passport and a visa? In any case, I brought her a passport size photo, and promised to come back in September when I finished my studies in Italia. Anything to go to Italia!

About a week later, on June 13, 1978, I was in my final week of the academic year when I was summoned to Signora Steganini's office. With a big smile on her face, she took out a passport and a ticket from her drawer, and informed me that I would fly to Nairobi the next day to catch Alitalia flight to Roma. Then, I would go to Milano by train to take another train to Gargnano del Garda, a small town along the shores of Lago di Garda [Lake Garda], located at about a two-hour ride from Milano in Northern Italia.

Signora Steganini also informed me that the school where I was to study Italian language and culture was called *Istituto di Lingua e Cultura Italiana* [Institute of Italian Language and Culture]. It was only for international students, and part of the University of Milano.

Signora Steganini added, *'Have a great time in Italia, Aklilu, and t forget not to come back in September. Good bye.'*

Little did I know that this would be the last time that I would see this lady.

A mix of pleasure, disbelief and uncertainty descended on me; I had never found myself in a situation like this before. I left the school and headed directly to *Enrico* Coffee house to meet my then-girlfriend (now wife, Menbere [Menby] Alemayehu).

I had met Menby back in 1976 in a small town called Begi, Wollega Province of Western Ethiopia, where we served in the National Development through Cooperation Campaign [aka *Zemetcha*]. She had just finished tenth-grade, and I had just completed third-year College, plus the one year Ethiopian University Service (EUS) at the time.

In any case, with a lot of anxiety and confusion of my own, I dropped a bombshell on Menby: I told her about my passport, tickets and the impending trip to Italia the next day. Needless to say we sat down quietly, lost as to what to do next. It was also in the wake of the Red Terror[5] [*aka Qey Shiber*] and all young people were at risk. In fact, Menby had actually been arrested once, albeit for a few weeks. I also have had a close call a couple of times but somehow escaped potentially disastrous encounters with security police.

*****

One such encounter could have easily cost my life. Rewind to August 1977, and it was the final week of my final year at Addis Ababa University. I was at home in my bedroom studying for my final exams. All of a sudden, at about 6 pm in the evening of one Friday, there was a savage knock at the main gate of my parent's house.

When someone opened the gate, a group of rustic looking soldiers, led by a mean looking corporal, swarmed-in without asking permission to enter. The shock was so great that the entire household stood at a standstill, since we all knew what the consequences of a slight mishap would be.

As soon as one of the soldiers saw me, he put his AK-47, a semi automatic rifle, against my chest and told me not to move, or else. A new experience, I obediently froze where I sat thinking what my fate would be next. The Red Terror, the first

---

5   A violent campaign by the Dergue against civilian opposition that killed tens of thousands of people in the country between 1976 and 1978.

thing that came to my mind, was in its full swing across the city. Perhaps for the first time in my life I felt the eerie sense of not having to live much longer.

The remaining soldiers started ransacking the house looking for 'reactionary' literature that they insisted were hidden somewhere in the house; after all, there was a young male living in the house. Only my mother was at the house at the time, and she went out of her way showing the soldiers every corner of the house to prove to them that there was nothing that would incriminate me or any member of the household. The soldiers kept on ransacking the house regardless, as if they had a national security mission at hand.

Frustrated that he could not find any incriminating evidence, the corporal came to me and asked who I was, and what I was doing. All meanness and sadism was clearly reflected in his mannerism. I politely told him that I was a fourth year university student and that I was studying for my final exams. The mere mention of the word 'university' was enough for him to label me as a counter revolutionary and eligible for a 'revolutionary action.'[6]

So, he ordered me to get up and start walking out of the house, with a soldier pointing a rifle at me - point blank; this time, at my back. I asked if I could change my pajamas and put my shoes on. The corporal responded in such a way that there was no need for me to do so, implying that I had only a few hours to live anyway. As he pushed me out of the gate, I could hear my mother frantically begging the corporal to let me go assuring him, and swearing with all the saints she knew, that I was never involved in any reactionary activities.

The corporal was not fazed. We were almost at the gate of the *Kebele* compound near our house, where many other young people were detained. I knew, once in that compound, my chance of leaving alive was slim at best. As a last resort to say goodbye, I turned around to see my mother, with our *Kebele* chairperson, Ato Girma, behind her. They were both frantically

---

6   That usually was death by a firing squad.

trying to catch up with the corporal, in the hope of changing his mind, before my fate was sealed.

Interestingly enough, I had never seen Ato Girma before. So, it baffled me when I saw him having a heated argument with the corporal on my behalf. I could hear him telling the corporal that I never participated in counter-revolutionary activities, and that he would be responsible - if he would only let me go.

The corporal pushed back giving Ato Girma a chilling warning that, if released, I would one day shoot him from behind. Ato Girma told the corporal that he would take the risk and, finally, I was let go. It was a rare event to see the corporal submit to pressure from my mother and Ato Girma. In any case, they saved my life that day.

Later that night, my father invited Ato Girma to our house for a drink, and we got to know each other a little bit. He said he had seen me somewhere, and thought I was taxi driver. But, it wasn't over yet!

Exactly a week later, I was driving home at about 7 pm, when I saw a commotion a few meters before I got to the house. The entire area was flooded with nervous and panicking security police, and I began to worry. I stopped to check what the commotion was all about, fearing the worst.

A bystander told me that Ato Girma, the chair of our *kebele*, had just been shot dead by a young man who managed to escape. Ato Girma, who quite possibly may have saved my life, was killed even before I got the chance to thank him properly. The prophecy of the corporal had turned out to be true, and I was in big trouble!

So, having nowhere to go, I proceeded to my house only to find my family disturbed and shaken; they already had heard Ato Girma's death. When I got home, they told me to immediately leave the house before security police surely came looking for me. I refused and, frustrated by the whole thing, went to my bedroom to be alone. Then, my aunt Etagu and my mother came to my bedroom and tearfully pleaded that I leave the house both for my own sake and for the sake of everybody else in the house. Go to a hotel for the night, they pleaded.

I finally gave in; I could not resist seeing my aunt and mother in tears. It was now about 9 pm, but where would I go? In those days one could be shot for being found in a hotel or in a house where he/she had not registered as resident, and with a Kebele ID card. So, I was out on the dangerous streets of Addis Ababa driving in every which way trying to decide frantically where and how to spend the night.

First, I thought about sleeping in the car somewhere on a street corner where it was dark. But then I knew, if found, it would be the end of me. Then, at about 11 pm, I thought of my close friend, Alemayehu Kebede, who was living near Arat Kilo with his wife, Tina Marino, and their newborn baby boy, Aseged. Their house was far from where I lived, and I thought maybe I would be safer there. So, I went to their house and told them what happened, and that I needed to spend the night with them.

The problem was that their neighborhood was being traumatized by a notorious government cadre called Girma Kebede (aka The Chief Executioner). He had been killing young people, including a pregnant woman, indiscriminately for the mere reason of being suspect reactionaries or anarchists. So, if he came to my friend's house by any chance and found me there, no one would survive. Tina and Alemayehu knew the risks involved, but they could not turn me down when I needed help.

Also, Alemayehu calculated that Girma Kebede had been to their house the previous night and it was very unlikely that he would come again - that would have been two nights in a row. So, Tina made me a make-shift bed using their sofa in their modest living room; and they retired to their bedroom at about midnight.

None of us actually slept that night, sometimes listening to shootings and painful screams throughout the night. It must have been a busy night for Girma Kebede and his friends that night and, fortunately for us, he didn't come to the house where I was.[7]

Very early the next morning, to minimize any risks, I thanked my hosts with all my heart, and went to the Lion Bar - our favorite hiding place at times of crisis. It wasn't open at the time, but I hovered around and stayed there the whole day, calling home once in a while to check on the situation.

At about 8 pm, I was told it was clear to come home; the government security forces were after a group of young men in the neighborhood as the suspects. I felt sad for the young men, probably innocent, who were being hunted for a certain 'revolutionary action' if caught. But I had to go home and prepare for my finals. Such is life, I sadly told myself.

*****

In any case, back to June 13, 1978, the hardest decision Menby and I had to make quickly was not whether I should go to Italy but whether I should come back in September; and we struggled a lot. The promise I had made to Signora Steganini to come back in September and the potential to be in harm's way if I came back was the albatross around my neck at the time, and for some time to come. Finally, after a lot of ups and downs and, considering the situation in the country at the time, we reasoned that I should not come back in September.

This was not an easy decision to make since. Even under those circumstances, I was worried about breaking my promise to Signora Steganini to return to Ethiopia in September. I also hated to be in a state of a limbo, which was a strong possibility, once I finished my studies in Italia. But, it was decided; and I was to make every effort to bring Menby to wherever I would end up after my studies in Italia. This, at the time, was more of a wishful thinking than a real possibility.

So, to help us with this effort, we decided to get married the same day. It was now 11 am on June 13, 1978; and we

---

7   Girma Kebede was later executed by the government for allegedly overdoing the killings and giving the government a bad image.

headed to Addis Ababa Municipality to ask for a civil marriage right away; we had no time. We were told to return at 2pm with four witnesses and 2 Birr for marriage registration fees. [8]

Left to right: My friends Tamrat Lakew, Asfaw Goitom and Tsegaye Beru, the bride, the groom, and Alemayehu Kebede. Addis Ababa Municipality civil marriage ceremony. June 13, 1978

We did and, less than 24 hours before my departure to Italia, we were husband and wife!

By 4 pm, our witnesses, who were our friends anyway, have left us. Now, we were faced with the unenviable task of informing our respective parents about what had just expired. I was first to go; I thought I would take care of my mother, which would be the easier thing to do, later. So I called my father from a public phone at his work place.

---

8   To this day, my wife is not amused when I tell my friends that my total wedding cost was 2 Birr. By the way, somebody needs to do a correlation between the amount of money spent at weddings and the duration of the marriages.

Aklilu: *Dad?*
Dad: *Yes, what do you want?*
Aklilu: *How are you?*
Dad: *I told you I was fine, what do you want?*
Aklilu: *Eh… I just got married!*
Dad: *What?*
Aklilu: *I said, I just called to say I just got married.*
Dad: *Good for you!* Click.

End of story; I actually did not expect too much hoopla from my father on the subject anyway. One of the characteristics that I like about my father a lot!

It was now my wife's turn to call her parents. Since her father was out of town, she called her mother, Amanelwa. Her mother, who already knew me by then, said she was happy for us but she would insist that I came home for dinner that same night. To make things short, I did have a great dinner at my new in-laws, said good-bye to my new wife, her mother and her siblings, and headed home to prepare for my early flight to Italia via Kenya the next day!

Once at home for my last night, I realized events had overwhelmed me by surprise. Only a couple of weeks earlier, there was no thoughts about me leaving the country, much less getting married. I was actually looking forward to my summer trip to my aunts in Dire Dawa or Asebe Teferi; but that was not to be.

Instead, alone in my bedroom, I was wondering what Italia would offer me that Gore and Addis Ababa did not. Even more importantly, I worried about what I would do once I finished my studies in Italia. I hated to be stranded, especially in a foreign country! But, I rationalized, I would deal with that when the time came.

*****

The next day, on the morning of June 14, 1978, I took Kenyan Airways to Nairobi; my first time ever to set foot out of Ethiopia. My brain was blank, and did not know what to think or expect. I had a few hours to see whatever Nairobi had to offer, most notably the Nairobi National Park. Compared to what I have seen in my own country, I was impressed. But, I could not but wonder why, unlike in Addis Ababa, most of the stores I saw in Nairobi were not owned by local Kenyans.

The Alitalia flight I took from Nairobi to Roma the next day was a long one - about 8 hours. I settled in my seat for a long flight, but not without noticing a few 'strange' things first. For one thing, I was never in a situation where an all-white crew served me. I wished my friends back in Addis, especially my twin friends, had seen when white flight attendants called me 'sir' and, upon my orders, brought me a cup of coffee or tea - or whatever I asked!

For another, here I was making decisions on my own as to what to say and do, with no one looking over my shoulders. In a strange way, I felt emancipated; a feeling I never felt before, although I had very little idea, if any, as to what the future had in store for me. But, it was the first indication of the path of transition from a local happy-go-lucky young man to a more international and responsible adult.

In any case, quite a few things went through my head as we were flying north over the Sahara Desert along the coast of the Nile, then the vast Mediterranean, and then the southern Italian landscape. At first I felt a strong sense of guilt that I was leaving my beloved ones behind, possibly never to see them again. The thought that I was also leaving them in difficult times was unbearable. To overcome and compensate for all this, I promised to myself again and again that, no matter what, I would return home, and as soon as I could.

I also feared that, in the coming months and years, my Ethiopian way of life, values and attitudes and, in short, my 'identity'- for whatever it's worth - was going to be tested, at best, and changed, at worst, in major ways. I wondered if I had it in me, through my upbringing or level of maturity, to withstand all the challenges I would be facing; and to remain composed and uncompromised as an Ethiopian.

Then, for a strange reason, instead of thinking about my future, my thoughts, one by one, drifted backward to my early elementary, high school and then my college years which I fondly remember clearly to this day.

Elementary school years

Staring down through the airplane window, I started thinking about my boyhood years in Gore, Illubabor. Although my parents were originally from Asebe Teferi (aka Chiro) Hararghe,[9] we had moved to Gore in 1955 when I (Meseret[10] Kidanu) was five years old. My entrepreneurial father, Ato Kidanu Wolde Giorgis, was to pursue his dream of growing coffee, and running a couple of other small businesses.

I was too young to remember my birthplace, Asebe Teferi, but later I found out, to my pleasant surprise, that it was one interesting mix of many religions, cultures and languages living together in peace.

Gore, is located at about 550kms west of Addis Ababa; it was the capital town of what used to be known as Illubabor Province. Its lush green surrounding area was blessed with many rivers, fertile soil, large cattle, plenty of honey and, of course, coffee. The local people, Oromos, spoke Affan Oromo and Amharic, in that order. But the official language, as it was throughout the country at that time, was Amharic.

Gore was also a historical town particularly noted as the bastion of patriotic resistance against the Italian occupation that began in 1935 and lasted for five years. Before Emperor Haile Selassie fled to England in exile in 1936, he had ordered that the government of Ethiopia be temporarily moved to Gore, where patriots loyal to the Emperor continued the resistance.

So, at an average elevation of over 2,000 meters and temperate climate, no malaria, no pollution, or no exposure to juvenile delinquency, Gore was the ideal place to raise children. But, I am not sure if my father had calculated all these

---

9   Before the re-structuring in the early 1990s, Hraraghe was a province in eastern Ethiopia where the ancient walled city of Harar is located.

10 Up until I was 18 and in my freshman year, my official name was Meseret Kidanu.

amenities when he decided to move his family to Gore. But, there we were.

*****

A few months after my family, which at the time was comprised of my parents and five siblings, moved to Gore, my uncles and aunts started to join-in with their children in tow. In a couple of years, there was one large household with several families and individuals living close to each other.

My father, being the oldest of his siblings who moved to Gore, was the vanguard and the godfather at the same time. He knew they had all come counting on him and understood he was shouldering a big responsibility on his shoulders. And, typically of him, he set out to meet the challenges wholeheartedly.

Celebrating my 12ᵗʰ birthday (center) with my numerous brothers, sisters and cousins in Gore, 1962. (Photo by Girma Zewdu)

Soon, my older brother Miemen and I, along our five male cousins[11]and some friends, formed a formidable team that took the small town by storm. We moved around town in a group as a wolf-pack, always looking for another local team to compete with. If one came along, we were more than happy to oblige!

Included in our group were two brothers, whose names I forgot, who were not so good in sports or in anything else for that matter, but had a very unique and unusual ability: they had figured out how to speak Amharic and Affan Oromo backward fluently - both the words and the sentences!

Imagine, if one were to say in English,

'Please give me the ball.'
He/she would say,
'Llab eht em evig esaelp.'

So, whenever they wanted to say something that the rest of us were not supposed to understand, they shifted to backward Amharic or Affan Oromo. They did it so easily and naturally that they did not struggle at all since they had mastered it from childhood. As a result, they had enormous power over us. None of us saw this coming, but we had to accept defeat, and helplessly watch them tear us into pieces in a language we did not comprehend!

I decided it was a skill that I needed to learn in order to protect myself!

But, in spite of all the efforts I made, I did not succeed; and the two brothers were not so helpful. Obviously, they did not want to give away their one strong point. So, after a number of futile attempts to do it by my own, I went to who I thought must be the source - their mother, an elderly lady I have known only from a distance.

---

11   Mekonnen Bekureyesus, Girma Zewdu, Kefale Gebre Giorgis, Solomon and Tedla Mulugeta. Girma was the ultimate pioneer who, in those days in Gore, had his own camera and studio that he used to support himself; and he also taught me how to ride a bicycle and drive a car.

My calculation was that she must have been the one who taught her sons how to do it, and she would be kind enough to teach me too. So I went to her house, and gave it a try.

> Elderly lady: *What brings you to my house today, my son? Aren't your parents Ok?*
> Meseret: *They are doing fine. How are you?*
> Elderly lady: *Aren't your sisters and brothers fine?*
> Meseret: *They are fine too.*
> Elderly lady: *Then, what brings you here?*
> Meseret: *Well, I just wanted to ask some questions about your children, the two boys.*
> Elderly lady: *Why? Are they in trouble again?*
> Meseret: *No no no, I just wanted to know how they were able to speak Amharic backward; did you teach them how?*
> Elderly lady: *No! It is a curse. I have nothing to do with it.*
> Meseret: *I don't think there is anything wrong with that.*
> Elderly lady: *I am telling you it is a curse; they are obsessed by the devil...what would people say when they hear this kind of talk.*
> Meseret: *I want to learn how to speak that way too.*
> Elderly lady: *I told you I had nothing to do with that; I don't want to hear it. May God be kind to them! I have nothing more to say!*

I gave up; I never learnt how to speak Amharic backward, and was a bit disappointed. But I still remember, since it left a scar, the nick name the two brothers gave me. As a young boy, I was a little bit chubby. So, instead of calling me *'duba'* in straight Amharic, they called me *'badu'* in backward Amharic!

They probably have forgotten by now, which reminds me of an Amharic proverb, when loosely translated into English goes: the person responsible may, but a stabbing survivor never forgets.

Always ready and happy to oblige. Back row from left to right: my cousin Solomon, my brother Miemen, my cousin Girma. Front row left to right: my cousin Kefale, my cousin Tedla and I. Gore, early 1960s (Photo by Girma Zewdu)

*****

Be this as it may, overall, we lived a happy and healthy life in Gore, albeit a bit risky one. Whenever we got the chance, particularly during the summer recess which lasted between early June and late August, we fully enjoyed what life in Gore had to offer; and it was plenty!

So, since there were no malls or shopping districts to hang-out at, our entire recreational activities were outdoors and organic; and often times pretty dangerous. Our childhood search for happiness and adventure exposed us to many dangers which we avoided purely by luck or by default.

So, as part of our urge to dispose of youthful energy, we wrestled each other endlessly, till one of us was too tired to continue. In the process, we established a hierarchy of authority among ourselves - an important factor to establish some kind of order among a mob of young boys.

We played soccer with competing local teams, often skipping lunch and our whereabouts unknown to our parents. Those of us who won a tournament would go around the town chanting and singing endlessly, carrying a makeshift trophy made of, usually, wood or paper cartons. If one ever felt on top of the world, those were the times for us. In the process, English soccer was instilled in our blood forever.

We played marbles non-stop - rain or shine. I do not know about my friends, but I was intrigued beyond description with the bright yellow and green colors inside the marbles. I would rather wash them, dry them up and keep them in my pockets than play with them on the usually dirty grounds. Also, I am not sure what it was that made us so obsessed with accumulating as many marbles as possible. Perhaps it was because, unlike most of our games, marbles could be converted into money. A couple of marbles may fetch five Ethiopian cents which, at the time, was a lot of money for us!

We rode horses without saddles and bikes without tires or brakes, and downhill, for that matter, in order to get the speed. We may have owned the tire-less bikes, but the horses were either wild or did not have owners. But, we did not mind either way. All this was without giving it much consideration that, if we broke some parts of our body, no one would come to our rescue.

On other days, we swam for hours in the nearby lakes without the ability to swim; only with the safety of old tire inner tubes which we inflated manually and plugged with a small piece of wood. No one knew or cared enough about death to understand that manually inflated inner tubes could give-in with disastrous results. The small pieces of wood which we used to prevent deflation of the tubes were the only things that stood between life and death!

We also enjoyed climbing tall trees in the forests to pick wild berries and fruits and, in the process, ran into snakes. Fortunately for us, most snakes in the area were not poisonous or would rather ran away than start a fight with a group of reckless young boys. Once in a while we would also run into places that looked like foxes' dens; but we never ventured to walk- in but ran away as fast as our young feet would allow us!

We hunted countless birds with slingshots for the sole purpose of impressing each other with our accurate but deadly shots. There was this poor bird that was targeted the most, however. The reason, as we were told, was that its feet when dried, ground and put in an envelope with a love letter, would help one 'get' the girl one was in love with - or so we thought. Apparently, we all must have had an issue secretly since we all went after that particular bird. I do not remember an instance when it worked, there probably wasn't any, but we still continued to kill the poor bird mercilessly.

We chased stray cats and dogs for hours only to corner them, usually inside a church compound, and stone them till they could not move anymore. Why these poor animals would be looking for a sanctuary inside enclosed church compounds, of all places, was beyond me; but we did not have any mercy or remorse regardless. Little did I know then that dogs, at times as many as four, would be my best friends during most of my adult life. Needless to say, I look back at this part of my life with regret and shame!

I may have kept a few harmless stories secret, but these were all fun activities which we immensely enjoyed as a group. However, one thing that we enjoyed the most was standing behind an airplane with stretched hands, as if we were flying, as it prepared to take off. In those days in Gore, there must have been daily flights from Addis Ababa in a DC-3, a twin-engine plane built in the 1930s. Whenever we did not have classes, we were mostly at the airport, standing behind the airplane at a safe distance, and waiting for the plane to take-off. There was no fence or guards to stop us.

As the two propeller engines roared just before take-off, we enjoyed the exhilarating feeling of being picked up by the strong winds, albeit for a few seconds, and be dropped several feet backwards. Then we would get up and pretend to chase the plane as it sped for take-off. There was no paved runway at Gore airport in those days, and the strongest among us would chase the plane the longest distance; which probably would not be much more than 50 meters. The rest of us would simply collapse one by one in the grass runway! Then, we all walk back home - each with as story to tell.

Talking about the rush to the airport, there was also this well built young man whom we called Bogale *Didaw* - a derogatory suffix for people with speaking disability. At that age, none of us knew better, of course, than to mock his disability. Not in front of him though, lest he would kill us.

So, frustrated because he was stigmatized and was not understood or supported by anybody, Bogale was quite violent. No one in his right mind would start a quarrel with him; or else, one would be the target of a barrage of stones that did not miss. In fact, those of us who were younger and knew what it meant to be struck by a fast moving piece of stone would step aside or change directions when we saw Bogale from a distance. He would acknowledge our deference to him by pretending that he had not even noticed us. And, it would be fine by us!

In any case, Bogale was a regular at the airport just like us - for a totally different purpose. He would run with us the distance to the airport and get there just in time for the pilot to notice him standing under the wings of the airplane. Invariably, the pilot would greet him; and Bogale would respond in his own way. Then the pilot would throw a couple of sandwiches down the cockpit window. Bogale would pick the sandwiches, devour them in a couple of bites, and then disappear.

Now, no one in his right mind would attempt to beg for, much less steal, the sandwiches from Bogale. We watched him from a distance with envy. But I secretly craved and always wondered what kind of sandwiches this young man was eating.

I never dared to ask at the time but, in hindsight after quite a few flights myself, it might have been tuna-fish sandwiches.

*****

Anyway, as young boys in Gore, although we were bad and wild but happy, we did not have the time nor did we develop the taste, unless kept secret, for girls, alcohol, cigarettes or *khat*[12], or any other 'vices' for that matter. It was unheard of for boys of our age, for instance, to talk to a girl, or to go into a tearoom to get a cup of tea, much less into a bar,

Interestingly, these unwritten rules did not apply to bars where they sold local drinks. Apparently, it was not against the social norms for us to drink local drinks, even if they were equally intoxicating. There were a few, even among our age group, who took advantage of this privilege; I wasn't one of them.

In any case, our parents knew only so much about how we spent our leisure time and did not suspect any unbecoming activities from us. On the contrary, when we got home in the evenings tired, hungry and dirty, our mothers would feed us, wash and put us in bed; a treatment that we took for granted.

Hence, our wildlife style largely took place without the knowledge of our parents; at least that was what we thought. Fortunately, nothing serious happened to us. We may have had bruised legs or ribs once in a while which we hid from our parents very well - except on one occasion.

This was the occasion which makes me shiver with terror even today. Yemane, my younger brother who was born in Gore, was only about four years old when we agreed to take him along to one of our 'swimming' expeditions; we just could not resist his tearful pleas. He bravely walked the one-hour distance to the lake with us, and earned his spot in our team as the youngest and least experienced member.

---

12 Khat is herbal stimulant, native to East Africa, with varying degree of potency depending on quality and amount chewed.

So, as we did for each one of us, we inflated an old tire inner tube, plugged it with a small piece of wood, put Yemane inside the ring and threw him in the lake. Having done our part, we soon forgot about him. On his part, for the first few minutes, he paddled around happily and energetically, as much as his tiny hands would allow, and then got tired.

By the time we have had enough to swim and were ready to leave and before we even noticed, Yemane had drifted further deep to the center of the lake; and beyond our reach. From a distance, we could see poor Yemane seemingly unconscious, locked in the tire ring, and drifting on the lake aimlessly in every which direction. We all started to cry helplessly.

When we finally got him out with the help of well-meaning local farmers, he had first turned dark and then, with the salty water, looked like he was painted white; and he was severely dehydrated. It did not occur to any one of us that we had put him in a grave danger of drowning. For that matter, since none of us was a strong swimmer, our lives had depended on how long the inner tubes of the old tires held-on without deflating.

We of course had to carry Yemane the trip back home. When we got home, my mother, who already was suspicious of our dangerous swimming adventures, immediately realized that we had taken the four-year old boy along with us. We had crossed her red line, and she was angry. She told my father about it; something that she would normally save as a last resort.

In fact, she had tolerated and even protected us from our father in many instances unbecoming of disciplined children. But, in her eyes, this one was the last straw that broke the camel's back, and it was an offense worthy of a higher authority - my father.

I never saw my father that angry before. He was mad because he had thought I should have known better than putting the life of my own younger brother at risk. In any case, after my father dealt with me in his own way which included a couple of spanking with his belt, I never went back to the lakes again. It was not the spanking that hurt me; it was that I contravened his expectations about me.

*****

Of course, there was school in Gore too. There were no extraordinary things in this small rural town school which, at the time, was called Haile Selassie I Elementary School; later a high school was added. But, there were four gentlemen who got stuck in my young mind, and lasted till today: our teachers of drawing, sports, our director, and our moral teacher. [13]

Our drawing teacher, Teacher Berhanu, was a tall, very quiet man who had tremendous skills - or so we thought - of drawing flowers and words in triple calligraphy. He had his unique and complicated way of drawing, which challenged us severely. For the first half hour or so, all we could see was his back since he would be facing the blackboard to do his drawings. When he turned around, usually 7suddenly, we would see a maze of flower drawings or letters in triple font, which we were supposed to copy.

None of us pleased him in our efforts, of course. None of us knew enough or had the inclination to learn art at that age. So, our attempts were far from encouraging. Quietly, he would go over our attempts, and finally leave the class with a sense of dissatisfaction, but a fatherly advice to try again the following class; which would not be any better. I eventually caught up with the triple scripts, and maintained it to this day.

Our sports teacher, Teacher Welkeba, was our favorite because it also meant outdoors for us; and weather conditions in Gore, almost throughout the year, were perfect for anything outdoors! Teacher Welkeba did not mean it, but he would always be cursing us or, worse, threatening to whip us for not stretching our hands properly; or for falling out of formation; or for whispering amongst ourselves; or if he thought we were laughing at him for some reason - which may happen once in a while. And he was always suspicious of us that we gave him due respect which he deserved!

---

13 Strange I could not remember any one of my academic subject teachers!

Interestingly enough, Teacher Welkeba would always show up in the same old blue suit which his lean and tall body supported beautifully. Since he would always be shooting commands at us and did not demonstrate by examples, he didn't see why, as a sports teacher, he should be dressed in something more appropriate than an old pair of suit. We were too young and frightened to ask, and he never reconsidered or offered to explain. But, privately, I waited in vain to see him wear a different outfit come next class.

Then there was our director Ato Gudeta. If I had ever seen a well-dressed Ethiopian man, it was him; at least at the time and in Gore. He must have just returned from a foreign country by looking at the smart suit he had on every day. As a small boy, his dressing habits must have impressed me, and that may be why I still remember him.

As to Teacher Gudeta's functions as the director of the school, I thought all he did was preside over the twice-a-day, one before classes in the morning and one after classes in the afternoon, ceremony of raising and lowering of the Ethiopian flag, always accompanied by the national anthem, which we knew by heart.

By the way, the country had since changed the national anthem twice, but the only one that I remember today is the one I sang in Gore as a small boy. Why some countries keep on changing national anthems, I have no idea!

But no other teacher was as puzzling to me as our moral[14] teacher, an elderly priest called *Membir* [teacher] Desta, who the school borrowed from a nearby church. He would always come to the school on a horseback, pulled by a servant who walked in front. With his all-white cotton traditional clergy uniform on, and a wooden crucifix always dangling on his chest, he had the charisma and demeanor that demanded the respect for a holy man; and he certainly acted like one - with much success!

Moral classes with *Membir* Desta took place every day. After all, it was regarded as one of the most important classes of all. So this elderly priest would come in and follow a routine that

---

14 A mix of religion and discipline.

never changed. He would first call out our names one by one, and made sure that every one of us was present; that took fifteen minutes off the class time.

I do not remember if *Memhir* Desta excused his Muslim students, which I doubt, but he would have all of us stand up and recite after him, as loud and as clear as our young vocal chords allowed:

God created light on Monday!
   Land on Tuesday!
      Plants on Wednesday!
         The stars, sun and the moon on Thursday!
            Animals on Friday!
               Man in his own image on
               Saturday! and
               God rested on Sunday!

Without really knowing what they meant or if they were true, we had learnt to memorize these statements and to recite them flawlessly. Of course, I was too young to question any of these but, secretly, wondered when God created 'woman.' Later, I was told, He didn't. 'Woman', we were told, was the product of a different process which, at the time, we were too young to be told. No further questions allowed!

Finally, in our moral class, it would be the Ten Commandments when each one of us would have the obligation to recite by heart. By then, the class would be over.

Then, *Memhir* Desta would have us stand up and watch him walk out of the classroom - proud with the satisfaction of having accomplished a major service to the moral and religious standings of his students. And, we obliged. As he walked out, brandishing his wooden crucifix at our faces as if to protect us from evil spirits till the next class, we knew it would be the same old thing all over again; but, no complaints on our part!

All along, though, my young mind would wonder why our pious moral priest-teacher would have a servant stand by his horse the whole time, rain or shine. And I began to think there was something wrong. But, as I was growing up, the social pressure to revere religion and the clergy was intense, and it worked to a large extent on my young and vulnerable mind. *'Do not ask questions'*, we were told, and we absolutely obeyed. And, I stood corrected by hook or by crook.

Similarly, like all children coming from Christian families, there was unconditional acceptance of the existence of God and the rest of the deity. But right from my early years, in spite of our insistent moral teacher and my parents' strong religious backgrounds,[15] my own inclination to religion was lukewarm at best. Later, as I was growing up, I wondered if one could not observe all the 'commandments' without having to belong to a religion or believing in God. I wanted explanations which I didn't get. Understanding the consequences very well, I would not yet mention this 'dissent' to my parents, of course.

But still, these four teachers, in addition to those I have failed to mention without bias, were among those responsible in instilling most of the values which stayed in me, in one form or another, for the rest of my life. Needless to say, I was grateful.

*****

And then there were my classmates; all kinds of kids mostly from poor rural backgrounds. One of them was called Habib Mohammed, whose father was a tenant on a farm just outside Gore.

Habib was a slim and quiet boy with twinkling eyes and with an incredible sense of loyalty to his friends; and I was lucky enough to be one of them. Every morning Habib would walk to school with his text books in his homemade khaki bag and his lunch tied in small piece of clean cloth.

On the days when I did not go to my house for lunch, which I would sometimes do on purpose, Habib took pleasure in sharing his lunch with me. And his lunch would always be fried corn or wheat packed tidily in a small piece of cloth; of course we always drank water. I enjoyed eating his lunch more

---

15   My father was a Coptic Christian; my mother is a devout Catholic, both from Hararghe province. They lived together in peace for 56 years.

out of the friendship and solidarity with my Muslim friend than the actual lunch itself; a trend that remained in me for all my life. In fact, there were times when I had thought if I ever had a son, I would call him Habib.

In any case, in my boyhood view, Habib's simple life, genuine friendship, and sincerity to his religion contrasted with the self-righteous and hypocritical attitude of our Christian moral teacher. As a matter of fact, I had thought many times that, if I must have a religion, I would consider Islam seriously. But then, as far as I was concerned, there was no need to have one. This, however, was not to discount any use of religion to those who believe in one; quite the contrary.

Of course I would not tell this to my parents or to anybody else for that matter, not in those days. But, come to think of it, my father would not have minded if I had told him. Because, I remember years later in Addis Ababa when my father and I went to see one of his many Muslim friends on a major Muslim holiday; I think it was Eid al-Fitr, the breaking of the Ramadan fast.

When we got to the house, a large group of people were about to feast on a home-slaughtered sheep, sacrificed and prepared according to Islamic laws. In spite of my views, but influenced by social stigma, I was a bit reluctant. But not my father, who came from devout Coptic Christian background. He immediately took his shoes off, sat on a mattress on the floor right at the center of the carpet table, and was ready to oblige. I followed suit, and found my own corner.

All along, I could not take my eyes off my father, who was sitting a few feet away from me, happily joining-in his Muslim friends and enjoying the dates and various sweets followed by lamb, totally indifferent to the religious barrier between him and his Muslim friends. I never asked him why he did what he did, but it was abundantly clear to me that, although he wouldn't say it openly, he believed religion was an artificial barrier between people; and I was taking notes.

*****

In any case, back in Gore, as if this small town had not provided us with enough opportunities to play and learn, two strange men from a far-off strange country showed up, marking for some of us at least, the beginning of a long journey into a world outside and far away from Gore: Peace Corps volunteers Floyd B Davis and Ash Hartwell. It was 1963, and I was thirteen and just joined grade eight.

Floyd B Davis was an African American. He was probably in his early twenties at the time, tall and always very formally dressed. In contrast to our local teachers, he was polite and extremely well behaved – meaning, he never punished or even scolded us.

I also remember he always put on a suit and a tie; it might have been a three-piece suit, complete with a bow tie! His clothing style caught-up in Ethiopia later in my early 20's and I remember I had at least one such suit. His shoes were big and always covered with rubber shoes (since there was a lot of rain in Gore), a condition that bewildered us for some time. Since, in the mentality of Gore men of those days, the smaller your shoes the more 'civilized' you were considered! He also carried an umbrella all the time, and I could almost swear he had a briefcase too.

Floyd's full hair was thinly shaved in the middle or slightly to one side; I guess it was the style at the time but it was also another condition that we struggled to understand. If I remember correctly, he would tell us he came from New Orleans, USA - as if we knew it was the name of a city. Or, maybe, he just talked a lot about New Orleans that we thought he was from there.

Floyd taught English and, among other things, he emphasized a fancy writing style with all the extensions on top and bottom of each letter. Using his name as an example, he would teach us how to carve the English letters perfectly in between two lines - both in small and capital letters - a habit that lasted forever with me since I must have written his name a thousand times! To this day, if I wanted to, I could still write in exactly the same manner he taught us how to!

Unfortunately for Floyd, one of his classes was on Friday afternoons. Now, half of the students in rural town schools like Gore came from the neighboring villages. So, on Fridays after lunch, they would slip to their rural villages for the weekend - only to show up on Sunday afternoons or Monday mornings.

Also, on Friday afternoons, some older students from the town itself had the habit of sneaking out to the nearby tej[16] [houses. With plenty of honey in Gore, this was part of the school culture. So, when Floyd came to his class on Friday afternoons, he wound find only less than half of the students - those of us who lived in Gore and were not old enough to sneak out for local drinks. So, Floyd would come in, stand in front of the class calm and composed but with some confusion, and would ask, *'Where is everybody today?'*

Of course, not anyone of us understood the question. Even if we did, I guess we would not have said a word. As for me, instead of answering his question, I would wonder quietly why he was saying 'everybody'. Doesn't that suggest all of us were not in the classroom? At least some of us would be in the class!

In any event, Floyd would be standing there for a while waiting for an answer. Then he would give up and continue with his teaching. I wonder if he ever knew why his Friday afternoon classes were always half empty![17] But, to this day, I maintained the habit of jokingly asking the same question whenever I get home.

*****

Ash Hartwell was, in a way, the flip side of Floyd. He was a white man with red hair; and informal in behavior and dressing. I never saw him with a jacket on. He was very young, not much older than the older students in the class. He probably was the first white person, other than the missionaries in town, whom we ever came to see or know close up. And we were excited!

---

16   Local intoxicating beverage made of honey.
17   Floyd is now a writer based in New York City, USA.

I do not exactly remember what subject Ash was teaching us, but he had a unique and creative approach. He was very eager to share knowledge, but his students were much more interested in his persona than in what he was trying to share. I remember in one of his classes he casually took off his shoes and socks to explain to us what a 'toe' was. I think he was trying to explain the difference between a finger and a toe.

Now, in a rural town like Gore, where teachers were considered next to God, it was unprecedented that Ash would take his socks off in front of his students – even to make a point. But, it worked! I know because I have known the difference between a finger and a toe since then. And, I clearly remember his snow-white feet as he took them out of his white socks!

On other occasions Ash would take off his contact lenses right in front of us, and put them on again. I do not know if he knew, but that scared a lot of us, albeit in a positive way!

Had they known, our local teachers would have caused a riot because of Ash's student-friendly but unusual, to say the least, approach to sharing knowledge. But we enjoyed them all the more.

Ash told us he came from Honolulu, Hawaii, USA. He probably spent half of the year trying to explain to us what it was and where it was. None of us, of course, knew where or what Hawaii was; but Ash was bent on explaining that it was an island, and he might also have drawn maps.[18] As a small boy, I was totally mesmerized by his account of Hawaii and Honolulu, and the life style he described. I fantasized that some time in my life, I would go to Honolulu.[19]

In any case, Floyd and Ash had volunteered to come to Gore, all the way from the United States, in order to share their knowledge with us in such a way that, almost fifty years later, I clearly and gratefully remember them and their teachings.

---

18 Ash is now a professor at University of Massachusetts, USA.
19 I actually did in 2004, and my effort to locate Ash was in vain at the time.

My parents

Back at home, my father Ato Kidanu Wolde Giorgis, was the undoubted head, patron, and godfather of the big household with multiple families and numerous individuals. Born in 1914 in a small farming community called Goro, somewhere between Asebe Teferi and Hirna in what used to be Hararghe Province, my father, at age 29, wed my mother when she was only 18. They had six children, I was the second.

His initial life started as a hand on his parents' farm in Goro, then as a small-scale trader, and eventually as an entrepreneur. He was particularly keen about growing coffee, which he eventually did.

My father was tall, and walked like a soldier. No matter what, he would always wear kaki jackets and trousers. His light brown shoes were always the same style, and must have shoelaces. I never saw him wearing a tie till he celebrated his 50th wedding anniversary; at a time when he was too soft to put on even what his grandchildren would demand of him. It is amazing how fathers soften-up over the years.

My father was also a very literate person, and spoke four languages: Amharic and Affan Oromo fluently; and Arabic and Italian fairly well. He knew the old and new testaments and the Ethiopian Civil Code in Amharic relatively well. In fact, he had once considered adding 'traditional' lawyer to his several trades; he loved to serve others with what he could, usually pro bono. Knowing that my father never went to a formal school, I had always wondered how he picked all the languages he spoke, and how he came to know the bible and the Ethiopian civil codes so well.

Coffee growing was their passion. My mother and father working on their coffee farm near Tepie, Southern Region, early 1970s, just before it was nationalized.

My father was also the type of person who would kill his own son if he believed it was the right and fair thing to do. He greeted and treated everybody equally. Whatever he did for his own children, he would do the same for his numerous nephews and nieces. At one time, since he wasn't able to buy shoes for all the children he supported in the household, he had all of us walk bare-footed; those were his rules. *'Besides,'* my father would argue *'most of the kids in Gore walk around bare-footed; how are you different from them?'* This would be the same argument I would use much later in life; albeit in a very different context.

My father also walked his talk - always. One day, one of my aunts came back to Gore after a brief visit to Addis. With her, she brought three pairs of shoes for her three children. So, as the rest of us were walking around bare-footed, my lucky three cousins were wearing brand new shoes - a violation of my father's rules.

So, I remember when my father went to his sister's house and demanded to have the shoes. My aunt gave him the shoes promptly but fearfully. As we all watched in horror, he put the brand new shoes in a toilet pit. End of story, and we all resumed walking around bare-footed.

On another occasion my father demonstrated, in front of my eyes, the type of person he was. In a small southern town called Tepie, he had lost his coffee farm during the 1975 land reform, but was allowed to keep his house with a large compound. At the time, frustrated by the government's action, my father had allowed an old friend, a *Belambaras*[20] and his family to stay in the house temporarily. My father has had his residence in Addis by then.

Later, in the early 1990's, with the new government in place, my father wanted to retrieve his house in Tepie. He politely asked the *Belambaras* to please hand over the house; the *Belambaras* refused, and the case went to court.

My father, who could also be as stubborn as the camel if need be, argued before the courts for ten years and won the case. In the mean time, *the Belambaras* had died and his widow and her children were living in the house. She refused to leave, '*Where would I go?*', she pleaded. But, the court ordered the police to evacuate the elderly lady and her family by force, if necessary.

When the police and my father went to the house for takeover, they saw a tent erected in the middle of the compound. One of the grown up children of the elderly lady, my father was told, had died suddenly. The tent represented the start of a 40-day of mourning period. My father, who knew this tradition very well, had the choice of having them evicted by force or wait until the mourning period was over. My father opted for the latter, and demonstrated not only the principle but also the humane heart he had.

When he returned to Tepie a couple of months later to retrieve his property, things have turned upside down. There

---

20 A social status title.

were new judges in place and the elderly lady had somehow managed for the case to be sent back all the way to the starting place. My father was getting ready to start from the scratch, and go for another ten years if necessary, when he was taken ill and died at age 90; and the elderly lady lives in the house to this day.[21]

Finally, my father always remained loyal to his friends - to the end and at any cost. I remember, in the aftermath of the Ethio-Eritrean war that took place between 1998 and 2000, one Eritrean gentleman who had been very close to my father's family since their years in Gore, was asked to leave the country. Having lived in Ethiopia for decades, the Eritrean had accumulated property and belongings that he had to stow away quickly before he was forcefully moved to Eritrea.

In a bold move that wasn't very popular at the time, my father allowed his Eritrean friend to store his belongings at his house; essentially locking one of the rooms shut for years. It wasn't until years later when the war was over, and both sides recognized the big mistake they had made in forcing thousands of innocent families out of their decades-old livelihoods, that the family members of his Eritrean friend collected their belongings.

It was a classic case of *'a friend in need is a friend indeed.'*

*****

Growing up in Gore, Saturdays were exceptional days for me; they were the days I would spend with my father. Every Saturday morning, I would leave home with him wherever he went, to help him with whatever he was engaged in. Usually, it would be providing pro bono arbitration services to couples who have quarreled; merchants who have crossed each other; or parents complaining about their children. I would sit right behind my father and watch with wonder as he first listened to both parties attentively and then deliver his decisions to the parties.

---

21 Some relatives had asked me to peruse the case, but I declined.

More often than not, as one of the elderly citizens of the town, his decisions would be happily accepted by the quarreling parties as the final ones. He was among a group of people considered wise and fair by community members.

On other occasions, it would be going with him to his coffee farm, a few kilometers outside Gore. There he would engage either in picking coffee or cutting shrubs or trees, right along with his workers and with equal strength and efficacy. Too young and unfit to do the same, he would hand me his hunting rifle and order me to stand aside – teasing me all along. I would carry the rifle with as much care as possible, but with a hidden fear in my heart. Another thing I had to worry about was watching the trees they were cutting, lest they fell on my head.

Revered senior citizens of Gore. My father stands at the far right. Early 1960s. (Photo by Girma Zewdu)

My prize for all these, which applied only for Saturdays, was the privilege of eating dinner with him while everybody else waited till we finished. My more subtle, but much more important prize, was that I watched real-time his values for hard work, his fair and just approach to life and treating people, love for his family, and respect for his wife. In fact, I never heard my father speak to my mother in a loud voice much less show any sign of disrespect.

Neither did he express his love for his family members with words; I never heard him say, 'I love you' to anyone, for example. No strange thing for men of his age in those days. But, there was no need for him to say so; it was abundantly clear that my father lived for his children, in particular, and the larger family members, in general.

The relationship between my father and I grew to the point where I associated all good things with him and wanted to be like him. In short, I worshiped him and nothing pleased me more than pleasing him. So, with all my glaring weaknesses compared to his compelling strengths, I also had the audacity to become just like him. But then, I had plenty of time to catch up, if I ever succeeded.

Also, in return, I suspect that he favored me over the rest of his children. Although my siblings may fiercely contest this, that much was clear to me no matter how hard my father tried to conceal it.

*****

My mother W/o Asegedetch Wolde Mariam, now 91 years old, is a very nice and religious lady brought up in the Catholic religion. As I was growing up, and as a typical Ethiopian boy, I really never paid a lot of attention to my mother. I had thought her job was to feed and take care of us, period. She did that very well, and we all grew up to be healthy adults. But, I knew very little about her.

In fact, for me and my boyhood friends and cousins in Gore, the opposite sex, including our own sisters, did not exist because we left no space for them in our activities. They had their lives, and we had ours; and we never mixed. We were also the victims of the social norms of the time that looked down upon women. Shamefully, it wasn't until I was in high school that I even realized that I actually had three sisters[22] who lived with me.

So, later in life after my father passed away, as if to catch up with all the opportunities I missed in the past, I cornered my mother at her favorite spot at her house and asked her to tell me about herself - beginning from the day she was born. She was 88 years old at the time and, at first, she resisted claiming that she did not remember anymore.

When I persisted, she relented and told me a truncated version of her story as follows.

I was born in 1928 in a small rural farming area called Hara, which is located in central Hararghe province, not too far from Asebe Teferi. I was the fifth child of seven. I had three older sisters to whom I was attached very much, an older brother, and two younger sisters. We spoke Amharic and Affan Oromo equally fluently; no writing though!

My father was a good man, and an accomplished farmer. He farmed sorghum and maize, for the most part, and had plenty of cattle and goats, and we lived a good and happy life. Then, my father passed away when I was only seven years old. The Italians had already invaded the county at the time.

So, as a prominent person in Hara, my father had gone to Asebe Teferi to talk to the Italians on behalf of the community. People in Hara had heard that unless you made peace with the Italians they would come and cause untold amount of damages. My father's mission was to prevent that.

On his way back to Hara, he fell off the horse he was riding and broke his ribs. His lung was punctured by the broken ribs, and a few days later, he died moaning with pain all the time. There were no modern doctors at the time. I was a little bit too young to remember clearly, but I still have some faint memories of my father.

My mother, a typical rural house wife, took over the burden of raising six children by herself. In addition to cooking, she taught us weaving to make netela and gabi. Those were the things which young girls needed to know. In the process, I grew very close and attached to my mother and sisters. But then, my two older sisters got married and

---

22   Hamelmal, Meheret and Misrak Kidanu.

left the household one by one; the third one, Shewaye, died due to illness nobody knew.

My mother standing at the center; to her right is her cousin Martha and to her left is her cousin Yewebdar. Sitting from left to right are my aunts Tiru Sera and Etagu.

Then *my mother died at the young age of forty, eight years after my father died. She did not even have a single white hair, and I heard she died from tuberculoses. I was only fifteen years old, and my oldest sisters had left the house.*

Devastated *without my mother, I went to Dire Dawa to live with my older sister, Tiru Sira, who was living there with her husband, Retta, and their young children. I enrolled at a missionary school where I learnt some Italian; although I have forgotten it now.*

A *couple of years later, the family moved to Addis Ababa and I enrolled at Zenebework School near Kazanchis. I think I was in the fifth grade and about 18 years old when our oldest sister, Etagu, summoned me to Mieso where she lived at the time. Unbeknownst to me, Etagu had decided to give me off to a young and successful businessman from Asebe Teferi; his name was Kidanu.*

It *was, of course, an arranged marriage and I never saw him before my wedding day. But your father went through every bit of traditional culture, including bringing the clothes and gold as the time required. He sent shimageles[23] to formally ask for my hands and, Etagu declared she was happy he asked.*

The church ceremony took place in Lega Arba, where my grandparents lived at the time. There was a big feast, but what I remember was the wedding songs. The one I remember till today is the one about having to raise a daughter only to give her away to a man.

After the wedding, I moved to your father's two-story building at the center of Asebe Teferi. It was called 'Kidanu Building' at the time; I think the signs are still there. Our first child was born within a year, and your father being a religious person called him Miemen.[24] It was just a delight beyond description for us.

Within nine years of our marriage I had given birth to five of you, and I was very comfortable in Asebe Teferi. All the children were very healthy except you.

On one occasion, for reasons we did not know, your body temperature and fever would get very high, and you were losing weight. After all attempts that the time allowed were made, many of us thought you would die. But, your father would never give up. Against all odds, he would swear that you would not die while he was alive. He spent his days at home sitting next to you; his nights were sleepless, praying and waiting for you to heal. Weeks passed in this manner, and we had almost given up on you. Then, almost miraculously, you started to feel better and gaining weight slowly but surely; and you eventually survived.

---

23 A small group of elderly men who would be sent to ask for the hands of the bride.

24 Miemen, in Amharic, is the singular form of the word 'believers'

My mother at age 21, brother Miemen at age 1 and my father at age 32. Asebe Teferi, 1949.

So, because of your illness, we paid extra attention to you; your father was obsessed. We coddled and pampered you to the point where you were spoilt; and you even slept with us in the same bed. I remember an incident I want to tell you. Your younger sister, Hami, was about six months old, and you were about three years old. You never liked to see Hami around me; she was your competition.

One night I was breastfeeding Hami in bed, and you were sleeping on the other side. I was sleeping between the two of you. Then, all of a sudden, Hami cried profusely, and we were at a loss as to what may have caused such an intense sobbing. We ransacked the bed looking for an ant or something that might have caused it. Your father feared some kind of sudden illness; but nothing was to be found.

Then, after a while, Hami calmed down but looked really pitiful. We made the bed again and went back to sleep; again I was in the middle of the two of you. After a few minutes, we were about to fall asleep when I heard you whisper, 'I got her!' Alarmed, I turned around to ask what you meant. You had actually gone behind me, without anyone noticing, and pinched poor Hami in the stomach as hard as you could. So we knew why Hami cried so painfully – you were the culprit but what could we do?

Your father was a very ambitious and successful man, but he also had a soft heart and helped a lot of people. After a while, he was at odds with the governor of the Asebe Teferi area and he decided to move to Gore where he dreamt to farm coffee. I do not know who told him about Gore, but he was convinced that his future lay there. We packed and left for Gore; you were about five years old.

I will stop here since you know the rest of the story.'

*****

In any case, back in Gore, now in the mid 1960s, the childhood activities along with the physical nature of the surrounding areas and its rustic population were slowly beginning to form my identity - both mentally and physically. I have been impacted one way or another at an early age by a lot of people who were close to me: my father, mother, siblings, cousins and friends; our neighbors, my teachers, Peace Corps volunteers, and the people of Gore. In return, I was slowly but steadily accepting and defining the place I liked and felt a belonging.

Yes, there was also much more to learn, experience and change, of course, but Gore was an important first base. By the early 1960's there was a high school in Gore but, for reasons I do not remember, when my older brother Miemen finished elementary school in 1962, my father had sent him to a boarding high school in Addis Ababa. He first went to General Wingate School but he later changed to Kotebe Haile Selassie I High School because his close friends were going there, and he wanted to be with them.

In 1965, when I finished the ninth grade in Gore, my father first thought about sending me to a high school in Addis, but he later changed his mind. Instead, he moved his entire family to Addis, while he still maintained his businesses and farms in Gore and the surrounding areas. My aunts, uncles and cousins had left Gore earlier, one by one.

So, in June 1965, my ten-year fun-filled tenure in Gore was over. I was fifteen, and left Gore and my friends with a broken heart, and with an intermediate level of Affan Oromo, the local language. The birds and cats and dogs of the town must have had a sigh of relief unless, of course, a younger generation of youthful mob replaced my friends and me.

A new life in Addis was about to begin!

Youthful Fun and Lessons

High school years

Still up in the sky over Southern Italia looking down at dimly lit small towns, my thoughts then went to my high school years at Medhane Alem School in Addis Ababa. This school has an interesting history. It opened its doors in 1931, during the reign of Emperor Haile Selassie, to provide academic and vocational training for about a hundred orphans of the country's local chiefs. By 1934, it had accepted many more regular students, most of whom received military training and ended up fighting the Italian invaders at the Battle of Maychew in 1936.

The school reopened in 1941 with a new name, *Balabat* [clan chief], and received students, mainly the sons of mostly martyred *Balabats* from the different remote parts of the country. In 1942, the name was changed back to Medhane Alem School. A high school was added in 1955, and the students' population increased to about fifteen hundred.

This was the high school that I joined in 1965, as a 10th grade student, and where I made my first 'real' friends, and my equivalent of 'urban life 101.'

A 'real' friendship for me was a relationship that one would jump into with both feet without doing any risk analysis. It was a state of being completely free and at ease, and not to have to worry about what to say or do. It is a simple, innocent and happy relationship. Such a relationship, in my view to this day, can be forged only at the high school age, perhaps with the exception of first year college.[25] As to my friends before my

---

25 Some friends of mine who I met after our freshman year may raise issues with this definition of friendship.

high school years,[26] I had simply thought of them as family members, my relatives. I am not sure I knew what 'friendship' was at that time, anyway.

So, having come from a small rural town to a relatively much bigger city, I was eager to mix. My wild, reckless but happy life style in Gore had now come to an end but not forgotten. It was now a new world, and it was now a different ball game; and I was game. My cousins Shimeles Retta, a maverick in his own right, and Melaku Rufael were kind enough to teach me the basic rules of the game.

Initially, it was not easy to adjust to the way of life in Addis Ababa. I had to deal with some urban culture that I was not used to while growing up in Gore.

My first real challenge came within a year of my arrival in Addis. My high school attracted all kinds of students from all corners of the city, including the *Mercato*[27] area, a place with a reputation for violence. Some students in my 10th grade class who had come from this area behaved like bullies, and the school's student population feared them. And, I was still a young rural boy with little or no idea as to how to deal with students from the *Mercato* area, and I was scared.

So, one afternoon, at the end of the school day, we were leaving our classroom to go to the stand where we would sing the national anthem while someone would lower the Ethiopian flag. And, while two girls were still inside the classroom, one of the bullies and his friends locked the door from the outside leaving them stranded inside. I noticed this, and went back to the classroom to open the door for the girls. Just as I was doing that, the school director, Dr. Leulseged Alemayehu, appeared and caught me red-handed. He accused me of committing the offense; I emphatically denied doing it.

When he pushed me hard, I told him that it was one of my classmates and his friends who did it. Upon the director's

---

26 Lema Kifle, Tesfaye Gurara, Adera Alemayehu, Abebe Kibret, Habib Mohammed.

27 Mercato was (or used to be) the largest open market in Africa; some students coming from that area were considered to be violent bullies.

instructions, I identified the students and disciplinary actions were taken against them. But, by so doing, I had committed the cardinal sin of exposing the offence of fellow students to the school director.

Needless to say, the bully and his friends declared me 'enemy number one.' They vowed, once the school year ended a few weeks later in June, I was dead meat.

*****

Fast forward to early June of the same year, it was the last day of school, and the 'school day' celebrations were about to take place. This was my first school day in Addis and I had heard that one of my favorite singers, Alemayehu Eshete and the Police Orchestra, would come and perform at the school. It would have been a first time for me to see him live, since we did not get such opportunities in Gore; and I resolved not to miss it at any cost.

But, I was not sure how to handle the threat of the bully and his friends who were known for stabbing people they disliked. I have only fought once in my life and I was badly beaten. I was never a violent person and I could not fight with bullies - with or without knives. And, I have never hit a person before. The only student from Eritrea who was on my side at the beginning of the incident had gone back to Eritrea. I didn't have friends who would help me, and I was only fifteen years old!

On the other hand, I really wanted to attend the school year and watch one of my favorite singers. What to do?

It was noon on June 8, and I was at home, and the school day celebrations would start in about an hour. I was dressed and ready to go, and the thought of missing the celebrations was unbearable. At any cost, I had to go. But I still wasn't sure what to handle the bully and his friends who threatened to 'stab' me on that same day.

All of a sudden, unsure of how the whole thing would end up, an idea came to my mind. My father had a revolver that he kept under his pillow in his bedroom. If I could only take the revolver to school with me and showed it to the bully and his friends, they will not come anywhere near me. Excellent idea, I told myself. I did not give it much thought as to what could happen if they called my bluff, and if things went wrong - terribly wrong.

So, without consulting anyone, I sneaked into my parent's bedroom, put the revolver in my trousers' pocket, sneaked out of the house, took a taxi, and arrived at the school promptly. My first task, of course, was to find the bully and his friends; and get the problem out of my way.

Sure enough, I saw four of them sitting in the middle of the school's soccer field. They saw me and started making all kinds of threatening gestures, while laughing at me all the while. I walked directly to them and, with a grim face and confident voice that surprised them and myself, asked to talk to them one by one. The bully stood first and mockingly volunteered to follow me to a nearby toilet where we would be alone; I had planned this out earlier.

As soon as we got to the toilet, I locked the door, pulled out the revolver and, from a safe distance of about five feet, I pointed the revolver at him and told him I would kill him if he and his friends threatened to harm me, let alone stab me. Then, remembering what my father had taught me to do years earlier, I unlocked the revolver and showed him the bullets in the rotating chamber to impress on him that I was dead serious. In retrospect, I wonder what I would have done if he had called my bluff; I did not have a plan B.

But luckily, like all bullies, he was simply a coward and he fearfully followed my orders.

As I looked at him, I got encouraged because I could see him sweating and shivering where he stood. He started mumbling words that sounded like an apology; but I, with the upper hand, was not impressed. When I was done, I followed him to his friends where I picked one of them and did the same thing. By the time I was done with the second one and out to the field for the next one, they had all disappeared. Then, with the feeling of a conqueror, I settled and felt the entire campus was left for me.

I did not see the bully and his friends anywhere near me the rest of the day.[28]

Soon, I forgot about the heavy revolver in my pocket or the bullies and his friends. Instead, I went to the hall where Alemayehu Eshete was singing, and joined the multitude of students who were having a good time.

I spent most of the money I had on buying refreshments to the singers which, at the time, was the thing to do. Each time there was a song that I liked, I would ran to the stage, plant a kiss on the cheeks of whoever was singing, pass on a bottle of Pepsi Cola or whatever was the cheaper drink, and ran back to my seat. I must have done this at least half a dozen times.

Throughout, I sang with the crowd, asked for popular songs to be repeated, and expressed my approval with loud applauses and whistles; I really had fun. I still remember that afternoon as one of the happiest days in my life.

When all was over, it was past 7pm. All of a sudden I remembered I had my father's revolver in my pocket. I frantically ran out of the school compound, took a taxi, and headed home.

Now, my father had a habit of going to the main road to look for anyone among family members who happened to come home late. Our curfew was about 7pm, when it got dark. He would also take his revolver with him. This time, of course, the revolver was not where it was supposed to be and, hence, he stayed at home wondering what in the world had happened to his revolver.

So, by the time I got home, it was chaos. The bed, sofa, dining table and chairs have been ransacked in search of the revolver. The entire family members, including my brother Miemen who had come for the weekend from his boarding

---

28 The bully left the school the same year; he later became one of the guards at Cinema Adwa and one of those who we would bribe to sneak- in with half the ticket price.

high school, were taking part in this frantic search for the revolver that had disappeared in thin air!

When I entered the house and saw the chaos, I stood frozen in front of my father; all eyes were now on me. Almost instinctively, my brother Miemen pointed at me and said it was I who took the revolver; I still do not know how he knew.

I didn't say a word, until my father walked towards me, took the revolver from my pocket, and checked if there were any bullets missing. Then I said something to the effect that I did not fire any shots and that I took the revolver to school to use in a play - as if it would make a difference. When he was sure there were no shots fired, my father put the revolver on the nearby dining table and turned around to face me at a distance of three feet.

Now, my father was a very strong man; and on several occasions on his coffee farm, l had seen him cut big trees with an axe single- handedly. So, there was no escape for me, and I did not even try. Before I knew what hit me, all of a sudden I was rolling under the dining table with pain. It was my mother's tearful plea that saved me another blow, which would have finished me.

My father, as far as I know, never mentioned this incident to anyone including myself, later in life. We always had our unspoken rules; but it was clear that I have made a disastrous mistake that could have resulted in much more disastrous consequences. I was simply lucky; that did not happen.

My father never said it in so many words, but I knew he had already forgiven me. In fact he may have privately said, *'Well done my son!'*

As for my brother Miemen who exposed me instead of covering for me, we made peace once he promised to take me to his high school dorm to spend a weekend with him. For some reason, I loved doing that! I think it was eating mass food at a large dining room, with tea in a large hot nickel cup in my hands, which excited me. His friends and I remember one in particular, Tefera Hailu, pampered me too.

Anyway, all by myself later that night, I congratulated myself, smiled the smile of a conqueror. But, I knew I had violated my father's trust in me, and I promised myself it would never happen again. Then, I gradually slid into heavy sleep.

Later in life, every time I listened to Alemayehu Eshete's songs, I remember the day, the events and the incident at my high school and shudder to think how badly things could have gone. I was just lucky.

*****

While still a high school student at age 15, another not less frightening incident took place. That was when I had to face Emperor Haile Selassie from a couple of feet; something unthinkable for a boy who grew up in rural Gore.

It was at the end of a school year and I was playing soccer with my friends in a neighborhood field when an official from my brother's Kotebe High School approached me and started throwing a series of questions at me.

Official: *What is your name?*
Meseret: *My name is Meseret.*
Official: *Are you Miemen's brother?*
Meseret: *Yes, I am.*
Official: *Where is he?*
Meseret: *I don't know. I think he is gone to Asebe Teferi or somewhere for the summer vacation.*
Official: *Ok, you are coming with me to the palace.*
Meseret: *The palace? Why?*
Official: *You need to take your brother's high school leaving certificate from the Emperor on his behalf.*[29]
Meseret: *Emperor who?*
Official: *Emperor Haile Selassie, of course; do we have any other emperor?*
Meseret: *From the palace? From the hands of the Emperor? Are you serious?*

---

29   In those days students from Addis Ababa highs schools who passed the college entrance examination would take their certificates from the emperor.

Official: *Yes.*
Meseret: *I don't think so; I am not even dressed for that occasion.*
Official: *There is no need to dress up, this is good enough. Besides, it is very important for your brother that you do so. Now, let us go.*
Meseret: *Ok then, let us go; anything for my brother Miemen.*

Along the way, the official kept on telling me that, when Miemen's name was called out, I would walk up to the emperor and take the certificate from his hands - while bowing really low all along. I agreed to do it, but I was scared. My thoughts were about all the rumors, surely unfounded, that I heard about the emperor including sacrificing young boys for some superstitious reasons.

One thing that bothered me in particular was the rumor that boys with eyebrows without a gap in between (a sort of a unibrow) were the main targets; and, sadly, I qualified. So, I started to blame my brother on whose behalf I was putting myself in danger's way.

In any case, when we got to the Emperor's office at the *Old Gebi,*[30] there were hundreds of mostly male students dressed up, and lined up in a huge hall waiting for the Emperor to show up. The official took me to the place where Kotebe High School students were standing in line, and put me somewhere in the middle of the line, sorted out, I suppose, by alphabetical order.

It was obvious that I was the youngest, smallest and least well-dressed young man in the crowd. I was terrified, but I felt much better when I saw some of my brother's friends I knew from my weekend trips to his school. They advised me to be calm and alert so I would respond promptly when Miemen's name was called out. 'I was not to miss that by any means!' I was warned.

Finally, after what I thought was an eternity, the emperor showed up and we quietly waited till names were called out.

---

30 The Old Gebi was the palace, built by Emperor Menelik II when he found Addis Ababa in 1886, that served as an office for Emperor Haile Selassie who, at the time, lived in the Jubilee Palace built in 1955.

Then eventually I heard my brother's name called out 'Miemen Kidanu.' I could see the emperor from a distance, seated in a throne on a platform. In my eyes he looked like a lion, albeit with a human face, ready to devour his prey – and I was one of them.

In any case, I took a deep breath and bravely walked straight up to him, stretched out both my hands while bowing as low as I possibly could. He handed me the certificate, but he won't let go the other end. I was holding one end of the certificate, scared to look up at the emperor who was still holding the other end. I kept on bowing as low as possible all the time, lest the emperor would notice my eyebrows, and I would be in big trouble.

Then, using a she-pronoun,[31] I thought I heard him asking me, *What would you like to become when you grow up?* Trembling under my pants, I was too freighted to respond. I kept bowing, looking down at what looked like carpeted floor, until he finally let go the other end of the certificate. I was spared; and literally ran back to where I was - right in the arms of my brother's friends who congratulated me for a job well done. I smiled a smile of fear and victory combined. After all, I had beaten the emperor!

I went home and told my parents and siblings that the emperor spoke to me, but no one believed me. They had no idea where I was that day. A few days later, the pictures of the emperor issuing certificates to me and many other students were displayed at the entrance of Ethiopian Ministry of Education; they stayed there for about a year.

I do not remember how many times I went there alone or with whoever would come along to see the picture. Needless to say, it was quite an experience at a very young age.

My identical twin friends

High school was also the turning point for me as well, and I suspect it would be the same for many other young people. The first couple of kids I ran into in the tenth grade, Banjaw and

---

31 A she-pronoun for very young boys is used to show affection.

Bezuayheu Tadesse, who also happened to be identical twins, ended up being my 'real' friends[32].

Born in the middle of the *Mercato* area in Addis Ababa, the twins had every aspect of juvenile delinquency at their finger tips - if they had opted to indulge in them. They did, in some of them, of course. And, how I, a rural kid from Gore, ended up being friends with identical twins from the middle of the *Mercato* area, was beyond me. It must have been the case of opposite ends attract.

Aside from our friendship, I was fascinated by how these identical twins operated. To begin with, I wondered how the two of them could have a common friend in me. Were they not supposed to be two separate individuals with separate interests?

Then I found out, maybe they weren't. They talked at the same time and said the same words simultaneously; if one of them started a sentence the other would jump-in uninvited and finished it; if one of them started a fight, the other one would join-in without knowing why. For all intents and purposes, I found out, they were one person!

In any case, the best treat for me, even today, was stirring up an argument between the two; like who was born first, or who was taller,[33] or who could ran faster; and then sit back and enjoy the drama. They could argue endlessly with either one of them having the upper hand, and I would be laughing the whole time. Finally, when they were tired in the course of their argument, one of them, and it didn't matter which one, would turn to me and, with a pretended exasperation, ask, *'Who introduced me to this guy?'* And, I would respond, *'You are twins, I guess you met each other in your mother's womb.'* I never knew there was so much competition, albeit short-lived and superficial, among identical twins.[34]

---

32 For sure I had other friends like Awgechew Kidane, Seifu Alemu and Zenebe Tamrat; but I hardly saw them after high school.
33 Both were very short and exactly equal in height.
34 I actually have fraternal twin sisters but, like most boys of the time, never paid much attention to them as we were growing up.

So, over the years, my twin friends taught me good things, which I absorbed; and bad things like smoking, which I resisted, unless I was tricked. Some of their influence on me, however, had long lasting effects, particularly in one area.

In those days, there were three famous cinemas in the old downtown Addis (aka *Piazza*): Empire, Ethiopia, and Adwa.

On Thursdays and Fridays, each cinema showed three movies between 12 noon and 6 pm - for fifty cents. On these days, after the ten o'clock coffee break, we would sneak out of school and walk the 45-minute distance to downtown Addis. Little did we know or care that our high school uniform was giving us away all the time.

Also, it did not matter if we had enough money since there were many ways of sneaking into the cinemas without paying the full ticket amounts. But, first, we would pull all the money we had in our pockets and see if we had enough to buy the tickets for all of us. If not, we would just bribe one of the guards to sneak us in. Whatever little money we had, it would still get all of us in. Lunch, of course, was a luxury that we could not afford or remember. But, I admit, there were rare days when we could afford to share one *pasta al forno* at the famous low-income Piazza restaurant called *Kibre Mengist*.

In any case, this bribing strategy worked all the time, and it helped that one of the guards at one of the cinemas was the same bully I had an issue with during my first year in Addis. Sadly, he had dropped out of school at the end of the same school year and become a guard at one of our favorite cinemas. Sad for him, but how convenient for us!

So, after three movies in a row, we would come out at 6 pm and walk home, with red eyes and a headache from all the cigarette smoke we consumed with the movies. All the way home, we argued heatedly about who did what in the movies we had just seen. My twin friends competed with each other as to who better mimicked the actions or speaking styles of the main actors.

That way, we must have seen all the major movies, some Indian, some Italian but mostly English movies that came to Ethiopia in those days. These included classic English movies of the 60s and 70s,[35] and we would know the names of the major actors in each film by heart; and we took some pride in that. There were also famous Indian movies like *Waqt* and *Mother India* which impressed our young hearts for a long time to come; we could still sing the songs[36] in these films with our own twists, of course.

In any event, our Thursday and Friday adventures in downtown Addis were not risk-free. I remember one day, as we were shuttling on foot from one cinema to the other to decide which movies to see, our school director was passing by in his car; and he saw us. We had put on our school uniform and, of course, the director recognized the twins immediately; something that would always put me at a disadvantage.

But, before he could park and get out of his car, we had disappeared into the neighborhoods - for the time being. Eventually though, this and other multiple 'crimes' by the twins resulted in their expulsion from school at the end of the 11th grade. I was spared but was left devastated without my twin friends at school. Yes, of course, we found ways of seeing each other outside school, but it wasn't the same.

Needless to say, none of us made it to college after high school that year. But, thanks to all the films we had seen, our colloquial English had improved a great deal. In fact, to this date, my twin friends speak English (or Amharic for that matter) like John Wayne, which is with a bent neck and twisted mouth. I didn't go that far; I had already gone far enough compared to what my childhood was like in Gore where I saw no films or listened to no English songs.

---

35 Like The Graduate; The Robe; The Great Escape; Spartacus; The Guns of Navarone; Taras Bulba; Lawrence of Arabia; The Godfather; Goldfinger; Bonnie and Clyde; The Three Musketeers; Dr. Zhivago; Patton; Kramer vs. Kramer; Love Story; Easy Rider; Rio Grande; Butch Cassidy; Guess Who is Coming to Dinner; The Thief of Baghdad; It is a Mad, Mad World and on and on and on.

36 Remember 'Aage Bhi Jaane Na Tu' in Waqt; 'Beete Re Bhaiya' in Mother India?

As if the films were not enough, we pursued western music with vengeance. Our main source, once again, was the cinemas. Films would usually begin at noon, but we were already in our seats at 10:45 am; the time in between was set for music. I never knew why, but all cinemas played English songs of the 1960s and 70s.[37] So, with one stone, our 50 cents, we enjoyed the songs and the movies. The musicians' names were like household names for us, and we knew them and all the lyrics by heart; and we still listen to them - when we are not singing them.

Of course, we listened to Amharic songs too, but there were no Amharic movies to see at the time. Beautiful, now classic, songs by Tilahun Gessese, Alemayehu Eshete, Mahamud Ahmed, Menelik Wosinachew, Bezunesh Bekele, Assefa Abate, Ketema Mekonnen, and Girma Beyene were the attractions at the time; they also lasted with us forever.

However, for reasons that must have had to do with youth and curiosity and the perceived social status that came with it, we were attracted more to western values, in general, and music and films, in particular.

My twin friends were also die-hard soccer fans and, in fact, in spite of their short height, played for San George's football team; probably the oldest and best team in the country. I, of course, used to play soccer in Gore. But my twin friends in Addis kept on reminding me that I was better-off watching them play than play myself; and, reluctantly, I had no choice but to oblige.

Sure enough, I became a fan of their club and constantly watched them play at Haile Selassie I Stadium (later Addis Ababa Stadium.) These were occasions that I enjoyed so much that I still remember some characters among the San George's fans who stood out. In those days, it was a different breed of

---

37 These usually included mostly songs like Inner City Blues; I Heard It Through The Grapevine; Don't Let Me Down; The House of The Rising Sun; Hit The Road Jack; Bridge Over Troubled Waters; Make Me Yours; I say a Little Prayer; What's Going On?; The Horse; Closed For The Season; Proud Marry; Can't Buy Me Love; You Can't Hurry Love; Some Day We'll be Together etc. etc.etc.

people who frequented the stadium; fans who behaved as if it was built for their exclusive pleasure. The jokes which flew around, usually at the expense of fellow fans, were hilarious. We were addicted!

So, all along, and thanks mostly to my twin friends, I was slowly adding to my vitae of an adventurous tree-climbing rural town kid, an urban movie-going teenager hooked to Motown music and Addis Ababa Stadium. Thereby, my comfort zone was slowly being defined: a rural identity with an urban twist. But still, Gore was where I laid a strong foundation that never cracked, as I was to find out later in life.

Of course, needless to say, my friends and I failed the Ethiopian School Leaving Certificate Examination (ESLCE). We did not understand the impact nor did we care at the time. And, unlike my brother Miemen, I was not invited to collect my high school certificate from the emperor. No problem, we believed we were not meant to be 'university material' in the first place.

In fact, the day we heard that we failed the exams, we went to a local *tej*[38]house called *Geftir*[39]and got drunk which, for me, was a first. It was a kind of celebration that we were spared from this frightening thing called 'college.'

Today, over fifty years later, nothing has really changed in our friendship. I still have difficulties telling who was who. Or, I would still be able to ignite a quarrel between them, sit back and watch, and have the time of my life.

But, for all the notoriety and the top-dog outlook they were known for, my twin friends were honest and I have yet to hear them lie, not even in self defense - a quality I and most people I know do not have.

They were not perfect either. Although I have hundreds of appointments with them over the years, I do not remember a single one to which they came on time. I also do

---

38   Tej is a favorite local wine in Ethiopia made of honey.
39   'Geftir' is an Amharic word that loosely translates into English as 'push to cause a fall.'

not remember a day when they had said they were sorry or apologized for a mistake.

But then, our friendship did not require such minor details. In our friendship, all misdeeds 'cured' themselves. End of story!

*****

High school was not a total waste for me, though.[40] Two subjects, Geography and English, had interested me at high school mostly due to our two Indian teachers Mr. Rodericks and Mr. Miller, respectively. That was in the 11th grade, and I wanted to do well in class for no other reason than to impress them - because I liked them.

Now, Mr. Rodericks probably was one of the most gifted teachers I ever knew. To begin with, within a couple of days of classes, he knew each one of us by name boosting the morale of his students - something which was a bit unusual in those days. He also came to class prepared and spoke very clearly and loudly. Hence, he made his lectures very easy and enjoyable to his students.

To impress him, whenever I could escape my twin friends, I would go to the American Library which was only a ten-minute walk from my house. There, I would read nothing but the atlases and globes that fascinated me beyond description. I gazed at the location of cities, especially those located at sea or ocean sides, for hours and fantasized the days I might go there. I located Honolulu, Hawaii, and wondered what my Peace Corps teacher Ash was doing at the time; naively, I thought he still lived there.

In the process, I studied not only the locations but also almost all capital cities of the world by heart. I could also draw the maps of the continents, especially Africa, and identify the location of each capital city. Unlike most of my friends, it was a skill I that had and was proud of, and I even showed off once in a while.

---

[40] I actually believe that education, and indeed one's fate, is determined at the high school level.

But, alas, all my interest in geography faded away when Mr. Rodericks left for South Africa after just a year's stay in Ethiopia as my geography teacher. Typical of a high school student, it was a classic case of abandoning a subject they liked - only because the teacher left the school!

So, with Mr. Rodericks gone, all my attention in the 12th grade was solely in the English language as a subject. Our teacher, Mr. Miller, was an Indian with British citizenship. Sure enough, although he looked like an Indian, his behavior and his English accent was very much British. He constantly and proudly reminded us that he spoke the 'Queen's English' which, whatever that meant, successfully made a lot of impression on us.

Mr. Miller, too, was a very good English teacher and was so confident of his abilities that he sounded a bit cocky at times. He was particularly upset when we mispronounced words, something which was very common at the time, and probably still is among many Ethiopians. '*Ask*', he would advise us with irritation, '*before you decapitate a word!*' None of us, of course, understood this piece of advice.

In any case, during our Friday classes, Mr. Miller would assign us a topic to write a composition on, which he would mark and bring to our Monday classes. I remember he was merciless when it came to marking our compositions.

One Friday he walked into the classroom with a mischievous smile, which was not uncommon with him. So, we didn't make much of it until he announced that he would not assign us a topic for the next composition. Instead, he said, he would allow us to choose our own topics; and no limits on the number of pages either. As we all froze with these instructions, he left the classroom with the same mischievous smile that he had when he walked in.

Ah! This is my chance to impress him, I decided. So, I went home and for the entire weekend I wrote a six-page composition about 'love.' It did not matter that 'love' was something I knew nothing about, save some meaningless childhood infatuations like all boys my age had.

In any event, before I submitted the final draft to Mr. Miller on the following Monday, I must have written and re-written the composition half a dozen times. I made sure that I wrote it with my best handwriting and that I used bombastic words - all to impress Mr. Miller.

When I submitted the composition, I was sure not only that he would give me the highest grade but that he would also single out my composition as the best in the class, and to be replicated. Come Monday class, when it was time to get our marked compositions back, my confidence had reached its height.

Now, Mr. Miller had the habit of returning our compositions according to the grade orders; in other words, the best ones were returned first - while everybody watched! So, I missed the first two, three, and four... and I was beginning to sweat. Finally, my composition was returned to me as 'second from last' with a grade of three out of ten; and I was unmoving!

My entire six-page composition was marked with red ink clearly showing the frequency of the mistakes I had made – to the degree that I didn't even recognize my own handwriting. At the bottom of the last page Mr. Miller had written, still in red and in capital letters, 'MESERET, DO NOT TRY TO BE TOO SMART!!' Clearly, he was not impressed, and I had failed with an exclamation mark. Such an embarrassment in front of my classmates was the last thing in my mind.

I do not remember how I survived what I thought was an assault by my own 'favorite' teacher. But, I went home unconvinced; with a broken heart, and quite a bit of boyish anger. My favorable outlook for Mr. Miller disappeared in no time. I told to whoever would listen to me that I had been wronged by an Indian teacher. I angrily argued that all Indian teachers would have to be kicked out of the country and be replaced by Ethiopian teachers. My family tried to cool me down a bit, but I didn't give them the chance.

Eventually, over the course of the week when things settled down a bit, I looked at Mr. Miller's red markings more closely.

I found out that he was actually right. To begin with, love was nothing I knew about and it showed that I did not know what I was writing about. More importantly, in my effort to impress him, I had literally copied what I thought were difficult words from a dictionary and put them where they did not belong, or where they did not make any sense in my composition. In modern day language, it was 'cut and paste.'

True enough, all the red markings that he put on my composition represented mistakes. Mr. Miller was absolutely right; I was just trying to be too smart.

Not that I never repeated the mistake, it was nevertheless the very first main life lesson I learnt!

The young man from Gojam

So, having failed the college entrance exam at a very young age, our group, including my twin friends who had failed the exam in another high school, went looking for jobs. Luck, or lack of it, has it that all of us, including my twin friends, were offered a job in one government office. Normally, no one in his right mind would hire a bunch of kids who failed to pass the high school leaving examination and showed very little, if any, maturity. But, it was a newly established government organization, a Mapping Institute, and they took all of us - as in a kitchen sink!

There, I met and became good friends with more young people.[41]One of them was Ayalew Admassu; a young man from Debre Markos, Gojam, in Northern Ethiopia. He was tall, shy and usually kept to himself. He was a little bit older but much more mature than us; he also came from a 'province', which gave my twin friends the license to harass him. It was like my favorite Chicago columnist, Mike Royko, would say: *When a chicken (Ayalew) walks into its den, what is a self-respecting fox (the twins) supposed to do?'*

---

41 Alemayehu Kebede, Mengistu Merkebu, Anteneh Belay, Rama Teklemariam, Getachew Gebre- to mention but few.

Having failed the college entrance exam, a Mapping Institute took us all. Standing: myself (second from left), the twins Banjaw (third from left) and Bezuayehu (far right) - or the other way round - Addis Ababa, 1969

So, no sooner had we been hired and stored in one large hall than my twin friends started terrorizing poor Ayalew. This would take place in many ways, but their favorite was the one in which one of them would play the role of an 'actor', and the other, the 'audience.' The actor would pick a 'weak' point which Ayalew may have, like his distinctly rural Amharic accent and tone, and start mimicking him.

The audience would laugh his heart out - all in the face of poor Ayalew.

A few minutes later the twins would change roles and with a new topic, like the way he walked or dressed, made Ayalew hate the day he came to Addis. I admit, I was part of this drama, albeit as an extended audience, since I couldn't but laugh at some of the cruel jokes the twins were making at the expense of poor Ayalew.

It wasn't just Ayalew who was the victim of the twin's cruel jokes. During our first six-months at the Mapping Institute, three highly trained and disciplined officers from the Ethiopian Army joined us to be trained as surveyors. One of them was a young man called Sergeant Tamiru. The first day they came to the Institute, while two of them wore civilian clothes, Sergeant Tamiru showed up in his full military uniform with his dark sunglasses on; a mistake he would soon find out and regret.

Now, Sergeant Tamiru was a little bit darker than most of us in his facial color complexion. So, the twins without bothering to know who he was, had one brief look at him, looked at each other quickly and, almost in unison, gave him a new name: Ojukwu.[42] Before Sergeant Tamiru could do anything about it, the entire group of rowdy teenagers, including myself, had started calling him by his new name. When the Sergeant found out that even our manager was calling him by his new name, he gave up.

But that was not the end of his misery. Sergeant Tamiru, perhaps in his early 30s at the time, made another big mistake: he told us he was married. Now, for most of us including the twins, he was the first married person we have come to know close-up. So, partly out of boyhood curiosity and partly out of jealousy, the twins wanted to know about his sex life - in detail! Of course, we all wanted to hear too.

So, almost every morning when Sergeant Tamiru walked into our common office, one of the twins would ask him if he had sex with his wife the previous night. The Sergeant, by now all of us waiting to hear the answer, would first blush and then respond mostly positively - which, for some reason, excited us all.

The twins would not stop there. Before the Sergeant recovered from the embarrassment of the first question, the next question would be about how often he had sex with his wife on a weekly basis, and on and on and on. And, to the chagrin of the Sergeant, we all listened to his responses with our mouths open.

---

42   Colonel Odumegwu Ojukwu, an Igbo, declared Biafra's independence from Nigeria in 1967 which prompted the bloody Nigeria-Biafra war.

When I think about it now, we were lucky that Sergeant Tamiru, an *arada*[43] in his own way, took it lightly. When exhausted with the questions, he would simply stare at the floor and shake his head.

Much later in life I ran into Sergeant Tamiru one morning. He had retired from the army, with the rank of a lieutenant, and was working as a security guard in one of the landmark buildings in Addis Ababa. Of course, he remembered the twins and, to my surprise, he told me he missed them!

*****

Back to Ayalew, finding himself in the midst of young men from the center of Addis Ababa, he was besieged. He observed a lot, but spoke very little; he wouldn't have gotten the chance anyway. So, one day, out of the blue, he came to me and started a conversation.

Ayalew: *Listen, Meseret, I want to advise you something.*
Meseret: *What about?*
Ayalew: *I have been watching you for a while. I do not think you belong here, and these twins are no good for you.*
Meseret: *Careful, you are talking about my best friends; and what do you mean I do not belong here?*
Ayalew: *I tell you I have been watching you guys, and the twins are up to no good. You are just too young to be working; you should continue your studies.*
Meseret: *Well, I did not pass the college entrance exam.*
Ayalew: *Ok, but didn't you say all you needed to go to the university was a 'B' in one of the compulsory subjects?*
Meseret: *Yes.*
Ayalew: *So why don't you register to take the exam for one of the compulsory subjects again. If you manage to get a 'B,' you are in college. I am going to do the same thing, and I will be happy to let you know when I go to register for the exams.*

---

43 Unlike the prevailing view, an 'arada' in my view is a person who is not excited easily; has quite a lot of skills but not in a hurry to show-off; knows his way around; easy going and always ready to help and share.

At first, I resisted Ayalew's advice, and believed he was doing it because he just did not like the twins. I also figured I was content where I was, a place where one was required to show little or no effort, and collect a salary. Besides, my twin friends, with a much less impressive college entrance exam results than mine, had given their approval that college was not meant for us. Or, we were not meant for college.

Then, I talked to my brother Miemen, who had come home on a vacation from his studies in Holland at the time, and he convinced me to give it a try. With all the goodies he had brought me from Holland, including a manual record player with one of Simon and Garfunkel's songs, *El Condor Pasa*, I would not and could not ignore my brother's suggestion.

In those days, in addition to two or more optional subjects, one was required to pass in all three compulsory subjects (Amharic, English and mathematics) to make it to Haile Selassie University; and, I had failed in Amharic. I had obtained a 'C' in English, a 'C' in mathematics and a 'D' in Amharic.

So, in order to make it to the university, I either had to improve the 'C' to 'B' in English or the 'D to 'C' in Amharic. I opted for the former because I figured, with all the English movies that I had seen, I might just stand a better chance.

My colleagues, the twins included, laughed at the idea, but the young man from Gojam persisted. So, I went along and registered and re-took the exam in English. And, to my surprise, I got a 'B' and ended up joining the university in September 1969; and so did my friend from Gojam who went to Gondar University in Northern Ethiopia.[44]

Thanks to Ayalew, I now became a very reluctant university student, with the minimum possible passing grade and enthusiasm.

---

44 Ayalew went on to receive his bachelor's degree in Public Health from Gondar University and his master's degree from Tulane University. Twenty eight years later in 1997, when I had to get the support for a study from the Ethiopian Ministry of Health, it was Ayalew who I had to speak to; it was the first time I had seen him since he gave me the life-changing advice in 1969.

Adulthood and Relationships

College years

Still up over the Mediterranean Sea flying north, my thoughts shifted to my years at Haile Selassie I University (HSIU).[45] I had joined the university at age 19 during the 1969/70 academic year and graduated with my first degree in English Literature eight years later at age 27, during the 1976/77 academic year. Due to the political upheaval, it was not uncommon in those days to spend 8 to 12 years to achieve one's first degree.

Initially, my thoughts went to the 1969/70 academic year when I first joined Haile Selassie I University. The previous three high school years in Addis had qualified me as an eligible young man to join the elite of the freshman lot. The freedom and the status associated with being a university student must have boosted my morale to the point where I may have become a bit cocky.

As our first few days in college were winding down, one thing started to bother me. Up until I finished high school at age 18, my official name was Meseret Kidanu. That was what my father called me at birth and, when it was time for me to start school at age five, it was the name my father used to register me.

Now, there was nothing wrong with the name except that it was predominantly used for females, at least in those days. I was totally oblivious to this fact until I got to college. Then, it started to bother me, and a series of incidents did not help either.

First, at age 19, I was just beginning to be seriously interested in girls. The problem, however, was that I was ashamed to tell them that my name was 'Meseret'- a girl's name. I could not remember how they reacted or if it made any

---

45   It started out as University College of Addis Ababa (1950 to 1962); and then it was re-named Haile Selassie I University (1962 to 1975); and later changed by the Dergue to Addis Ababa University (1975 to present).

difference but, at that age, I was petrified to introduce myself to girls mostly because of my 'feminine' name.

Then, at the beginning of my freshman year, I could not find my name on the list of students assigned to the dormitories on campus. I read each name one by one, and my name was nowhere to be found. So, frustrated, I went to the registrar's office and complained that I wasn't able to find my name on the list. The Registrar asked my name, looked at some papers and, with a smile I did not like, told me that my name appeared on a separate list for female students. I had been assigned to a girls' dormitory, and I have had it! I decided to change my name immediately.

The next day, without consulting anybody, I went to the courts and demanded that my name be changed. At first, the judge made fun of my request, and people in the courtroom laughed at my expense. Then he saw I wasn't laughing and, after enquiring as to why I wanted to change my name and listening to my answers - to which he was not convinced - asked me what name I would like to be called by instead. He put me on the spot, because I hadn't gone to the court prepared with an alternative name.

After a few blank moments, I remembered my older brother Miemen had another name, 'Aklilu'[46] which one of our maternal aunts, Etagu, used to call him by. So, I told the judge that I wanted to be called 'Aklilu'; it was a pattern of taking away something from my brother that endured for a long time to come.

The judge told me that I could change my first name, but not my second name that would remain 'Kidanu', because it belonged to my father. I agreed, since I did not intend to or could not change my father's name in the first place. After some paper work, which took a few weeks, and sometime in my early freshman year, my name was officially changed to

---

46 Usually in our family, children had multiple names used by different family members. My other names were mostly nick names not appropriate for official documents.

'Aklilu Kidanu.' All relevant documents in college adopted my new name.

My friends found out in due course. Some accepted the change; some laughed at me and kept on calling me by my old name to tease me. As long as they were not girls, it did not matter to me.

But, subsequently, I had mixed feelings about the whole thing. On one hand, I was happy that I could now interact with girls without having to worry about my name; although it did not necessarily make a lot of difference regarding success. On the other hand, especially as I got older, I felt bad that I changed the name that my father gave me at birth. He may have had a reason to call me 'Meseret' which, when loosely translated into English, means 'the foundation.'

My father never asked me why I changed my name nor did he get stuck with my old name. Within a few days, he was already calling me by my new name; he probably was among the first ones to do so. As to my brother Miemen whose extra name I stole, I did not care how he felt. In fact, I had always enjoyed taking anything that belonged to him, when I could. He did not care either, and started to use my new name. Half of my die-hard family members and boyhood friends still call me 'Meseret', sometimes just to indicate to me that I may have made a mistake by changing my name without at least consulting them.

Now, that I am a married man, it is fine with me by whatever name I am called. In fact, I might go back to my original name one day and hope it would not be the same judge who had fun at my expense while formally changing my original name decades ago!!

*****

Anyway, in those days, freshmen would be welcome to campus at Haile Selassie I University with a freshman party organized by the students' union. I remember the one for us was held during the first week of the 1969/70 academic year.

Freshman year at Haile Selassie I University, with my friend Tewodros Gebre Michael (right). Sidist Kilo campus, 1969/70 academic year

It was an afternoon to evening party conducted at Christmas Hall that also doubled as a dining hall as well as the main venue for political rallies; and everybody was invited. The band was the Royal Imperial Guard, and the lead singer was the renowned Tilahun Gessese. It was the perfect opportunity to meet new and old students, and, if lucky, maybe some girls too.

In those days, being one of the few universities in the country, students came from all over the country to join Haile Selassie University. Those who came from outside Addis would try and associate with us, urbanites, and learn a few tricks about how to dance, dress or meet girls. But, unbeknownst to them, we would divide up the female students amongst ourselves. The problem was that there was one female student for about twenty male students. Even that would be true only if the older people with jobs, who to our chagrin drove into campus in cars, would save some for us.

So, some of us in desperation, would turn our attention either to the nearby Empress Menen School or Nazreth School - both girls' schools where we had a better chance, or so we thought. Even a better bet for many of us was the chess sets at the famous campus café where we spent an untold amount of hours playing or watching others play chess; with loud music all over the place as background.

I remember the day when we spent the whole night competing with each other and finally just watching quietly for hours when the final two played till dawn. Once we determined the winner, we went directly to the dining hall for breakfast and continued arguing about what move should have been made or not. [47] Those were the good old days!!

*****

In any case, I started my concentration in English Literature, with philosophy as a minor, beginning in my second year; and one of my closest friends, Tsegaye Beru, joined me. In our time, we had till our second year before we declared our majors. So, given all the English films I had seen, I thought English Literature was an easy subject to pursue for my degree; but I was dead wrong.

On the other hand, someone had also told me that if I really wanted to be 'literate', I would study literature; he was, in my view, dead right.

As English majors, we had to read and critique numerous English and American novels[48] in short periods of time; it was a killer. Our teachers were mostly British, and they were really good. Also, with Dr. Hailu Araya at the helm, we read a few West African novels including *Things Fall Apart* and *The Arrow of God* by Chinwa Achebe; and a series of poems and plays by a Nobel Prize for Literature winner (1986), Wole Soyinka.

---

47 One thing I have always wanted to say about chess was that it should be given as a required course at the high school level. Not only because of its recreational values but also as a game that teaches students how to think three, four steps ahead; anticipating what the opponent would think. This helps not only in the game but also in future real life decision making.

48 Classic works like Wuthering Heights; Great Expectation; Emma; The Adventures of Huckleberry Finn; The Scarlet Letter; The Canterbury Tales; Robinson Crusoe; For Whom the Bell Tolls; Pride and Prejudice; Animal Farm; The Grapes of Wrath; Gulliver's Travels; A Tale of Two Cities; The Sun Also Rises; The Merchant of Venice etc. etc. etc.

Eventually, I came to enjoy literature immensely. My thesis advisor was Dr. Hailu Araya, who had just returned from abroad, and who successfully guided me through my bachelor's thesis[49] and my graduation. For a lukewarm student like me, he did a great job.

Also, as a minor in philosophy, I took classes that introduced me to logical thinking for the first time.

Man is an animal,
Kebede is a man,
Therefore, Kebede is an animal.

It made perfect sense to me. Unlike what I was told by my moral teacher way back in Gore, it was simple and clear - no abstractions, no complications.

In any case, our main philosophy teacher at the time was Professor Claude Sumner, a Canadian Jesuit who must have been at Addis Ababa University forever. He also authored, among many others, the book 'The Philosophy of Man.' I remember Professor Sumner liked to talk about Ethiopian philosophers like Zera Yakob. I also remember his humor, his tall and grandfatherly figure and his perfect English - with distinct French accent.

One other philosophy teacher in those days was Dr. Fouyas, a Greek, whose older brother was the Patriarch of the Greek Orthodox Church in Addis Ababa at the time. Dr. Fouyas, always with a boyish smiling round face, was supposed to teach us about the connection between politics and philosophy. But, he ended up talking mostly about Athens and its numerous attractions, like the Acropolis, that he argued we must see one day.[50]He also took particular pleasure and pride in impressing us about his older brother, which was fine with me since I did the same thing all the time.

---

49 My Bachelor's thesis was on symbolism in the West African literature.
50 Dr. Fouyas was right; much later in life I took my immediate family to Athens and concurred with his adorations of his city.

Dr. Fouyas was also genuinely proud that he was part of a culture and history that produced so much knowledge, thanks to his fellow citizens like Aristotle, Diogenes and Socrates, and presented it to the rest of the world. I had read some of the works of these philosophers and was impressed that Dr. Fouyas had so much knowledge about them.

So, one evening he kindly invited us, about ten philosophy minors, to dinner at his residence near our campus, which was also the residence of his older brother, the Patriarch. We sat around a huge but elegant wooden table in an even more elegantly decorated room which, to us poor university students, looked like a mini-palace. As we were eating a combination of strictly Greek dishes, Dr. Fouyas kept on telling us that every head of state who visited Ethiopia had eaten at the same table, as the guest of his brother. I wondered which world leaders had sat on the same chair I was sitting on. I felt strange and a bit uncomfortable.

In any case, for those of us who were used to eating our meals at Christmas Hall of Sidist Kilo Campus, not only was this welcome departure in quality of food but also a boost to our moral. We were also impressed by the importance of the Greek Orthodox Church in world politics, at least according to our professor.

Then there was one other professor I always remember, Professor Andreas Eshete, who sometime during the 1973/74 academic year, was back in Ethiopia teaching a course on philosophy, 'Marxian Thoughts', I think it was. In any case, that was what the course guide indicated. And so we knew only that much about the person and the subject.

Now, before classes started in September, we, a group of cocky and boisterous third-year students, had seen a new young man on campus. Little did we know or suspect that he was going to bring us down to earth one day. Without knowing who he was and given his young looks, afro-hair style and bell-bottom trousers with black turtleneck sweater, we had concluded that he was just another new freshman we had never seen before. In fact, we wondered what planet this young man, who out-did us in every way, showed up from; and we were a bit jealous too.

So, when it was the first class time, we were all in the classroom waiting for Professor Andreas to show up, as indicated in the course guide. Instead, the young Afro-man who we saw on campus came in and walked directly to the blackboard. I thought he was one of those students, usually from outside Addis, who thought they were collecting favors by cleaning the blackboard before the professors arrived.

Well, sure enough, the young man cleaned the blackboard, picked a piece of chalk from the table and started writing in large letters: *ANDREAS ESHETE!* Then he turned around, faced us squarely, and said, *'That is my name!'*

If there was a hole beneath my chair to swallow me, I would have been more than happy to oblige! Then, with painful humiliation, I turned around to look at my friends and saw that they were equally dumbfounded; wide open eyes and jaws dropping in awe.

Then, while we were still trying to recover and as if he knew about our predicament, the professor started a series of lectures that I thought were the best, both in style and substance, which I was ever lucky enough to attend.

I had learnt my lessons the hard way: never to underestimate someone, especially by the looks, again!

*****

Other than our studies, there was also life outside the university's Sidist Kilo campus for those who dared. Some of us explored this life once in a while.

So, one Friday evening, our core group decided to go to a night club which was a thirty-minute walking distance from campus; nothing new since we have done it many times before. But this time, there was this guy[51] who came to the university from Gondar, a regional town, and he wanted to tag along. He

---

51 He would kill me if I mentioned his name; he is now a successful businessman in Addis.

took pleasure in sticking with us, the urban elites, and learn a few tricks in the process.

When we got to the club, most of us were interested in the music and dance. We danced our hearts out, competed with each other and didn't even need female partners. Not this guy who tagged along; he was attracted to one of the girls who worked at the night club. That, for all we knew, might have been his mission in the first place. We didn't see him try, but he felt he didn't impress her with his charm at all.

So, against our advice, he decided to walk back to campus all by himself, refresh, and come back to the nightclub and try his luck again. By the time he came back an hour later, with a borrowed jacket and plenty of cheap perfumes on, the girl had left with another man. Our friend looked pitiful, but we laughed mercilessly all the way back to campus. Our dejected friend from Gondar did not utter a single word; it must have been a long walk back to campus for him. Once in a while I would look at him and tell him he had at least tried his best!

On another occasion, sometime between our second and third years, a group of us decided to camp a weekend at *Sodere*, a hot spring bath and swimming resort about 120 kilometers East of Addis Ababa. We brought our tents, sleeping bags and other gears. We drove in two small cars, a Fiat 127 and a Renault 4, on a Friday afternoon. When we got there we looked for an appropriate location and erected our tents, settled, and started to think about food. One of us suggested that we got a goat from one of the surrounding villages and grilled or roasted it for dinner. The idea, in principle, sounded appetizing.

So, good idea, we all agreed, and four of us set out in the Renault 4 to the local village looking for a goat. One of us was a young British friend of ours, Michael Miller, who had come to the country about a year earlier to set up Oxfam UK. In any case, we drove uphill to a small village where we found a goat. After a lot of pretty bad negotiation skills, we purchased the goat.

Now, a Renault 4 doesn't have a roof rack or a trunk, a fact that did not dawn upon any one of us till then. Even if it did, the alternate car we had was a Fait 127, a much smaller car than the Renault 4. So, we had to put the goat inside the car in between the two of us who were sitting at the back seats. Our friend Asfaw was driving and Michael was sitting in the passenger's seat. Myself and one of our friends, Daniel, were sitting in the back seats with the goat in between us.

So far so good; but the drive back to Sodere was down hill. So, once in a while Asfaw would hit the brakes slowly and the goat would lean forward just a little bit; and come back to its place. But, at one point, for reasons not clear to us, Asfaw hit the brakes real hard, and the goat dived forward right into the front space between Asfaw and Michael - with its four legs pointing upwards, and kicking frantically.

Asfaw, not sure what to do, kept on driving.

The chaos and laughter that followed was painful. In fact Michael was laughing so hard that we thought he would choke to death. For an Eton[52] educated young man from England, being in the same car with an animal, much less with a goat turned upside down and kicking, was more than he could take. He would later say he would never forget this event; neither would we.

Finally we got to Sodere, and proudly presented the goat to the rest of the group; some of us were still laughing. The group congratulated us on a job well done, and we immediately started to plan how we were going to skin and roast the goat.

There was this guy from Somalia, Ahmed, a rather stubborn guy who had befriended us through Michael, who insisted that he would do it if he got some help from us. The tasks, he explained, were simple: skin the goat, build a fire, put the goat in a rotisserie, and cook. Sounded easy enough, and no one raised objections.

But, as we all watched in horror, our Somali friend failed miserably in all these tasks: when skinning the goat, he left half of the meat on the skin to begin with; then he had the makeshift rotisserie (a metal pipe which he stole from a nearby construction site) melt and spoil the meat. Whatever was left

---

52   A very prestigious school in England.

after our Somali friend was done was not something fit to see much less eat. We threw the entire meat away after a couple of uneasy bites.

All the commotion, the excitement, and the money we spent to buy the goat went down the drain; and we ended up eating our dinner in a nearby restaurant at the resort - outside our financial plan. Some of us, not always jokingly, threatened to send Ahmed back to Somalia. He didn't even show an iota of remorse, much less apologize; nothing new, since none of us would have done differently.

As if that was not bad enough, all along, the treasurer of our trip, Teddy, had drifted away and found a group of vacationers playing cards for money by the poolside. He would tell us; first he sat and watched, then he started playing, and eventually lost all our money. None of us had enough extra money to sustain us the two nights that we had planned to spend at the resort. After the first night, we borrowed money from the same people who Teddy lost our money to, and headed back to Addis.

Again, of course, true to the Ethiopian tradition of the time, nobody admitted mistakes.

*****

However, as a student at Haile Selassie I University in the early 70's, politics must have been the most profound experience of all. In my view, between 1970 and 1974, the student body was divided into three distinct political/social groups: the Revolutionaries (or, the *Revos*), the Saboteurs (or, the *Sabus*) and the *Jollies*.

The *Revos* were divided into two groups; the leadership and the cadres or the agitators. The leadership was a group of committed and energetic young people who sacrificed a lot in life and spent several years in prison for what they believed in. I had nothing but a lot of respect and admiration for them.

The cadres, however, were a different breed of people. They carried Mao's Red Book in one hand and a bunch of revolutionary slogans in the other; and *khat*, always conspicuously visible, was their trademark. They were the agitators but, when push came to shove, they were nowhere to be seen; they did not want to sacrifice in any form. They believed in labeling, intimidating and bullying anybody who did not agree with their views.

I remember one day a group of us were standing outside the Arts Building of *Sidist* Kilo campus waiting for the next class to begin. A couple of cadres walked toward us and, all of a sudden, one of them asked if any one of us knew what 'dialectical materialism' was all about.

It so happened that none of us knew the answer. Then, a barrage of insults and intimidation descended upon us. One of the cadres went as far as saying that we had no business being on campus if we did not know what 'dialectical materialism' was. If I had the courage, I would have asked the cadre to tell us about it rather than insulting us. It probably would not have made a difference!

Then, there were the *Sabus*. The *Sabus* carried books in one hand a *gabi [a traditional blanket made of cotton]* in the other. They were bent on finishing school and getting a job - no matter what. They were not interested in campus politics or student union meetings. Instead, they studied day and night; and missed no classes. And, they never complied with the resolutions of the students' union to boycott classes or to withdraw from campus because this or that student demand was not met.

For this, the *Sabus* suffered the most. They were despised, stigmatized, intimidated, bullied and labeled 'saboteurs' - a harsh label for young people whose only crime was to want to finish their studies. I know many so-called saboteurs who, more than forty years later, are still scarred from the experience.

Then, there were the *Jollies*. The *Jollies* (and I was one of them) always had an album in one hand and chess set in the other. With the Afro hairstyle and 32-inch bell-bottom trousers as their trademark, life for them was music first, chess second, and parties third. Classes? What classes?

The *Jollies* actually were supportive, albeit lukewarmly, of the changes that the *Revos* were instigating, and tried to understand their arguments. The *Jollies* agreed that land should belong to the tiller or that the Emperor had stayed in power for too long. They just did not appreciate the tactics that the *Revos* and their cadres applied to attract followers, which was mostly through bullying, ridiculing and intimidating the student population.

The cadres had mixed feelings about the *Jollies*. On one hand, they hated them because they thought the *Jollies* were having fun while they weren't; or the *Jollies* never took their revolutionary slogans seriously. On the other hand, they liked them because, should there be a students' union resolution to withdraw, the *Jollies* would be the first people to line up to complete the withdrawal forms - for their own reasons.

I also suspect that the occasional contributions the *Jollies* made - by hook or by crook - for cigarettes and *khat* had positive impact on sustaining uneasy truce between the *Jollies* and the cadres.

*****

In any event, whenever we withdrew from campus upon the instigation of the *Revos*, for our core group which included Tsegaye, Daniel, Teddy and myself, The Lion (aka Leon) Bar, located near the train station and the National Theatre in Addis, was the refuge. When I think about it, we owe this bar a lot.

First, every time the university students' union decided that we should withdraw from campus for one reason or another, our destination was the Lion Bar. The half-dark, eerie and smelly basement at the Lion Bar was the perfect location for us to hide.

Second, at the basement, there were three billiard tables, two pool tables and two table tennis tables. There were no chess sets, but there was enough to keep us busy. Some of us developed the skills and the addiction to playing billiards, sometimes for money.

Third, with an affordable restaurant specializing in pasta dishes, the Lion Bar was the perfect place for us to camp from morning to night, and every day except on Sundays. It was not uncommon for us to stay inside the basement without having to see the daylight or breathe fresh air for stretches of hours.

But, alas, the security police, tipped by a disgruntled client of the bar, found out about young university students spending a lot of time in the basement. One day, when none of our core group members was present by pure coincidence, the security police raided and rounded-up everybody in the basement. They arrested many and executed a couple of young men, including the young son of the owner of the bar, in broad daylight; we escaped but stayed away from the Lion Bar for good.

It wasn't until much later one day in the early 2000s that I went back to the Lion Bar, and down to the basement, only to come out with tears in my eyes triggered by the smell and the memories of the 1970s.

My American friend

Still on the Alitalia plane flying north, my thoughts then drifted to one of the persons who affected my life significantly. It was Richard Caulk who, at the time, was Professor of Ethiopian History at Haile Selassie I University. I met Richard in 1972 at the Ghion Hotel swimming pool in Addis Ababa. We were both doing the back- stroke in the opposite direction, and we collided head-on. I swam to a corner and started evaluating the pain in my head. A few minutes later Richard, who was an ardent and expert swimmer, came to me and apologized for what happened.

I came to know that Richard, an American of about 35 years, had finished his Ph.D. (From School of Oriental and African Studies, SOAS, in the United Kingdom) and was a professor of history, specializing in Menelik II, at Haile Selassie I University. And I was, about 22, a second year English literature student; and we connected.

Richard was a pleasure to be with. He was meticulous, brilliant with a lot of humor and a great taste for good food and wine. He immediately realized that I was not a brilliant student by any stretch of imagination, but that I had my own strong points: some charm and social skills, and the potential to be good in the English language.

Three things he told me over the years remained in me forever:

> *'It is not enough just to be charming.'*
> *'Nothing impressed Americans more than a non-native who spoke good English.'*
> *'You will never regret being to as many places/countries as possible.'*

True enough, although I may have had some strong social skills, I never was a good hardworking student, much less the scholarly type which Richard was. It had taken me three long semesters to get out of the academic probation that I got into as a freshman! Richard had read me very well, and he worked on my strong points.

He introduced me to the small American and English expatriates living in Addis Ababa, like Mrs. Innes Marshall, editor of Haile Selassie I University Press at the time; the lady who later would introduce me to Signora Steganini at the Italian school; and to Michael Miller who later joined our core group of university friends.

I remember Richard encouraged me to read as many books as possible, loud and in front of a mirror when I was alone at home. He made me translate Amharic history books like *Yetarik Mastawesha* [*Remembrance of History*] by *Dejazmatch Kebede Tessema,* into English.[53] The length of the books killed me, but it also improved my English and my confidence to speak it immensely; in hindsight, I believe he did it on purpose.

---

53 This was for Richard's purposes only.

Richard Caulk. Prof. of Ethiopian History, Addis Ababa University. 1972-1976

Over the years, until about the end of 1976, my then-girlfriend Menby and I were constant guests at Richard's wonderful lunch events at his Salcost apartment in Addis. Menby eventually picked his food tastes while I picked, or tried to pick, his conservative but elegant dressing habits.

Listening to his album collections, which included Simon and Garfunkel, Aretha Franklin and Diana Ross, became a habit and, later, an obsession. My tastes and, indeed, life-style were being re-shaped, and Menby was joining in.

Richard also enjoyed our company, especially when he was distressed about something. He would call us for a coffee at one of the coffee houses in Addis and would simply be chatting non-stop. Menby and I, with youthful innocence and laughter at his incredible humor, were his therapy. He genuinely enjoyed our company. In his eyes, we were simple, unpretentious, youthful couple and ready to burst with laughter at any time.

Some of the humor was at our cost too. He once told Menby who was 50 kgs at the time, '*Menbraa*', he would call her out in his own way, '*if you get any skinnier, I may not be able to see you without my glasses.*'

Another day, we were sitting next to a huge fat man by the Sodere swimming pool. Richard did not know if the fat man spoke English or not, but that did not stop him from telling the man, '*Mister, if you are planning to explode, I suggest you move a few meters away from me.*'

Yet another day, a group of us including Richard, was having lunch at a traditional Ethiopian restaurant. Richard, who was not particularly fond of *injera* and *wat*, was struggling to use his fingers to feed himself. So, exasperated and in his routine humorous way, turned to me and said, '*You know, Aklilu, if my father saw me eating with my fingers, he would faint.*'

I took my time to respond, and said, '*You know, Richard, if my father saw me eating with a fork, he would faint.*' I may have exaggerated, of course, but I got even! We laughed at our jokes!

In any event, it was in late 1976 that Richard had to pack and leave Ethiopia. It was the time of the socialist revolution in the country and all westerners, particularly Americans, were declared *persona-non-grata*. I remember his last few days in Addis; he was raging with anger - he was leaving the country and the job he loved.

Richard left and eventually took a job at Rutgers University, near Philadelphia in the United States. Later in 1978, when I was in Italia waiting to hear from the American Consulate in Milano about my visa application to the United States, I knew it was Richard (and my brother Miemen) who was doing things behind the curtains.

Later in the early 1980's, Menby and I visited Richard a couple of times while he was teaching at Rutgers. He was not very happy and yearned to go back to Ethiopia. He went back in 1982, only to come back to the United States with pneumonia about six months later.

One summer morning in 1983 when we were in Chicago, I got an unusual call from the University of Illinois Urbana campus. It was Professor Donald Crummey, a friend and colleague of Richard's back from their Haile Selassie I University years. Since I never got a call from Professor

Crummey before, I feared there was something wrong, and it was promptly confirmed: Richard had died of pneumonia; he was 46 years old.

Professor Crummey and his wife were to drive to the funeral in New York; I went along. We drove about 1,300 kilometers from Urbana, Illinois, to New York City in one day. There, in the presence of his parents and sister, I witnessed the cremation of one of the most important persons in my life - a person who affected my life so positively and profoundly!

The drive back to Urbana the next day was one very long silence.

University service year

My thoughts, still up over Southern Italia, shifted back to the 1974/75 academic year when I was serving my one-year Ethiopian University Service (EUS) program. This program, which included teaching at government schools, was a requirement for graduation.

So, I was assigned to teach at a junior high school in Shire Inda Selassie, a small town in Tigray Region. The town, located at about 900 kilometers north of Addis Ababa, had a population of about 3,000 at the time. I camped in a small hotel, which consumed about 80% of my monthly income of 180 Birr a month.

I started teaching the English language and civics in earnest with a lot of youthful energy; I was 24 years old. And, I enjoyed it immensely. I interacted with my students, some of whom were only a couple of years younger than me, freely and with a lot of interest in their semi-rural culture and behaviors. This was something which reminded me of my own upbringing in Gore; but Gore was much greener and more rustic. There were also marked differences in how people dressed and behaved. Due to its location on a major road, Shire Inda Selassie had many urban amenities which Gore did not have.

I immediately recruited Tsehaye, one of my 9th grade students (probably the oldest one in the class) to teach me Tigrigna after classes and on Saturday afternoons. Our weekday

Tigrigna classes, which would be accompanied with a few glasses of the famous Shire Inda Selassie *tella*[54] went well. The Saturday afternoon classes, however, were hilarious.

We would all go to the *tella* house after the regular Saturday afternoon soccer games. That was when we were more interested in quenching our thirsts than quenching a desire to learn Tigrigna. Quickly, any instruction of the Tigrigna language would disappear and would be replaced with a hot discussion of how the soccer game we had just finished was won or lost.

In the end, I struggled, but I learnt 'tolerable' Tigringa, and I even dared to speak it. Tsehaye, my student and teacher at the same time, became a good friend of mine, but I never saw him again once I left Shire Inda Selassie in early 1975.

Talking about Shire Inda Selassie *tella*, my first experience was a few days after I arrived in town. The school director, Ato Gebre Selasise, in typical Tigray hospitality, took me to the most famous *tella* house in town. As we approached the place, I could see a few clubs and guns lined against the outer wall of the house - with no one guarding them.

With a little bit of not-so-well-hidden shock, I asked my host about the guns. He casually told me that they belonged to the customers who came to drink *tella* and, since they were not allowed to take the guns in, they left them outside. I asked if some people would not steal the guns. He laughed and assured me that, since everybody knew each other, no one would dare steal the guns. End of story.

As we walked into the *tella* house, I could see quite a few people sitting against the inner wall that formed a big circle. In the middle, there was a huge pole that supported the structure. In a small side-room, I could see the *insera* [clay container] out of which the *tella* was supplied. In front of each person there was a metal cup [aka *Shashati* or *Menelik*] big enough to contain three times the size of a regular beer glass. I noticed that the ever-busy female hostesses would fill the cups to the maximum and more as soon as they were emptied; no questions asked or permissions required. Those were the unspoken rules.

---

54   Local beer made of 'dagusso' or millet.

Upon our entry and recognizing the senior teacher and acknowledging the 'outsider' who was with him, the entire crowd stood up and exchanged pleasantries in Tigringa that must have lasted for a good five minutes. I was introduced as the *Memhir* [teacher] from Haile Selassie I University who would be staying in town for a year teaching English and civics.

From that day on, my name was *Memhir* which I found to be a bit strange considering that I was sharing the same title with my respected moral teacher back in Gore. The reverence that came with it was overwhelming, and my introduction to the local culture was taking shape.

In any case, we found our seats after a lot of offers by the patrons of the house to take their seats, and ordered two cups of *tella*. Within seconds, our cups were in front of us and overflowing. At first, I had a hard time picking up the cup with one hand; and then, I was faced with the second challenge: how was I going to finish it? I noticed my host and the people sitting near me would have no trouble drinking a couple of cups every fifteen minutes or so. That first day, I managed to drink about half of the cup in a matter of about two hours; my host had about half a dozen.

It turned out, by the end of the first semester at Shire Inda Selassie, I would manage to drink three cups in one sitting - which would last for an average of about an hour. My student-teacher Tsehaye would have about two dozen. He once told me, in a good afternoon, he could drink up to eighty (yes, 80!) cups. I wasn't sure whether I should believe him.

My classes went very well; and my students were more than eager to learn. During the 1974 Christmas break I teamed up with my close friends Berhane and Daniel, who were doing their EUS in Axum and Mekele, respectively, and ventured to Asmara and Massawa by bus. It was the first time I had seen a sea, the Red Sea, and large ships, not to speak of the beautiful cities, at least compared to the then-Addis Ababa, of Asmara and Massawa.

But, soon after the start of the second semester in early 1974, a revolution broke out in the country and we were ordered back to where we came from, which in my case was Addis Ababa. I figured if I had stayed the full ten months in Shire Inda Selassie, I would have mastered Tigrigna and would have emptied at least six cups of *tella* in one sitting. But, that was not to be. I left Shire Inda Selassie with many memories including the reverence I was shown by my students, colleagues and the entire community.

Also, in Shire Inda Selassie, a passionate love for teaching was implanted in me forever.

In any case, I finished the rest of my EUS year at Wosen Seged School in Addis Ababa in the middle of the *Mercato* area. Unbeknownst to me, my future wife, Menby, lived only a few meters away.

Yes, I completed the EUS program[55] but, during the same time, the government was secretly planning a two-year 'campaign' which steered my life, and many others', in a direction that I never imagined or volunteered for.

Zemetcha years

The two-year Development through Cooperation Campaign (*aka Zemetcha*) was one of the most significant events of my university life, as it probably was for many others. About sixty thousand university and all high school students above grade ten as well as teachers were deployed all over the country, to help '*promote land reform and improve agricultural product and to teach peasants about the new political and social order.*'
Our task was to 'educate' the rural population in the 1974 revolution and the land reform, and all the benefits it entailed to the farmers, in particular. I was sent to a small town called Begi, Wollega Province, about 650 kilometers west of Addis Ababa. There I joined about 120 young boys and girls, aged 16 to 27, with different social and economic backgrounds.

The students had come from all over the country but mostly from the surrounding areas. Most of them were high school students from grade ten and above; five of us were from

---

55   Our batch was the last EUS program participants.

Haile Selassie I University. Our manager was a young marine lieutenant with no or little experience of managing 120 young people from varying walks of life.

We settled in two large makeshift halls, one for girls and one for boys, that served as dormitories. Since, by then, I was used to sleeping in a room with multiple occupants, I did not mind. Food was plentiful; we would kill an ox every Saturday and there was plenty to eat. The sanitary situation, however, was a totally different story; that is when I learnt that human beings adapt and adjust no matter what. Then, I settled.

Posing gleefully in a Zemetcha gear. Begi, Wollega, 1976

We soon divided ourselves into several committees. One of them was the committee that would organize students into small groups and send them to remote villages, sometimes hours away from Begi. The idea was to teach the 'peasantry' whatever we knew about the land reform and the need for peasant associations. Talented students helped prepare the speeches and delivered them in Affan Oromo; those who did not speak Affan Oromo used student translators. In spite of our differences in background and depth of understanding the objectives of the *Zemetcha*, we achieved some success.

Also, due to my relatively older age and my stature as a third year university student, I was elected chair of the discipline committee. There were three members, and one of them was a young beautiful girl of about 18 years who later would become my wife.

So, as the chair of the disciplinary committee, I had to preside over quite a few disciplinary issues.

*****

There was this young boy, the youngest in the group who had just finished tenth grade, who was a regular. He would slip out of our camp almost every other evening, go to a local *tej* [honey wine] house, and come back drunk. He would then walk directly into the girls' hall and, with both hands in his pockets, start lecturing them in English, on subjects nobody comprehended. Since this happened so often, the girls had learnt to simply ignore him.

Why Ethiopians, when drunk, resort to English, of all languages available in the country, is beyond me!

So, having given his lecture to the girls, this young man would then go to the boys' dorm and sleep quietly; he would not dare disturb the boys, even when drunk. I heard that they had once warned him that they would put him in a barrel of cold rain water, full and waiting outside, if he ever bothered them.

In any case, I would see him in the morning and give him my advice not to do it again; but he would.[56]

Another disciplinary problem took me by surprise, considering the status of the student involved. Almost across the street from our camp, there was a community clinic run by a white 'missionary lady', as we called her. She was a stout lady with no nonsense in her demeanor. The local people respected, if not feared, her like a saint. We were no exceptions!

One day, out of the blue, I saw her walking to our manager's room yelling all kinds of curses so loudly that one could hear her from a distance. Our manager referred her to me, and I knew there was going to be a disciplinary case; and a big one.

So, she came to me and told me feverishly that one of our students had insulted and embarrassed her publically, and she demanded a strict disciplinary action. 'Or else', she said, 'I would close the clinic and go back home.' I knew the clinic was the only one in town. So, I apologized for what happened and politely walked her back to the clinic promising that we would take a strong disciplinary action against the perpetrator. She demanded that she be told about the punishment, and I said I would.

I found out that the student in question was none other than Feleke Kebede, a third year Haile Selassie I University student and a rather brilliant and respected member of our group. He was also someone I had known from my boyhood years in Gore! All the while Feleke, a bit short on temper, was watching from a distance. I called him to a quiet corner and asked him to tell me about what happened.

Feleke: *I was not feeling well and I went to the clinic for help.*
Aklilu: *What was the problem?*
Feleke: *I guess it was something I ate, I was having diarrhea.*
Aklilu: *Did you see the missionary lady at the clinic?*
Feleke: *Yes, she was the one.*
Aklilu: *So, what did she tell you?*

---

56 I will not mention names, but he now holds a high government position.

Feleke: *She told me I needed a test, and asked me to bring my stool in a small plastic cup that she gave me.*

Aklilu: *So, what was the problem with that?*

Feleke: *The Problem? As I turned around to get my stool, she yelled, as everyone was listening, 'Don't bring one kilogram, Eh!'*

Aklilu: *One kilogram of what?*

Feleke: *One kilogram of my stool!*

Aklilu: *So what happened?*

Feleke: *So, I turned around, told her 'bullshit!'*

Aklilu: *You told the missionary lady 'bullshit?' I can see you were angry, but she is the only one who provides health services around here!*

Feleke: *Yes, still, she is bullshit!*

Aklilu: *But, you took her literally. When she said one kilogram, she did not mean one kilogram.*

Feleke: *Then, what did she mean?*

Aklilu: *I am sure she meant to say not to bring too much. Now, would you apologize to her?*

Feleke: *No way! She is just a mean woman, imagine me carrying one kilogram of shit around. She is bullshit!*

There was no hope and, all along, I was trying very hard not to laugh at the matter. But, after a while, I couldn't control it and I burst out with laughter. Feleke laughed with me for a while and said, '*Now Aklilu, do you have some coins on you? I need to go and get some cigarettes.*'

End of story; there wasn't really much I could do. The missionary lady refused to treat our students for a few days, and then things went back to normal.

*****

Then there was this young man, Kejela. Probably in his late teens, rather short and sturdy, and with two passions: playing the harmonica and staying clean. I may, with all due respect, add another one: womanizing. I wasn't sure which school or town he came from, but he had a warm and sociable personality, and always smiling from ear to ear.

So, Kejela would go to the nearby river every other afternoon to wash his clothes and himself. If anybody among us had dirty clothes or needed a bird bath, he would be more than happy to wash them too. Whenever he showed up for breakfast every morning, he was as clean as crystal with glowing skin and shiny hair which reflected the amount of hair oil he had put on. I actually liked Kejela, a harmless womanizer.

One early evening, after dinner, our manager came to me with a somber face, which did not surprise me, and engaged in the following conversation with me.

Manager: *Aklilu, you need to do something about this guy Kejela.*
Aklilu: *What did he do?*
Manager: *I hear he is roaming around the neighborhoods on Saturdays and Sundays, singing and playing his harmonica.*
Aklilu: *So what is wrong with that?*
Manager: *The problem is that he is using his songs and harmonica to seduce women.*
Aklilu: *So what is wrong with that?*
Manger: *Sometimes it is married women.*
Aklilu: *Well that may be a problem, but I do not think this is part of my job description as the chair of the discipline committee.*
Manager: *I think it is.*
Aklilu: *Surely you do not expect me to follow Kejela to every house or bedroom he goes, and monitor what he may be doing!*
Manager: *I did not say that; but it still is a disciplinary issue.*
Aklilu: *Maybe; in my view, he is an adult and the women are adults too. Why should I interfere with this? It may be done with mutual consent.*
Manager: *But it is not good for our reputation or safety. How would people react to this? We are already seen negatively by the public, and Kejela's deeds are adding fuel to fire. It is part of your responsibility to stop him.*
Aklilu: *I really cannot do that; besides, he may have some natural needs to satisfy. If you like, you can tell him to stop it yourself.*

Our manager was disappointed at me; but, I stood by my decision. In a way, I was taking side with Kejela. After all, he had washed, if not me, my clothes a few times - voluntarily, of course!

So, one day, I ran into Kejela and mentioned the issue with him in passing. *'Has any woman complained so far?'* he asked me. Honestly, not to my knowledge!

In hindsight, I actually had seen Kejela in Addis a few weeks before I went to Begi. As I waited for my turn, I would sometimes go to *Jalmeda,* the wide open field from where the *Zemetcha* was launched, to see my friends off to their assigned locations. Every day I went there, I would see this guy sitting on the tall brick wall that enclosed *Jalmeda.* He would be blowing a huge horn and making unsolicited loud encouraging speeches to the unhappy students who were leaving for their assigned locations in a convoy of buses.

Parents would cry as they saw their children off, despite this guy's frantic efforts to comfort them. But, the noise that came out of his horn and voice were irritating to say the least. Nevertheless, the huge smiles and twinkling lights in his eyes were captivating. *'What a naughty boy!'* I would ask myself with some disdain and interest combined.

So, the day it was my turn to take off from *Amist Kilo* for Begi, in a bus with about sixty other students, this guy was nowhere to be seen. The place was quiet and peaceful, and I thought he must have already been sent off to his assigned location; a relief. Then, we boarded the bus and took off.

After about fifteen minutes into our two-day journey, while we still were within the premises of Addis Ababa, I suddenly heard the familiar horn, accompanied by a loud voice, from a distance of about five feet. When I stood and looked back, I saw the same young man a few rows behind me in the same bus! With half of his body out through the widow, he was doing his thing! I was told his name was Kejela, and was assigned to Begi! *'How am I going to survive with this guy in Begi?'* was all I could think of the whole day.

In any case, much later one afternoon and a few months after the *Zemetcha* collapsed, I ran into Kejela on the streets of Addis. I jokingly asked him if he left all the women he seduced in Begi behind. He laughed in his usual way, joked that he had brought a few of them with him, and walked away; I have yet to see him again.

*****

Another potentially disastrous disciplinary problem was yet to come soon, though. This was when one of our two armed guards had a quarrel with one of the local area students called Edjigu Kabata. As a member of the food committee, Edjigu had introduced an in-house rule where whatever leftover food after our meals would be put on a large serving dish and given to the local kids who would hang around during meal times.

One day, one of the guards violated this rule and gave his leftover food to a kid he favored. Edjigu tried to explain to the guard that he was not supposed to do that; and the guard got irritated. In a few minutes a serious quarrel had begun between the two; and we were all watching the scene.

Edjigu was a very polite and quiet person, but he had to defend himself and he was strong. One day, for instance, I saw him throw a piece of stone so high into the sky that I almost did not see it for a while! I had said to myself on many occasions that if they had trained this guy he could easily get a gold medal in the Olympics throwing javelin, discuss or shot-put.

Anyway, Edjigu literally pulled a pole from a nearby fence and landed a huge blow on the guard's back. Knowing that he was no match for Edjigu, the guard went looking for his AK-47; as semi-automatic machine gun which that he kept in his bedroom. Those of us who were watching from close-by anticipated what was about to happen and scrambled for cover every which way. Edjigu stood his ground.

Our manager, the marine lieutenant, who was a much more trained officer than the guard, was also observing the events from a close distance.

The guard was on his way back with his machine gun when, our manager who had actually beat the guard in the scramble for a gun, stopped him before he got to Edjigu, and perhaps to all of us. He pointed his gun at the guard and ordered him to kneel down with his hands up. The guard, who obeyed the order almost automatically, was taken away and arrested; we breathed a huge sigh of relief.

We had actually thought our manager was a weakling just because he was skinny, soft spoken and we resented, for no good reasons, that he was our boss. But, from that day on we showed him a little more respect; after all, he may have saved our lives!

A bunch of young people from different backgrounds. Zemetcha participants: Edjigu (second from left) and Moges (third from left). Menby is standing at the far right. Begi, Wollega, 1976

*****

Now, parallel to all these, my relationship with Menby was getting deeper and deeper. On weekdays, we would walk for several kilometers in the farmlands around Begi, together with a bunch of other students; to perform whatever *Zemetcha* related tasks we were assigned. In the process, we explored and learnt about the livelihoods of poor farmers; their needs, aspirations and their challenges. We talked to them but, in reality, offered very little.

On weekends, Menby and I explored the natural beauty of Begi and its surroundings. The lush green fields, the wild natural mango trees, the soothing sound of the rivers, and the acrobatics of the monkeys in the trees captivated us. The pleasantly cool weather, the full moon and multiple star formations in the clear skies of Begi filled our imaginations. Our romance, in short, blossomed.

In all these, one striking factor in our relationship was the constant presence of the soul and spirit of a lady, Kershi Jimato Aredo, in Menby's life.

Kershi was a character to reckon with in her own right. Born in 1904 in Abichu, Semen Shewa, her father, Jimato, spoke no Amharic while her mother, Medina, spoke no Oromifa. That did not prevent them from having six children, and Kershi was the third.

Kershi, who couldn't have her own children, left her husband and moved to Addis Ababa and started a small business: selling butter which she bought at reduced price from farmers around the city. She became so successful that in a few years she had added a famous *tej bet* to her business ventures, and bought large tracts of land at the center of the Mercato area in Addis Ababa, a farmland in Arsi, and a large coffee plantation near Jimma. In fact, the very land where Anwar Mosque in Addis Ababa is now standing belonged to Kershi. Yes, she got an equivalent plot across the street in compensation where she built her residence, and much more.

In addition to her growing businesses, Kershi had one obsession: her brother Lidetu, Menby's paternal grandfather. In the mid-1930s, Lidetu, a father of three children, had gone to Maychew, northern Ethiopia, to fight against the Italian aggression. Ethiopia lost the battle and Lidetu never returned home. Kershi conducted extensive search for her brother, travelling for weeks in Tigray region, whenever she would hear hearsay that somebody called Lidetu was living.

But, all her attempts were in vain, and Kershi was heartbroken. Then, as if to compensate for her brother's loss, she took it upon herself to take care of his children, particularly the only son - Alemayehu, Menby's father.

Kershi was tall, very well built and always defiant. She would never accept defeat even if it meant carrying a revolver in her bra to fend off any potential trouble maker. When she ran her *Tej House*, there were times when she would brandish her weapon or even fire at people who did not know better than bullying a lady. She wanted all women to do the same but was disappointed to find out that she was the exception.

So, when Alemayehu was old enough to go to school, Kershi believed that he, as the son of a martyr, should go to Teferi Mekonnen School in Addis Ababa – with free food and lodging. She knew that the only way she could achieve this was by getting direct access to Emperor Haile Selassie.

So, one morning, with a long letter in her hands, she waited for the Emperor on the road he would normally take to go to his office. Just as the Emperor was passing in his car, he noticed her frantically trying to tell him something. The Emperor's car stopped, and Kershi boldly delivered her letter. Next thing, Alemayehu was admitted to Teferi Mekonnen School.

But, after a while, this didn't settle well with her. She was an independent business woman and she wanted her 'son' to be like her too. But, first, she figured she should find him a wife.

So, with a lot of push from Kershi, Alemayehu wed Amanelwa in Addis Ababa, when she was only fifteen. Losing Alemayehu to Amanelwa, Kershi waited until Menby was born a year later, and she claimed her. Kershi successfully argued that Amanelwa, who was only sixteen at the time, was too young to raise a child. So, Menby was only four months old when she started calling Kershi her 'mother.'

Menby's parents, Amanelwa and Alemayehu. By age 21, Amanelwa has had five of her six children. Addis Ababa, 1967

Over the years Kershi and Menby bonded and worshipped each other; nothing would separate them. Kershi raised Menby to be a highly disciplined and thoughtful young lady. She also managed to teach her the merits of hard work and self-confidence, but couldn't get her to carry a revolver in her bra!

Kershi, with strong traditional values, poured unconditional love and wisdom on Menby; and Menby reciprocated equally strongly – in her own ways! In fact, we still cherish some of the wisdom which Kershi passed over to Menby directly, and to me and our daughters, indirectly.

One of them, which was Kershi's fundamental outlook of life, when loosely translated into English, goes like this:

> *If it works, it works.*
> *If it doesn't, we will see,*
> *And go to where it works.*

But, alas, the 1975 land reform nationalized all Kershi's hard-earned properties, with the exception of one residential house. It left her devastated, and she finally succumbed to liver cancer in 1980 at the age of 76. Menby was devastated, but she carries to this day most of Kershi's values and personality, again short of carrying a revolver in her bra!

*****

Now, back to Begi, within a couple of months, it was an open secret that Menby and I were dating. The rest of the students accepted it, and wished us all the best. This was particular true with Menby's newly found *Zemetcha* friends.

Our manager, however, did not like that at all. He felt we were setting a bad precedence and, soon, we would have several babies roaming around our camp!

So, one day, taking advantage of a general meeting, our manager raised the issue. Without mentioning names, he told us his concern that he had seen boys and girls sneaking out of our camp, sometimes in the evenings, and hand in hand. Of course, we all knew who he was talking about.

A typical weekend day, friends at the Zemetcha; our camp at the background. From left to right: Sophie Mekuria, Senait Seyoum, Menby, Mimi Tamrat and Christine Seifu. Begi, 1976

Now, there was this young student called Moges who somehow had developed a particular liking to Menby and me; like many other students in our camp. He was hot tempered, and also hated any resemblance of authority. He was so combative and impatient that his actions would always precede his thoughts.

'What are you trying to say?', Moges asked with a frighteningly bulging eyes staring at our manager. Our manager calmly repeated his concern. Then Moges fired back in his usual defiant manner. *'Don't pretend as if we do not know you. No one among us runs after women more than you do; you are just jealous!'*

I wished Moges would stop, but didn't; the rest of the students burst out with laughter, which also doubled as a show of support for Moges and for us - by extension. Our manager stood frozen with this reaction, regretting his decision to raise the issue in the first place. He calmly walked away.

I have no idea where Moges dug the information about our manager from! But, nevertheless, I was appreciative of his support.

Our manager may have had a point. A private moment with Menby in the jungles of Begi. Zemetcha, 1976

*****

In any case, within six months of my stay in Begi, things were getting from bad to worse. The initial excitement gave way to fear and disarray as the local police, aligned with the local chiefs and landlords, violently responded to the students' agitation and the objectives of the *Zemetcha*; and there was no one to protect us. Particular targets were university students who were considered to be the primary causes for the disinheritance of land and property of the local ruling class.

One evening rumor had it that a police force from the nearby district town of Assosa was on its way to Begi to arrest university students, who were believed to be instigators of all evil. I was advised to flee Begi, since I was one of those targeted to be arrested. At first I resisted, but the pleas of my then-girlfriend Menby and many others who argued that they would be safer without university students amongst them convinced me to flee.

A high school student from Hawassa, Getachew Mengistu, decided to join me; not sure whether he wanted to accompany me or whether he had his own reasons. In any case, he was welcome and we planned to flee together and our destination, Addis Ababa, was over 650 kilometers away!

According to our plan, we would leave Begi very early in the morning and walk the 40 kilometer distance to a town called Mendi, where we hoped to find a truck that would take us to Nekemte and from there, we would take the bus to Addis. So, one early morning, with little money that we raised from our friends and some dry bread, we took off to Mendi on foot, as planned.

The dirt road from Begi to Mendi meandered through savannah type thick grasslands and scattered trees and shrubs. Since it was the rainy season it was hot and humid; and we were also told there were lions and other wild animals living in the tall savannah grasses. But, that was not the only danger. Once in a while we would see local people walking in the opposite direction, usually with their spears ready to attack at the slightest provocation. And, we were not sure what provoked them and what did not.

Now, Getachew was the typical 'arada' and the de facto leader of the team of the two of us; and I would follow his orders, whatever they may be. Upon seeing threatening looking people walking the opposite direction towards us, Getachew would quickly step aside as far as possible and, with a bent head looking down, would let them pass by peacefully; and I followed suit. It worked each time, and we kept on walking alive.

At about half way, we heard a vehicle coming towards us. We figured it would be the police vehicle, and Getachew issued an order to hide in the tall grasses a few meters from the road. We stayed there until the car arrived and, sure enough, we could see a pickup truck through the grasses with about six armed police and heading towards Begi. When all was clear, we came out of the grasses and, after breathing a big sigh of relief, we resumed our journey to Mendi.

Just before we got to Mendi, it was getting dark and we had to find a place to spend the night. Luckily, we located a small farm and a *tukul*.[57] When we slowly and quietly walked in, we found an elderly farmer and his wife, in the simplest residence I have ever seen. Basically, it was a one-room small mud house. The room had a partition made of *Netela*,[58] one half was the place where the couple slept, and the other half was where they kept their roosters and two cows. We were pointed the part where they kept the roosters and the cows as our bedroom; we gratefully accepted.

For dinner, we shared our bread with them, they gave us some of their food in return. When we finished dinner, with a lot of gratitude, we covered ourselves with an old blanket they gave us, and slept on the dirt floor in our designated corner of the mud house. If they had wanted to harm us, they could easily have done so. But, after having walked the 40 kilometers for about 12 hours under very difficult weather conditions, we were just too tired even to worry about our safety.

We slept like a log until it was time for the roosters to crow! What I knew was that roosters crowed just before day light; not these ones! They started soon after midnight and did it continuously till it dawned! Apparently, it did bother neither our hosts nor Getachew; but I did not sleep after midnight.

---

57 A hut made of mud and thatched roof common among villagers in Ethiopia.

58 Ethiopian hand-woven textile made of cotton.

Early in the morning the next day, no breakfast served, but we thanked our gracious hosts and sneaked into Mendi, avoiding any detection by police or government cadres. Or else, we would end up in jail. Luckily, we ran into a loaded truck that was just about to leave Mendi for Nekemte, some 300 kilometers miles away. We managed to convince the truck driver, a middle aged Italian, and his Ethiopian assistant to allow us to climb and hide ourselves under the canvas cover of the load.

The truck took off at a very slow speed and, somewhere between the two towns, it started raining. That was not necessarily a problem for us since we were properly insulated from the rain, sleeping under the heavy canvas. Then the truck got stuck in mud, as it was going uphill. No amount of maneuvering by our experienced Italian driver could result in getting the truck out of the mud.

So, at about 6 pm, our tired and frustrated driver left us where we were stuck and walked to a nearby village where, we were told, he had a mistress. As he was enjoying the night, we shivered under the wet and heavy canvas till morning. When our Italian driver arrived refreshed, he had a group of young male farmers who pushed the truck out of the mud.

We continued our journey to Nekemte, and we got there just before dusk; at this point, we hadn't eaten for about 48 hours. In any case, we got off the truck just before it went into town, and hid in a nearby eucalyptus forest. When it got dark, we sneaked into the town, ate our dinner, and collapsed in a small cheap hotel; Getachew was still in charge.

Very early in the morning the next day while it was still dark, we went to the bus station and made a deal with the assistant of the driver. Accordingly, we would start walking towards the direction of Addis, and they would pick us up on their way. So, we made the payment in advance and, while it was still dark, we started walking towards Addis. Sure enough at about 7am, the bus came behind us; blowing the horn to alert us. We quickly boarded the bus and took seats far from each other to avoid any detection by security police or an informer.

The journey to Addis, which was about 325 kilometers away, commenced in that way.

At the time, government media were warning about students who might be running away from the *Zemetcha* on foot or public transportation. But, the driver and some of the passengers somehow knew who we were, and helped us conceal ourselves from the police or political cadres. In fact, one elderly Muslim gentleman in the bus gave Getachew his headscarf, which, along his beard, was the perfect camouflage for him. I sat between two elderly ladies, and looked like I was part of the family. Some passengers even prayed for us!

That way, we escaped two checkpoints; the third and last one was the main one just before we got into Addis. Fortunately, it rained heavily and the police did not care to get wet; so they waved the bus driver to proceed into Addis. Again, we all breathed a long sigh of relief!

When we got to the main bus station in Addis, it was about 5pm, and Getachew and I had to split. I gave him all the money I had which he needed to spend the night in Addis and travel on to Hawassa the next morning; we agreed it would have been too dangerous to invite him to my house just for the night. So, we hugged, wished each other all the best and went our own ways.

When I got to my parent's house, it was about 6pm. My mother opened the door, and almost fainted when she saw me. To begin with, I was not supposed to be there given all the government's warnings about students who ran away from the *Zemetcha*. I also looked terrible; I had lost weight, had not washed for several days and my clothes were dirty.

Once settled, I told my parents why I had to leave Begi, and they understood. But, I was advised to keep a very low profile to avoid detection by security police.

A few days later, I heard news that Getachew had been arrested in Hawassa and brought to a police station in Addis for interrogation. In spite of all the advice against it, I went to the police station and managed to see him; he looked terrible with bruises all over his body. He was happy to see me and appreciated the risk I had taken to visit him in custody. With all the things he did for me, I told him I wished I could do more.

In any case, it was the last time I saw him until about 30 years later when I ran into him on streets of Addis, close to a cinema. He had become a successful actor and showed me a couple of posters where he was one of the lead actors. I was happy for him; but it was short lived. A couple of years later I learnt that Getachew, my comrade-in-adventure, had died and I was not even sure from what.

*****

Within a year of the kick-off of the *Zemetcha*, most students, including my then-girlfriend Menby, had returned back to their respective homes. There was one full year before schools reopened; so Menby and I enrolled at the Alliance Française Addis to study French, and graduated with intermediate French.

As for the *Zemetcha*, things went from bad to worse, and it finally collapsed for three good reasons, in my view.

First, the *Zemetcha* was a non-starter right from the outset. The whole program was organized hurriedly for the main purpose of keeping the students' population out of urban areas, especially Addis Ababa, where they would have posed trouble for the military government that overthrew the Emperor and stuck to power.

Second, in spite of their efforts, the students who took part had come from different backgrounds and understandings. Most of them did not know what they were talking about, much less educate the peasantry about the benefits of the land reform and the formation of peasant associations.

Third, and more importantly, local police aligned with local chiefs and landlords stacked against the students, considered the vanguards of the unwelcome changes. Obviously, they weren't about to sit down and watch as the students encouraged the peasantry to keep land and the produces to themselves. They threatened and, in some instances imprisoned the students; in some areas, students lost their lives. Many students were back home, and hiding, within a few months of the campaign.

And, at the end, although we may have achieved some, we had all essentially lost two of our most productive years. This, of course, was a small price to pay compared to those who lost much more, including lives, in those unsettled times.

Later on, when all was said and done, I would joke with my friends that the only good thing that came out of the *Zemetcha*, as far as I was concerned, was that it introduced me to a girl who later would become my wife of 40 years and counting. It was true!

*****

My final year at the university, by now re-named Addis Ababa University, in 1976/77 was uneventful: the *'Revos'* were gone, the *'Sabus'* had graduated before us, and the *'Jollies* 'have mostly kept a low profile, and some even refused to re-join the university out of respect for the martyred fellow students.[59] A few close friends and I decided to get it over with, and enrolled.

But, the campus had become a quiet and strange place - even for us. It was also the height of the Red Terror; when the country lost its potentially most productive young men and women. Several thousands were imprisoned or forced to flee the country. It was a sad and gloomy campus; all the good times have evaporated.

So, after eight years in college, EUS and *Zemetcha*, we licked our wounds and just wanted to graduate; and we did. The irony was, in spite of all the opposition and sacrifice, we were made to receive our degrees and diplomas from none other than the Chair of the Dergue,[60] Colonel Mengistu Haile Mariam. Many students stayed away from the graduation ceremonies in

---

59 One of them was my close friend Tsegaye Beru; it took him 11 years to eventually graduate with his Bachelor's degree.

60 Coordinating Committee of the Armed Forces Police and Territorial Army composed of about 120 soldiers below the rank of major that ruled the country between 1974 and 1991.

protest, but many more, including myself, with some pressure from scared family members, opted to attend.

As if this was not bad enough and for reasons that may have to do with alphabetical order, I was the first to receive a degree from the Colonel. Photographers scrambled to document this 'history' when the Colonel issued degrees to university students for the first time.

To add insult to injury, my photograph with the Colonel issuing me my degree, appeared on the front page of Addis Zemen[61] the next day.

Despite the misgivings, receiving my bachelor's degree from Colonel Mengistu Haile Mariam. Addis Ababa, September 1977

I remembered, about ten years earlier, I had a similar experience with Emperor Haile Selassie on behalf of my brother Miemen. But that wasn't such a bad experience compared to the chagrin and embarrassment of having to receive our degrees from a person who we considered to have been responsible for the loss of many of our friends and

---

61 Government-owned Amharic language daily newspaper which I still have a copy of.

classmates at Addis Ababa University. Einstein, of course, was right: *everything is relative.*

So, *'Ces't la vie'*, I told myself, and over the skies of Southern Italia, I dozed off.

Chapter 2.

EXPOSURES AND ADAPTATIONS

And so, at age 28, I concluded what looked like my first phase of life; equipped with an identity profoundly influenced by a rural upbringing and intertwined with an urban twist. With a new wife and deep-rooted passion for literature and teaching, I was ready for the second phase, in whatever form it appeared, and there was much more to live and learn!

'You live in this world only once; don't live it like a coward!'

New Ways of Life and Challenges

First exposures and impressions

When we landed at *Fiumicino* International Airport in Roma on June 15, 1978, it was dark, and a bit hot and humid; a condition entirely new to me compared to the high altitude and temperate climate I was used to in Gore and Addis Ababa. Nonetheless, my first reaction was *'Roma and Italia; here I come!'* My young and free spirit was curious about and eager to see what Roma had to offer.

Also, in my view, I have come to a faraway land to a different people and country as a 'guest' for a brief period of time. Back in my own country I had always considered non-Ethiopians living in Ethiopia as my 'guests' and, as such, I always tried to treat them with respect and the pride of being an Ethiopian 'host'- for whatever it's worth. My outlook to my Peace Corps teachers and the expat professors at Addis Ababa University were cases in point. Hence, perhaps naively, I did not except anything different from the Romans when I got to Roma. In any case, I said to myself, *'I will live and learn.'*

With no idea what hotel to go to, I had to struggle to ask my taxi driver to take me to an affordable hotel near the main train station; I had planned to take the train to Milano a few days later. After a forty-five minute ride which I thought was endless compared to the ten-minute ride from Bole Airport to downtown Addis, I ended up in a hostel close to the *Termini,* the main railway station in Roma. The hotel was comfortable enough but can't remember if I had dinner; I soon collapsed in my bed in deep sleep.

Waking up in Roma in a mid-June morning promised a great few days in this incredible city. So, I was having coffee in a nearby coffee-house and planning my first full day in Roma on a piece of paper with the help of a tourist guidebook, when a young black lady approached me with a huge smile and an English accent I never heard before. I returned her smile and waited till she started a conversation, wondering what language she was going to attack me with.

Lady: *Hello my dear, where are you from?*
Aklilu: *Ethiopia, and you?*
Lady: *I am from Nigeria, are you staying in this hotel?*
Aklilu: *Yes.*
Lady: *Is this your first trip to Roma?*
Aklilu: *Yes, it is my first trip to Italia, and you?*
Lady: *I have come hear several times; how long will you stay here?*
Aklilu: *A few days, then I will go to Milano.*
Lady: *Is it better in Milano?*
Aklilu: *I do not know, but I have to go there to study Italian for a couple of months.*
Lady: *So you are a student?*
Aklilu: *Not really, I have come for a summer seminar; what about you?*
Lady: *Me, I am a business woman, no school for me.*
Aklilu: *What do you do?*
Lady: *I am a business woman.*
Aklilu: *Really, what do you do?*
Lady: *I buy cloth here cheap, and take them to Nigeria and sell them for profit.*
Aklilu: *You do this all by yourself?*
Lady: *Why not?*
Aklilu: *Where in Roma do you buy the clothes?*
Lady: *Flea market, real cheap.*
Aklilu: *Used clothes?*
Lady: *So what? I wash them when I get to Nigeria.*
Aklilu: *How often do you do this?*

Lady: *It depends; three or four times a year. It is all legal, if you are wondering. There is one such market called Mercato Ponti nearby, you want to go with me?*
Aklilu: *No thank you, I have other plans. Besides, I wouldn't buy anything. All the best, though!*

I was already impressed! The story of this young Nigerian woman who dared to come all the way to Europe by herself to buy clothes and take them back to Nigeria and make profit was incredible to me. But, I also wondered how it was that, in my first full day in Italia, the first person I ran into was not an Italian but a Nigerian woman!

I suppose it may have been the emergence of globalization, and Nigerians have already gotten used to it! But for me, it was the beginning of a series of exposures to events outside the realm of my identity which was formed growing up Gore and, later, in Addis. And, I was ready to learn more.

In any case, I admired the entrepreneurship spirit of this Nigerian woman and wondered if my fellow Ethiopian women or men were capable of doing the same. I saw her a couple of times in the next few of days ferrying huge suitcases full of clothes up and down; I wondered how she was going to take all those suitcases to Nigeria and by plane! I never saw her again, but it was my first introduction to Nigerians, which would continue in different ways, in the future.[1]

*****

So here I was in Roma, someone who two weeks earlier was planning a trip to Dire Dawa in Eastern Ethiopia, literally walking from one wonder of the world to another. My honeymoon in Roma, although a brief one, had begun and no

---

1   Later in the early 80s, I met a wonderful Nigerian, Godfrey Okoye, his wife and two children, who were like family to us until we went our separate ways in 1984; they actually returned to Nigeria after Godfrey obtained his degree in electrical engineering. Given his ambitions, he must be a wealthy businessman by now.

amount of words or exaggeration would describe how dumbfounded I was by what I saw in Roma.

Granted that I never had been outside Ethiopia or seen anything like this before, the closest being the Axum[2] obelisks and the cities of Harar, Gonder, Asmara and Massawa, but Roma was and still is one city with a fascination I still could not get over with - no matter how many times I visited later in life.

I also remembered, when I was young, I had read legendary stories about how Roma was founded over a thousand years ago by twin brothers, Romulus and Remus, who were raised by a she-wolf. Wandering among the wonders of the ruins, I felt like I was in Roma to verify this myth myself. The guidebook that I purchased '*Ancient Roma, past and present*' introduced me to ancient Roma; some of which I have seen in movies during my high school years with my twin friends.

These wonders included the Colosseum, The Pantheon, Trevi Fountain, Monument of Victor Emmanuel II, Spanish Steps etc.; the attractions in Roma were endless. The sculptures and paintings looked so real that I would gaze at them for extended periods of time waiting for a muscle to move or an eye to blink. Of course, nothing moved, but I would still do the same thing next time I saw another sculpture or painting.

Throughout the day I would walk in Roma from one attraction to the other, indifferent to the deep Italian culture and history embedded within the art or sculpture; only admiring the craftsmanship as they appeared on the surface.

My most favorite spot in Roma, completed in 1626, was St. Peters Basilica at the Vatican, and I wondered how my Catholic mother would have felt if she had seen it. For some reason, when she got the chance, she opted to go to Lourdes in France, a pilgrimage site for Catholics with over five million visitors a year. To this day, I hear stories from my mother about the miraculous healing power of the holly water at this holy site; I dared not disagree.

In any case, the cultural and religious aspects at St Peter's Cathedral meant very little, if any, to me. But, I just could not

---

2   Axum is a historical city in the highlands of Northern Ethiopia.

believe human hands made the paintings, the sculptures and the mosaic I saw at this Cathedral, as well as in many smaller churches spread throughout the city.

Also, interestingly enough, the fact that Italians had once briefly occupied my country back in the 1930s and caused untold amount of suffering to fellow Ethiopians never interfered in my admiration of what I saw in Roma. It may be that amazing things were neutral to one's biases, regardless of who made them. But, be that as it may, the exposure to numerous and varying physical wonders that a city like Roma could offer was something that got me at a young age. It never faded away, much less disappear.

Then, there was the latte' macchiato and the array of Italian cuisine, something I was not a total stranger to. Growing up in Addis Ababa in a middle class family, one cannot help but be addicted to Italian-introduced macchiato, pastries and pasta dishes; and I was no exception. As young people, my friends and I would deliberately seek for restaurants in Addis that specialized in Italian food. Places like Lombardia, Oroscopo, Enrico and Cremerie were our favorites, mostly because they were good and affordable by our standards.

Castelli's, however, considered the best Italian restaurant in Addis (some say in Africa), was beyond our budget except for the few times when somebody else would be paying.

That somebody else who enjoyed treating her students and friends to lunch at Castelli's once in a while was none other than Mrs. Innes Marshall. After the lunch, she was the only person who was allowed to have beer in her own personalized beer mug which she kept at the restaurant. Not that I liked beer at the time, but I watched from a close distance with envy. A ten Birr tip at the end, considered extravagant by our standards at the time, is still stuck in my memory and vision. Lucky waiter, I would think silently.

Anyway, I had come to Roma, my first foreign trip, with the background of a rural kid, albeit to some extent modified by an urban culture, but with a deep sense of local Ethiopian identity packed in my head and heart. Still, I was impressed and intrigued with what Roma had to offer, and I also found out Romans, although a bit short in English, to be very warm and friendly people.

I realized it was the beginning of a series of exposures to cultures different from mine. It was also a learning curve for me. But cultural shocks, adaptation or transformation were yet to come, if at all.

*****

After a few amazing days, I left Roma for Milano by train, which at the time took about six hours. I enjoyed the train ride a lot, although it had very little resemblance to the train trip experience I had in my country, which I enjoyed immensely too.

As a teenager in Ethiopia, I remember the times when my cousins and I would be sitting on the open door-sills of the speeding trains singing, or eating fruits and enjoying the breeze all the way from Addis to Dire Dawa or Mieso, or wherever we ended up going in eastern Ethiopia. No matter how long these trips took, usually about twelve hours from Addis to Dire Dawa, we sang and ate fruits nonstop. We would even help contraband merchants hide their small size merchandise items like watches or radios in our pockets or t-shirts just for the thrill of outsmarting the finance police. Little did we worry about what would have happened to us if we were caught!

So it was actually true that those of us who come from Hararghe originally have a special attachment to trains. But, the train trips in Italia were pleasant and enjoyable in their own separate ways.

In any case, when I got to Milano's *Centrale* Train Station, my cousin Roman and her husband Yoseph, and their small daughter Kidist, were there to meet me. They kindly hosted me for a few days, and I got to know them more. Yoseph was a character I never figured out; I remember he was fast and spoke fluent Italian, which for me was miraculous at that time. There were also times when he wouldn't answer his telephone calls, and I had wondered.

My cousin Roman was a kind-hearted lady who seemed to have gone through a lot by the time she got to Milano. Their daughter Kidist was a darling. Their two-bedroom apartment, which was at a walking distance from the *Galleria*, a very famous glass covered shopping center in Milano, and other attractions, was just perfect for my purposes.

I had a great few days in Milano visiting historical wonders when it was time for me to proceed to my school at Gargnano del Garda. Yoseph and Roman were kind enough to offer me a ride that I happily accepted. But, before that, Yoseph made sure that I experienced three things in Milano.

First, it was the Milan Cathedral, also known as the *Duomo*, built in the late 14th and 15th centuries. This fabulous Gothic architecture was too complex for me to even try to understand, much less explain. But, I was simply flabbergasted.

Second, it was the *La Scala*, an opera house considered to be among the best, if not the best, in the world. Once inside and looking at the architecture, a rush of history that was foreign to me but common to humanity, went through my spine, exacerbated by the wonders human beings were able to accomplish at their best.

Finally, it was The *San Siro* Milan Stadium, of course, where we saw a team from Brazil play either A.C Milan or Inter Milan, I just couldn't remember. Most of the audience was so preoccupied with shouting and singing or with other activities that I wondered if they ever watched the game itself! Nothing like what I saw at this stadium happened at Addis Ababa stadium where my twin friends played; and I really hoped they were with me to see it. As an ardent fan of soccer, particularly the Ethiopian San George soccer team, I was eternally grateful to Yoseph for this incredible treat.

So, the ride from Milano to Gargnano del Garda was two and half-hours long. Yoseph's tiny fiat, even by Ethiopian standards, was 'flying' on the highway. I have never been on a highway before, or been driven at that speed. Although Yoseph was driving as if it was no big deal, I was scared but managed not to show it. But, as we drove through the landscape, I was totally mesmerized by the beauty of Northern Italia. As an Ethiopian who grew up in the mountains of Gore, the landscape of northern Italy was a pleasant surprise that made me homesick.

Also, Yoseph and Roman had planned the trip in such a way that we would stop at a couple of small towns along the road to visit some Ethiopian friends. I suspect the friends were told in advance about our arrival because, at each place, I remember we had what could pass for authentic Ethiopian food; the first time since I left Ethiopia and I was impressed. We finally reached our destination in one piece.

A small town by the lake

The small town of Gargnano, built over seven hundred years ago, had about 2,500 people at the time. It was located at the shore of Lago di Garda, the largest lake in northern Italia and among the most popular and beautiful holiday locations. The lake and the hills and the mountains surrounding the town complimented each other, while the alleys reminded me of Harar, the historical town in Eastern Ethiopia.

Of course, like in any town in Italia, Gargnano had its famous landmarks including the historical church of *San Francesco*. It also once had its notable resident, Benuto Mussolini, the dictator who invaded my country in the 1930s, reside during his fading years. What a coincidence I had come to this town! Didn't I grow up in Gore where patriotic Ethiopians resisted Mussolini? I figured it was definitely something I had to tell my father, when I got the chance, and hear what he had to say.

In Gargnano, for the first time in my life, I saw people sailing and windsurfing. I even saw hydroplanes, aircrafts that could takeoff, land and float on water. I was fascinated beyond belief and all I was thinking about was the time when I would tell all this to my twin friends back in Addis - if they believed me.

In any case, in Gargnano, I stayed with an Italian family that lived close to the school. It was a three-story old building and I had my own private corner in the attic with a bathroom.

In fact, I hardly saw my hosts and, when I did, it was all smiles, which we mutually agreed replaced a conversation. Nevertheless, staying with a family other than my own, much less an Italian family in Italia, was definitely an experience for me to try out, and I was ready to live and learn.

The school itself was a medium size historical villa built along the shores of Lago di Garda. There were a total of about 25 students, who had come from mostly Western Europe, to study Italian language and culture; I was the only one from Africa. We ate together at the school's cafeteria, and the food was just great, especially compared to what I was eating at Christmas Hall of Addis Ababa University. I reinforced my taste for Italian food, which had begun back in Addis some years earlier.

I had to be told some eating manners too. One morning, as we were eating breakfast at the school's cafeteria, one young lady from Switzerland who was sitting next to me and who has been observing my table manners struck a conversation with me.

Swiss: *Aklilu, why are you doing that?*
Aklilu: *What did I do?*
Swiss: *You are putting the jam on the toast first.*
Aklilu: *Yes I am, and then I will put the butter on the jam.*
Swiss: *But that is not how you should do it. You put the butter first and then the jam.*
Aklilu: *Why? What difference does that make?*
Swiss: *You put the butter first because the warm toast will melt it, and then you can put the jam. The butter will not melt if you already cover the toast with jam.*

At first, I was offended for no other reason than a young girl was commenting on my eating etiquettes. But, when I thought about it, she was actually right. All those years at Addis Ababa University of eating bread, jam and butter for breakfast, I never knew or cared which one went first.

I swallowed my pride and accepted the unsolicited advice.

It also took me a while to notice that I was the only black person in this group or in the town for that matter; I just wasn't oriented in that way. I had already noticed that the cooks and cleaners at the cafeteria were all white people. This was a situation that I had never seen or experienced before. Again, I couldn't wait to tell my twin friends about white people cooking for and serving me; at this point this would have just been a fun story to tell my friends!

Life went on and, during my first couple of weeks at the school, there was this five-year old son of the director of the school. Every time he saw me, he would look up at me and ask, *'Perché è Lei bronza colore? È seduto molto nel sole?'* Of course, I had no idea what this kid was talking about. But he would ask me the same question every time he saw me.

So, one day, I asked his father what the kid meant. The father laughed a hearty Italian laugh and told me that the kid was asking me if I had been sitting in the sun a lot and had become black. Then I knew the kid, and almost everybody else in the small town of Gargnano, had not seen a black person before.

So, all of a sudden, I noticed the color of my skin was different from all the people around me. For the first time, at age 28, I was a minority, based on my race. I realized it was a new world and a new way of life that I have come to, and I had to cope with it one way or another.

It is not that I felt 'inferior' in any way, but I realized that living as a black person among a multitude of white people, was going to be my fate, at least for some time to come. But, while in Italia, I still had to face either personal or institutional racism; a concept I had little firsthand experience or knowledge about to begin with.

*****

Back in our classes in Gargnano, for those who came from Spanish or French speaking countries, Italian was a piece of cake. Most of us, however, struggled but not as much as this young man from Great Britain. I did not know what part of Great Britain he came from, but it was as if he was speaking an entirely different language when he tried to speak Italian, which none of us understood.

In fact, I was having a hard time understanding what he was saying in English, much less in Italian. Back at home, I was used to laughing whenever I heard or saw something that I thought was funny. So, true to my Ethiopian upbringing, I would laugh out loud when I heard this English young man try pronouncing Italian words. And, it didn't help that I was sitting next to him. The guy was clearly offended. A few weeks later, all of a sudden, he stopped coming to class, and I really hoped I was not the cause.

Nevertheless, I wondered why native English speakers would have such a hard time pronouncing Italian words. As for me, I realized that the trick of learning or pronouncing Italian was to stress every letter of every word as forcefully as possible - and, it worked!

Anyway, classes actually combined basic Italian language and cultures. I was doing well with the former, picking a few more words and phrases and sentences every day. The latter, which involved visiting cultural and historical spots in Northern Italia, was what I liked more. We traveled to places like Florence, Pisa and Parma just to see the cathedrals, museums and the cultural festivities.

One such trip which I always remember was our trip to Siena, a city where we watched the *Palio*, a day-long festivity which concluded with a horse race. The *Palio*, which has been going on for over one thousand years, is a special occasion for the residents of Siena city. It represented centuries old traditions that honored the deity in the Catholic religion. The race would be among participants organized in ten teams, each representing a part of the city with its own colorful flag.

Although, back in Gore, I had spent a lot of dangerous times on a horseback without saddles, what I was about to witness in Siena was something far beyond our boyish adventures in Gore. The race itself involved three fast and dangerous laps around the cobble-stoned *Piazza Del Campo* located at the center of the city.

But, before that, an interesting religious ritual would take place. Early in the morning, the horses and the jockeys and their fans will gather inside a church where the priest would conduct a mass which would be open to the public. I, too, sneaked in; I have never seen a single horse, much less a bunch of them, inside a church before.

Then, they will all assemble at the main square of the city, The *Piazza Del Campo*, where a large number of singing and dancing spectators would be waiting - beer, wine, pizza and Italian sausages in abundance!

Then, attendance of the participants would be taken and, some time in the afternoon, the race takes off! After about two hours, the winner, the first comer, could be a horse with or without its jockey. Once the winner was known, they would all go back to the church for prayer of thanks, marking the end of the festivities.

Satisfied with the wonders of the *Palio* and its rituals, everybody would scramble to go back to where they came from. But, in our case, we had to spend the night in Siena, roaming throughout the night from one party to another.

*****

Life at the school and my exposure and familiarity to this ancient country continued. During my spare time, following on the advice of my good friend Richard Caulk, I would take the train to see as many places as I could; places like Venice, which I believe is the most beautiful city in the whole world. It was my conclusion that Italians, notwithstanding the invasion of my country a few decades earlier, must be or must have been the most talented people on earth.

I wondered frequently why Italians would ever leave their beautiful country at all, as I was told that was the case in the previous decades.

In the meantime, my older brother Miemen, who was studying in Chicago at the time, had initiated a process that would mean yet another major shift in my life. In a series of letters, he would insist that I should not return to Ethiopia; that he would get me a college admission and bring me to Chicago, the United States.

I knew school in Chicago meant a long wait before I went back home. In spite of the decision I had made while in Ethiopia, I still was not sure if I did not want to return home. For one thing, I have left my wife and friends and family behind. For another, I had promised Signora Steganini that I would return in September, although that had actually seemed less and less feasible.

On the other hand, the pressure on me not to return to a very dangerous situation in Addis was intense. I was also curious to see what life looked like in this all-too-important United States. The dilemma I had put aside when I came to Italia was beginning to bug me as my days in Italia were winding down.

True to his word, with the help of my friend Richard who by now had returned to the United States to teach at Rutgers University, my brother Miemen got me an admission (aka, I-20) to the Graduate School of English at the University of Illinois, at Chicago, on condition that I was to take GRE[3] once I got there. He sent me the I-20, and urged me to go and apply for a student's visa at the United States Consulate in Milano.

I was reluctant to do so at first, but with an encouraging letter from my new wife, Menby, I took the train to Milano in mid-August to apply and see what would happen.

Consul: *Mr. Aklilu Kidanu.*
Aklilu: *Yes.*
Consul: *Can I see your papers please?*
Aklilu: *Yes, of course.*
Consul: *I understand you want a student's visa to study in the United States.*
Aklilu: *Yes, I do. I have been admitted to a graduate school.*
Consul: *Yes, I see that, but the rules are that you need to go back to your country and apply for visa from your country.*

---

3   The Graduate Record Exams (GRE), a requirement for admissions to most graduate schools in the United States.

Aklilu: *But, I am here.*

Consul: *Why didn't you apply for a visa while you were in Ethiopia?*

Aklilu: *That was three months ago. I didn't think I would go to the United States at the time, I didn't plan to; this is a new development.*

Consul: *So, why do you want to go now?*

Aklilu: *Well, as you can see, I have been accepted to a graduate school in Chicago now.*

Consul: *Haven't you seen the hundreds of Ethiopians and Eritreans standing outside waiting to get visa? There are too many of you applying.*

Aklilu: *Yes, but how is that my fault?*

Consul: *I didn't say it was your fault.*

Aklilu: *Well then, I have applied. If you give me the visa fine, if not...*

Consul: *If not what?*

Aklilu: *If not, I will go back to my wife, and my country; I still have those.*

Consul: *Is that right?*

Aklilu: *That is right.*

Consul: *Well then, go back to your school; we will let you know.*

Aklilu: *How?*

Consul: *We will call you, bye.*

Aklilu: *Ok, thank you, bye.*

And, to be frank, I had mixed feelings about getting the visa. On one hand, deep inside me and regardless of the situation, I knew I had a country, a home to go to if things did not work out. On the other hand, although I did not fully comprehend what the country stood for, I did not see the possibility of going to America lightly. So, I had told the consul the truth. Yes, I had wanted to go the United States, but I wasn't about to lie to him in order to stay away from my wife, my home, my twin friends, my country, my identity etc. etc.

And, I suspect that the polite but firm consul had sensed that and understood me. But I didn't expect a call at all.

*****

Back in Gargnano, in the main building of the school, there was a long narrow lobby at the middle of which was fixed a telephone booth. It would ring once in a blue moon, and nobody would pay attention. One afternoon, during a lunch break, it rang and it so happened that the same student from Switzerland who had given me her unsolicited advice on how to butter my toast was passing by, and she picked it up. A few minutes later, I heard her calling out, '*Aklilu, Aklilu ... it is for you.*' I ran to the telephone booth and answered the phone.

> '*Mr. Kidanu, this is from the United States Consulate in Milan, you may come and collect your passport; you have been given a student's visa. Congratulations and good luck!*'

I do not remember how I responded or if I responded at all. I only remember hearing the words '*good luck*' and the 'click' sound.

Standing by the telephone booth in bewilderment, I felt my life turning in a direction that I never anticipated a couple of months earlier. It was a mixed feeling of joy, apprehension, uncertainty, and anxiety all at the same time. Strangely, the fact that I was given a visa took me to square one and to the muddle of making a decision all over again.

But now, at least I had two clear options, and I recognized I had to make the most difficult decision of my life: should I proceed to the United States to go to the safety of a graduate school or should I go back to Ethiopia, to my wife, to my job, to my twin friends; but also to a predictably dangerous life.

I had a few sleepless nights. Finally, a letter from my wife convinced me that I should proceed to the United States; she argued, maybe just maybe, she would join me there one day. Then, I rationalized that there will always be a time to go back home. So I decided to go the United States, but only to study and return to my country as soon as possible. I told this to myself again and again to the point where I promised I would leave no room to consider any other option when I completed my studies in the United States - whenever that may be.

*****

My Gargnano school closed sometime in early September, and we had a farewell party at a local club. We were dancing throughout the night with loud songs like the then-popular 'Saturday Night Fever' by the Bee Gees, and drinking plenty of cheap Italian wine. My dancing ability, especially compared to the lots around me, was enviable, thanks to my African beat and my jolly years at Addis Ababa University.

We were having a great time and a bit tipsy, when all of a sudden somebody came up with a crazy idea where each one of us would put the most valuable thing we had on a blanket that was spread on the dancing floor. Then, blindfolded and the crowd screaming '*go! go!*' we would each reach into the blanket one by one and pick whatever came into our grips, and keep it for good. It was supposed to be a reminder of the person who owned it after we had all gone our separate ways.

Now, before I left Ethiopia, my maternal aunt, Etagu, had given me a huge triple-ring to remember her by, and I had it on my index finger. Granted that I wasn't too comfortable with it and, with the influence of wine and Ethiopian pride (or vanity) and a deafening scream that went '*Aklilu go! go!, Aklilu go! go!*', I took the ring off my finger and put it on the blanket on the floor.

Before I realized the huge mistake I had made, somebody had picked it up. My aunt's precious gift, more for the social value, was gone. But, as a source of consolation for me, I found out that the person who got the ring was again the young lady from Switzerland who answered the telephone when the Unites States consul from Milano called. I rationalized that if it were not for her picking up the phone, I would have missed the call. So, I thought perhaps she deserved to get my aunt's gold; and I felt slightly better.

My aunt never asked me about this ring when we saw each other again years later. Maybe she forgot or, knowing her, maybe she did not; maybe she just did not want to hear bad news.

*****

So, before I left Italia, there was one thing I had promised to do: visit Signora Steganini's mother in a small village town near Genoa, Northern Italia. One Friday morning I took the train and arrived in Genoa; I was to stay there for a couple of days. The elderly lady was at the train station waiting for me carrying a sign with my name in huge letters; her daughter had informed her I was coming.

With her broken English and my broken Italian, we got along well. After we exchanged greetings, she asked me to follow her, which I did promptly but it was not easy. This lady was a human machine; she walked so fast that I had to jog along to stay on par with her. Of course, this was going to be a totally new experience for me, a 28 years old Ethiopian man, to spend a couple of nights at the house of an elderly Italian lady I have never seen before.

In any case, as we headed to her house on what looked like a small hill, she would tell me life in Italia was always *'corore, corore. pagare, pagare* [run, run... pay, pay]. I asked her what she was paying and why she was running all the time. She told me rather bitterly about all kinds of bills and taxes she was paying. Typically Ethiopian, where we do not do much *run, run* or *pay, pay,* I didn't know what she meant, but acknowledged her predicament with some sign of concern on my face.[4]

Signora Steganini (Sr.) had planned to show me around. One of the places she took me to was Portofino, a small harbor town built over six hundred years ago, not too far from Genoa. First, we went to a hill by the famous church of *San Giorgio.* From there Portofino could be seen bustling below, providing a most beautiful scene of a small town blended with water at the front and green mountains at the back.

Then we went downhill into the town's famous Piazza where we had yet another delicious Italian food. We saw a few attractions of the city while, all the time, we were chatting with a mix of broken English and Italian.

But I carefully avoided the subject of going back to Ethiopia, when I finished my studies in Italia. I was sure her daughter would have told her about me, and about my promise

---

4   Many years later, in the early 2000s, I found out that Ethiopia collected less that 15% of the total local taxes it should have collected.

to return to Ethiopia once I had completed my studies in Gargnano. I felt bad and ashamed that I was hiding something important, given her exceptionally warm hospitality.

Signora Steganini (Sr.) took this picture of me at a small town (Porto Fino?) along one of the lakes of northern Italia. Early September, 1978

Her daughter had trusted me enough to send me to Italia and I had promised to return to Ethiopia. To this day, I consider this breach of trust as one of my biggest regrets of my life. I swallowed my shame, thanked my elderly lady host with all my heart, and headed back to Gargnano del Garda, never to see her again.

Heading to the United States

The trip

My first and brief exposures to non-Ethiopian culture and way of life in Italia were for the large part additional learning experience mixed with a lot of excitement and wonder that exceeded my expectations. My interaction with the local population in Italy was scant and superficial and, hence, there was very little, if any, major cultural shocks, adaptations and learning curves that I experienced during this initial exposure. This had to wait until I got to the United Sates.

A few days after my visit with Signora Steganini (Sr.), it was time for me to leave Italia for the United Sates. But, I did not want to fly directly to Chicago; I wanted to see Paris and London - two cities I have heard about all my life and looked forward to seeing as much as I could.

Using the money my brother Miemen had sent me wisely, I planned my trip to take me from Milano to Paris and, a few days later, to London by train; then take a one-way flight to New York; and finally take the train to Chicago.

So, a few days before my trip kicked off, I must have gone to the French and British Consulates in Milano to obtain my single entry visas to each country.[5] My goal was to be in Chicago by September 12, in time for registration of classes at the University of Illinois, Chicago.

Soon, I was on the train from Milano to Paris with a backpack and a small carry-on that I packed my entire property in. The nine-hour trip from Milano to Paris went through the Alps Mountain range and small beautiful towns whose name I could not remember. The ride was scenic and comfortable. But, as whenever I was on a train, I remembered the Addis-Dire Dawa train trips I used to make when I was a young boy. European trains were comfortable, spacious and orderly; the Addis-Djibouti trains were crowded, chaotic, but a lot of fun for young people.

By the way, I still do these trips, sadly by car[6]; and one such trip was memorable. Fast forward to the late 2000s when one morning, my wife Menby and my cousin's son, Danny, drove to Asebe Teferi, the birth place of everybody on my parents' side.

---

5   I still have my original passport where I had my visas for France and England, but I do not remember going to the respective embassies or consulates at the time.

6   It looks like I would soon get a chance to make the trip by train once again.

The main purpose of our trip was to see a church in the farmlands near the town of Asebe Teferi where I planned to move my father's remains permanently from its current burial place at Holy Trinity Cathedral (aka *Kidist* Selassie Church) in Addis Ababa. His entire ancestors lived, died and were buried in the vicinity.

So, we got there in the afternoon and, after we checked in our hotel rooms, walked to pay a visit to my then 94-year old aunt, Abaye Beleyu Wolde Giorgis. Abaye was pleasantly surprised to see us, and insisted that we stay for dinner. She lived alone in a simple and clean compound which she preserved like a curator would an art gallery. In spite of her age, she was relatively healthy and strong, with some hearing loss.

When she knew we would not stay for dinner, she insisted that we had breakfast at her home the next morning, and we agreed. So, in the morning the next day at about 6 am, Menby and I went out for a walk on the main road of Asebe Teferi; we were the only two people on the streets. Then, as we were walking in one direction, we saw another lean person walking in the opposite direction across the street from us. We did not recognize the person until it came close enough; it was Abaye.

Abaye had left her home at 6 am to go to the market to buy the ingredients for our breakfast. We pretended not to have seen her, and she did not look in our direction either. When we went to her home about two hours later, she had prepared the best Ethiopian style scrambled eggs and the best tea I have ever had in my entire life.

The lesson was that this elderly lady had made a commitment to prepare breakfast for us and nothing, not even her then-94 year old body or the morning cold in Asebe Teferi, stopped her from carrying it out.

What a generation it was!

*****

Back on the train, when we got to Paris it was late afternoon, and I immediately called my cousin Dr. Mesfin

Retta,[7] who at the time was the Charge De Affair at the Ethiopian Embassy in Paris. He gave me instructions to his apartment by the city train, which I followed without much problem. Mesfin and his wife, Bruktawit, hosted me in Paris for a day, and showed me around, but not much because I was there just for the night. I remember they took me to the movies where we saw one film.

I realized how expensive the tickets were, much like everything else in Paris, and thought about the small amounts we paid at cinemas in Addis - for three films for that matter.

When I was ready to leave for London the next day, the one incident that I remember about Paris was related to a bag of pepper powder that I was supposed to take to my cousins in New York. My cousin's wife in Paris had put the pepper in a plastic bag which I conveniently put in my small handbag, and forgot about it.

So, after bidding farewell to my cousin and his wife, I took the city train to the main train station where I would take the inter-Europe train to London. The city train was a bit crowded, and I found a narrow space just enough for me to stand.

A few minutes into the trip, people started sneezing; and those who were close to me were sneezing violently, and I started to wonder why. I had totally forgotten about the pepper powder in my bag, until I started sneezing myself. Then, I smelt the pepper, and I knew I was the culprit and I had to leave the train immediately. Looking at how the passengers of the train were being affected without knowing why, I felt bad and the three or four minutes to the next stop was like an eternity.

Finally, the train stopped and I left the train, and found a trash can nearby where I dumped the plastic bag full of pepper. Then, I took the next train with confidence. My cousin and his wife never asked me if I delivered on my mission to take pepper to New York. And, I didn't offer to inform.

---

7   All in all, including my siblings and myself, we are sixty-two first cousins.

In any case, the train-ferry-train trip from Paris to London in those days took about eight hours[8] and involved three phases: The first phase was a three-hour train ride between Paris and Calais, France. The second phase was a two-hour ferry ride crossing the English Channel from Calais to Dover, England. The third phase was a three-hour train ride from Dover to London. I somehow braved all that and arrived in London's Victoria Station in early evening of September 3, 1978 -safe and sound.

Not bad for a kid who grew up in rural Gore, I congratulated myself!

*****

As usual, once in London, I asked a taxi driver to take me to an affordable lodging just for the night. He took me to a hostel run by Young Men Christian Association (YMCA), which I thought was quite affordable and comfortable.

In the morning, I woke up to find out the hostel was full of young people, boys and girls, who had come to visit London or who were on their way back to their respective countries. They were mostly Americans and carried their entire property in their backpacks. I was a little bit older but managed to strike a conversation with a couple of them, and marveled at their curiosity and adventures. They have come to Europe to visit and learn - I was a bit jealous.

Then, with a small tourist guide in my hands and the Anglophone advantage, which I didn't have in Roma, I set out to accomplish two missions in London. First, as an English literature major, I wanted to see Westminster Abbey, an old but marvelous Gothic Church where many of my favorite authors, from my Addis Ababa University years, like Charles Dickens and Geoffrey Chaucer, were buried.

Once I got to the church, I was expecting to see tombs very much like I knew at home. Instead, I found out that some of the tombs were actually small marks on the floor of the church.

---

8   The current high speed Eurostar train trip from Paris to London through the English Tunnel takes just 2 hours and fifteen minutes.

So, in a way, I was literally walking on the graves of these literary giants, and I was amazed to say the least.

Anyway, it was getting around noon and I was ready for my second mission in London which was to call Mr. Miller (Sr.), the father of our good old friend in Addis, Michael. I called using the contact number I got from Michael, and Mr. Miller responded in a very polite, sophisticated and formal English that I had heard somewhere before. I was reminded of my Indian high school English teacher in Addis, also called Mr. Miller by coincidence. So, that was what he meant by the 'Queen's English', I told myself.

In any event, although it was a bit difficult to understand his English, Mr. Miller gave me the directions to his office which t I followed easily. It was about lunchtime when I got to his office, and he received me very well. He looked about sixty-five, well-built and genuinely happy to see me. He obviously had heard from his son Michael about me, our friends, and my planned trip to the United States via London.

So Mr. Miller asked me to return at 4:30 pm, and he would take me to his house to spend the night - before I headed out to New York the next day. I had a few hours to see more of London which t I used to quickly visit the Big Ben and The London Bridge. I promised to myself that I would come back some other time and see more, and at 4:30 pm I was at Mr. Miller's office once again.

We took the train from London and headed to a small but affluent looking town called Dorking, Surrey - an hour away from London. This town, I was told, was known for its art galleries and boutiques. I did not get a chance to visit any of these but on our way, I could not but notice the lush green mountains that surrounded the town. Again, I was happily reminded of my upbringing in Gore where the green mountains and valleys and forests were our sanctuary as well as our playground.

Mrs. Miller was waiting for us in a Jaguar at the Dorking train stop. Her greetings were very warm and full of smiles. She drove elegantly and on the right, which amused me a bit.

Besides, I had never been in a Jaguar before, much less seated at the back seat and driven by an elegant white middle-aged lady with snow white gloves on.

When the gate at their house opened, it was clear I was in the hands of a wealthy aristocratic family. I was shown my bedroom on the first floor of what seemed to me more like a castle than an ordinary house. The furniture and accessories in the house was like nothing I had ever seen before, and a far cry from the YMCA hostel where I spent the previous night. Not that it would have made much difference, but I wondered why Michael never told us about his parents' English aristocratic background.[9]

Soon it was dinner time, and I sat by the huge wooden dinner table joined by Mr. and Mrs. Miller, and Michael's younger sister who was warm but spoke very little. I cannot remember what we ate exactly, but it was clear Mrs. Miller had prepared for it. Over dinner we talked about their son Michael in Addis, and how we met and became good friends.

I also told them about some of the things that Michael and his friends in Addis did, which mostly was going to bars, playing chess or trekking around Addis. At one point, I thought about telling Michael's parents about the incident in Sodere back in our college years when we had a live goat kicking upside down in a car where Michael was a passenger. I didn't think his parents would ever imagine such a thing, and I gave the idea up.

All the same, they were happy and grateful that we 'took good care of him', using their words. I expressed my gratitude for having me in their house, and their warm hospitality. Eventually, we all retired to our bedrooms and I prepared, mostly mentally, for my New York trip the next day.

Mr. Miller and I went back to London the next morning the same way we came to Dorking. Once in London, I thanked Mr. Miller with the bottom of my heart, said goodbye to each other,

---

9   I found out from his parents that Michael studied at the elite school of Eton in England; but we would not have known even if he had told us.

and I headed to Gatwick Airport while he went to his office; never to hear from him again.

So, my brief encounter in Europe was about to end, I have learnt a lot and was ready for the United States, for whatever it had to offer - with some apprehension.

I had been told by one of the young tourists at the London YMCA hostel that if I went to the airport early enough, I might be able to buy the cheapest one-way ticket to New York. It turned out to be true, but it also required queuing in line at the airport the whole night. What do I care, I figured, I had plenty of time. Besides, I could use the money I saved.

It was on September 5, 1978, and the airline was called *Skytrain*; and the ticket price for one-way trip from London's Gatwick Airport to New York's John F Kennedy Airport was fifty dollars, or about thirty-five English pounds given the exchange rate at the time. This was a deal I could not pass. So, at about 6 pm, I stood in line with my light luggage in tow.

In front of me, there were dozens of young people who have just finished their vacations in Europe and ready to go back home to the United States. Soon, there were tens of young people behind me, and I was the 'outsider' in the middle.

This was the first time that I saw so many citizens of the United States, mostly students, at one place. Three things intrigued me immediately.

First, there were as many female students as there were male students; second, they were all very vocal, loud but friendly, and within a few minutes we were talking; third, as the queuing time dragged from one to two to three to four hours, I wondered why, even young people from the richest country in the world, would stand in line for so long to save money, like a poor Ethiopian like me. But, in the course of our chat with those near me, I was told that they had set out to travel in Europe about three weeks earlier, and that they operated under a tight budget.

While we were still standing in line, my new friends near me would occasionally ask me if I could watch their luggage while they went to get something to eat. When they came back with some sandwiches, it would be my turn to ask them to return the favor, which they did happily. So, over the course of the queue which lasted over six hours, we took turns several times to go to the bathroom or to walk around and stretch a little bit.

Our perseverance paid off and after hours of standing in line, we got our fifty-dollar one-way ticket to New York; we congratulated each other, and went our ways till we boarded the plane. It was not until late morning the next day that we boarded a huge Boeing 707 for a non-stop flight to New York. I do not remember if we were assigned seats or how many passengers were aboard but, once inside, the plane seemed more like inside a huge hall than a flying machine.

I closed my eyes as it sped on the runway hoping it would take off safely with the entire load it had carried. For a brief moment I also wondered what it would have been like to stand behind the plane as it sped for takeoff - just like we used to do in Gore years ago behind the DC-3 airplanes.

It probably would have been a totally different story!

*****

The flight from London to New York was a very long one, about 12 hours in those days. I was tired from standing in line most of the previous night, and I slept the first half of the flight soundly. During the second half of the flight, I was mostly awake. The fact that I was heading to the United States, something that was not in my mind only three months earlier, started sinking-in slowly but surely.

Unlike during the flight from Nairobi to Roma when I thought about my past, my flight to New York was also filled with thoughts, but of my future. I reckoned I was about to start life in a foreign country for an extended and unspecified period of time, and I was worried. I was worried because, by age 28, I had already developed an Ethiopian 'identity', for whatever it's worth, and I did not want to lose it.

My childhood in Gore, added to my boyhood in Addis, had instilled values, good and bad, in me that went right through my heart. The question in front of me and that I dreaded was if my continued exposure to new cultures and ways of life would change me so significantly that they would separate me, perhaps permanently or for most of my life, from the country and people that I have grown to accept as mine.

Surely, my stay in Italia was too short for me to understand and learn about the full impact of living as a minority black man in a white man's world. That was yet to come. In fact, Italia was really a treat in terms of the wonderful culture and handcraftsmanship, not to speak of the food and hospitality, which I was lucky enough to enjoy. The few Italians who I came to know were warm and friendly and have lived up to my expectation from a 'host'. I was not sure, however, what would have happened if I had stayed much longer. Neither did I want to stay and find out!

Similarly, whatever opinions I had about the United Sates at the time were mostly positive. I have heard so much about the country, much of it from my Peace Corps teachers in Gore and the movies I saw as a high school student in Addis. Surely, I was eager to see what the country and the people looked like.

At the same time, I was aware of the racism that prevailed in the United States, although I did not know exactly how it expressed itself or how deep-rooted it was. But, this was my chance to find out and I was ready with an open mind, primarily as a 'guest' - as I would always like to be seen when outside Ethiopia.

*****

As I struggled with these issues, we were told the plane was about to land at JFK Airport in New York. When we landed, it was getting dark. My first encounter was with immigration officers who I found to be very professional and welcoming. I could not but also notice a few African Americans at close range, which reminded me of my Peace Corps teacher in Gore, Floyd B Davis, when I was thirteen.

When all was cleared, just like I did in Roma and London, I asked a taxi driver to take me to an affordable hotel where I would stay for the night. The taxi driver was an African American who spoke very little and, when he did, I honestly could not understand a word of what he was saying. And, I thought I spoke English. He somehow understood my request, parked in a drive way, took out my luggage and said *'Here you are bro!'*

A bit confused by the way he addressed me, I paid my fares and entered a structure where I was met with another African American, the receptionist apparently.

I ended up in an attic bedroom on the third floor of an old building, in a hot summer night with no air conditioner. It was not very comfortable. Before I collapsed in heavy sleep, I wondered why an 'affordable' hotel in Roma, not to mention the YMCA hostel in London, would be better than an affordable hotel in New York. After all, wasn't the United States the wealthiest country on earth? My first impression was already in place.

In the morning, it was my chance to discover more. New York of the late 1970s took me by surprise, considering what I heard about the city as a young boy. The subways were full of threatening graffiti, and the streets were not so clean. Even the places that were clean and impressive were threatening in their own ways; and I did not feel comfortable. The tall buildings, noise and rush were just too much for me to handle, and I was ready to proceed to Chicago, hoping it would be better.

In the afternoon, I met my cousin Yeshi Retta, who was living in upper Manhattan, after a long and frustrating effort to locate her apartment. I spent a couple of nights with her, and she was kind enough to show me the better face of New York, places like Times Square, the Statue of Liberty; and I felt much better about New York.

The honeymoon

Then, on September 11, 1978, I took yet another train from New York to Chicago. This was the last leg of my travel plan which, so far, had gone perfectly well. I arrived at Chicago Union Station on a hot Sunday afternoon in mid-September, one day before registration for classes. My brother Miemen and two of his Ethiopian friends, Dereje and Fikre Mariam, met me at the train station. We proceeded to his apartment on

Fullerton and Clark avenues, close to Lake Michigan and its beaches. I noticed how relaxed and happy my brother and his friends were, and I could see why, at least superficially.

In any case, it was a pleasure to see my brother after about three years. My brother had a nice two-bedroom apartment, and a common balcony at the entrance of the building. No sooner had we put my luggage in my bedroom than we all went out to the balcony and resumed drinking beer. So far so good, I told myself. After all, I like that idea of drinking beer on a balcony. I was to live with my brother till I found something that would make me more independent.

Regarding the graduate program in English literature I had come to pursue, I was as reluctant as I was during my freshman year at Haile Selassie I University, nine years earlier. But I knew I did not have much choice but to brace for the long haul as a graduate student in the United Sates. Even if temporarily, I told myself, I better learn the Chicago vernacular.

Chicago, my first major metropolitan city to live in, impressed me infinitely and I was excited. In those days, the 108-story Sears Tower was the tallest building in the world; O'Hare Airport was the busiest; and Michigan Avenue was the richest one-mile. There was also the Lake Shore Drive where the Drake Hotel, the hotel that had once hosted Emperor Haile Selassie, was located; the Lincoln Park Zoo and the numerous Chicago museums were all impressive land marks at a walking distance from my brother's apartment.

Add to all these, the small Italian community near campus that sold the best Italian subs, sausages and pizzas. Our favorite joint, especially after my wife joined me, was Papa Charlie. They served by far the best pizza and pitcher beer I had ever tasted. So, once in a month or so depending on our budget, we would treat ourselves and take the train ride home a bit tipsy. I still use Papa Charlie, not sure if it is still there, as the standard for good pizza and beer; I actually liked Chicago a lot.

In addition, at the time, Chicago had a small but tight Ethiopian community[10] that met for the Ethiopian holidays or Super Bowls. I also had a special Saturday afternoon session with Nega Beru, who at the time was a doctoral candidate in biochemistry at the University of Chicago, when we played chess for hours at a joint called Sam's Club in Southside Chicago. Once in a while and in the middle of a game, Nega would make his move and ask to be excused so he could go and check his lab at his close-by university while I contemplated my next move. We enjoyed these Saturday sessions immensely and, with glasses of beer in our hands, most of the time Nega would beat me hands down.

Add to all these, a nice Ethiopian restaurant called *Mama Desta,* owned and run by a close friend of my brother's, Tekele Wolde Gabriel, I was beginning to feel at home in Chicago.

I also realized early on, while in Chicago, that the ordinary Americans who you met at places like laundromats or groceries were simple, straightforward and very helpful. They dressed casually and practically, kept their boundaries and respected your opinions, and did not interfere in what you did - unless you asked for help.

Many would be eager to know, and give you the benefit of the doubt to the point where they would believe you if you told them, without any evidence, that you were the oldest son of Emperor Haile Selassie. But, when they tell you about them, usually it was in a very modest and honest way. Hence, I had wondered many times if most of the politicians of the country were drawn from the same population or if they were a separate breed of people altogether!

But, I found out soon enough, that that was only half the story. My honeymoon in Chicago was about to end - inevitably. Little did I know that the following weeks and months were also to be marked with a series of cultural shocks, which I never experienced or prepared for.

---

10 Notably, Lema Kifle, Nega Beru, Dereje Eneyew, Dawit Getachew, Tekele Wolde Gabriel, Adisu Gessese and Efrem Kifle.

They shook me to the core!

Cultural shocks and adaptations

I did not, of course, expect to continue my daily Ethiopian routine in Chicago; I already had a break in my routine about three months earlier. I did not have any dietary problems since I was used to eating non-Ethiopian food as I was growing up. Neither did I have significant interaction problems since I spoke English fairly well, although there were times when my English accent, added to my looks, was mistaken for Spanish or Puerto Rican.

One day, about two months after I arrived in Chicago, one of my professors invited me to a Thanksgiving dinner at his house. He and his family lived in one of the northern Chicago suburbs, on Howard Street. I got to the suburb by train, and started looking for Howard Street, but I could not find it. So I was desperately walking up and down when I saw an African American gentleman fixing something in the engine of his car.

So I got close to the gentleman and, in a very polite way lest I disturb what he was doing, asked if he could please tell me how to get to Howard Street. The gentleman looked up at me curiously and said, *'Man, I don't speak no Spanish.'*

A bit confused, I replied that I didn't speak Spanish either. Then, he got frustrated and yelled, *'Man, I say speak to me in Ingles, no Espanol!'* I left him alone, but felt some kind of pain or chagrin in my stomach. Then I paused for a moment and jokingly wondered if I had learnt 'forged' English at Addis Ababa University! I eventually located Howard Street and my professor's house. It was my first Thanksgiving experience with all the history and culture surrounding it, as I was told by my good professor.

In any case, the fast pace of life in Chicago, compared to what I briefly saw in New York, did not bother me much either. But it was clear my 'honeymoon' in Chicago was about to end abruptly and inevitably, in the form of severe cultural shocks. I believe these shocks were exacerbated because I had not come to the United States prepared to change countries or ways of life, but to accomplish a purpose - go to school.

Yes, I was open to some changes, but my thinking was that my Ethiopian identity, culture and the way of life, may give way temporarily, but would remain steadfast in the long term.

*****

The first shock came during my first few days in Chicago, when I was moving around the campus of the university trying to finalize registration for classes. At one fateful point, I happened to be walking in a hallway where, on each side of the hallway, there were photographs of gay and lesbian students demonstrating for their rights; some photos showed same-sex couples posing in compromising positions. Of course, I had heard about gays and lesbians before, but I never thought I would be facing them as real and at close range as I did on this day.

Given my background in a predominantly patriarchal Ethiopia and as a male of 28 years, my first reaction was total disgust. My understanding, also influenced to some extent by several left-wing literatures that complained about this group of people, was that they were reactionary and among the final outcomes of a decaying capitalist society; I was already becoming disoriented.

Another related cultural shock took place when, one night a few days after I arrived in Chicago, my brother Miemen and I went to a bar on Clark and Fullerton streets, not too far from our apartment. We were talking and laughing when, all of a sudden, a strange conversation ensued between us.

'Aklilu, do you see that woman sitting over there?', my brother asked pointing to the stool at the bar.
'Yes, I see her, what about her?', I asked.
'It actually is not a woman.'
'So, what is it?', I asked.
'Aklilu, I am telling you it is not a woman.'
'Well, Miemen, I do not know what you are seeing or talking about, but what I see is a lady', I responded with confidence.

'It is a man.'
'Are you trying to test me or what?'
'Well, Aklilu, if you are going to live in this country even for a short while, you might as well learn a few things.'
'Yes, but this is not learning', I replied.
'Just take a close look at her', my brother insisted.
'Miemen, let us not talk about this anymore', I said with a clear sign of frustration.

He smiled and tried to change the subject; it was clear he wanted peace. But I could not help but wonder about what my brother was talking about. I stole a couple of glances at this lady and could clearly see her lipstick, her dress, her hair (or hairpiece) and behaved like a woman and my brother had the audacity to tell me it was a man!

In the end, my brother was actually right; but I was lost in a 'strange' culture.

*****

There were also other less significant examples of cultural shock, which I had to learn to deal and contend with.

For instance, as much as I loved swimming, I did not know how to handle standing stark naked in the men's shower room, in full view of everybody twice - both before and after swimming! Exposing myself like that, I felt it was a violation of my privacy. And, I knew no one of my friends back in Ethiopia would ever do that! But, eventually, when I saw my other *habesha* friends do it at the university's swimming pool, I did it too; but it was not easy for a rural kid from Gore!

In yet another example, one day, my brother politely advised me to put deodorant on. Of course, I was a young male of the 1970's and no self-respecting Ethiopian would in his right mind use deodorant or aftershave in those days. Not even our girlfriends demanded it. So my brother gambled to his dismay.

'Aklilu, can we talk?

'About what?'

'It is hot and humid here in Chicago in the summer', he explained very politely, *'and it might be a good idea if you put deodorant on. I have plenty, here is one.'*

'I never had to put on deodorant in Ethiopia, and I was fine', I responded with some irritation, my pride was hurt.

'But it doesn't get as hot in Ethiopia, and maybe there was no need. But here it is a different situation', he responded.

'I am not going to put any deodorant on; in fact, I feel sorry for you for putting deodorant and perfumes all over your body like a woman', I told my brother with some controlled anger.

My brother shook his head and quietly walked away; he was used to me and my behavior by this time.

But, with all these 'anomalies', my initial excitement of coming to the United States was beginning to fizzle and, in a few days, I was already sorry I had come to the United States. I blamed my brother who, after all, was responsible for bringing me to the United States. I took every opportunity to make him feel bad or guilty for separating me from my wife, my twin friends, my country, and putting me in this kind of predicament, where I had to wear deodorant! I told him, if he had advised me about all these feminine things before, I would never have set my feet in the United States.

But my brother knew that I would eventually adapt, whether I liked or not. Returning to Ethiopia was not an option at the time; so he kept a low profile knowing time would resolve problems. Typical of my older brother, when it was a matter of disagreement between the two of us, he would shake his head and quietly walk away which, in fact, made me even angrier.

That was how my brother was, and this is true to this day. He is two years older than me and he always deferred to me as if I was the older one. Our mother once told me that that had always been the case since the day I was born.

In any case, I had adamantly refused to apply any deodorant or aftershave or anything that I believed violated my manhood. I was impervious to the polite signs that my classmates or colleagues at my part-time job at the university's mail office showed me in this regard. I now in hindsight also remember that some of my female classmates were changing seats if I happened to be sitting next to them; but I was simply too insensitive to notice.

But, one day, one of my African American colleagues at my university part-time job, Smithy, told me bluntly.

> *'Hey Ak!',* he called out using the nick name he had given me, *'come over here.'*
> *'What do you want Smithy?',* I asked as I approached him.
> *'Here, I am going to give you some brotherly advice',* he responded.
> *'What advice?',* I asked.
> *'Listen up! You better put this damn deodorant on before you learnt to do it the hard way!',* he yelled at me.

It was the same deodorant issue again, I did not respond; needless to say, I was intrigued and hurt.

Smithy, probably in his mid-30s at the time, actually was a person I really liked. He was nice and funny, and very articulate. He once told me on a Friday afternoon, in front of his white colleagues, that he could not wait to go to his Southside Chicago home and spend the entire weekend without having to see a single white person. Not sure why, since I did not fully understand the race dynamics at the time, but we all thought what he said was very funny and laughed our hearts out.

On another occasion, a few months after I arrived in Chicago, Smithy asked me how I crossed the English Channel on my way from Italy to the United States. I innocently responded *'by ship'*; but that was not how it sounded to Smithy. So, he started laughing and making bleating sound while I struggled to read his mind, and where I made a mistake. I actually was not angry at him since, back in Ethiopia, I always used to make fun of my expat friends, especially Michael Miller the British, when he spoke even one word of Amharic.

'So you crossed the English Channel by sheep?' Smithy would ask me with more bleating sound; and I would still respond positively.

Finally, when he and our other colleagues got tired of laughing, he explained to me the difference in pronunciation between the words 'ship' (with a short 'e') and 'sheep' (with a longer 'e'). I, obviously, used the long 'e' which prompted Smithy's cruel jokes. I now know how poor Michael felt! So, now, every time I see a 'sheep', I think of Smithy; I guess I must have been scarred!

In any case, I was hurt a little bit by his advice on the deodorant issue. I did not know what he meant by the 'hard way', and I was devastated that my good friend Smithy would say such a thing to me. I went home a bit angry, and I felt my pride, for whatever it's worth, was on the line.

But, after some reflections, I put one (my brother's) and one (Smithy's) advice together and decided to try the all-too-important deodorant. After all, I figured it would not kill me or my good old friends in Ethiopia would not see me. So, the next morning I ran into my brother in the bathroom on purpose and asked him to give me a deodorant. With a notorious smile, he handed me one.

*****

Talking about cultural shocks, I remember a joke (or it could be a true story!) which one of my close Eritrean friends told me while in the United States.

So, an Eritrean gentleman who had just come to the United States goes to a Mc Donald's with his friend to eat something that he had heard a lot about, but never eaten: hamburger. Neither had he ever ordered food at a fast food restaurant before. So, as he waited in line to order his food, he was a bit nervous. His Eritrean friend was standing right behind him.

When he finally approached the counter, one of the sales girls and the Eritrean gentleman started a brief dialogue.

Sales girl: *So, what can I get you sir?*
Eritrean gentleman: *Hamburger.*
Sales girl: *Ok, sir. What would you like to have in it?*
Eritrean gentleman: *Meat.*

Sales girl: *Yes, of course, there will be meat. But, what else would you like to have in the hamburger?*
Eritrean gentleman: *Meat.*
Sales girl: *I heard that sir; but what else?*
Eritrean gentleman: *I told you meat!*

After a few more futile attempts, the sales girl threw her hands up in the air in despair, perhaps regretting the day she decided to work at Mc Donald's.

The Eritrean gentleman, equally frustrated, turns to his friend and, in his native Tigrinya, complains, *'Ewai...why is this woman giving me so much trouble? Isn't 'siga'*[11] *translated as 'meat' in English? I told her three times; let us go somewhere else!'*

Such things happened a lot. I remember it took a long time for my wife and I to order meals other than those we were very familiar with; especially when we did not have enough money to spend on food which we may not like. And, that was the case more often than not!

Learning curves and social consciousness

In any case, now that my deodorant problem was solved, I still had to figure out how to address the issue of gays and lesbians. Having spent eight years at Addis Ababa University, even if I had belonged to the 'jolly' group of students who were considered as liberal as one could be in Ethiopia, nothing had prepared me for what I was faced with at the Chicago campus.

Neither did I have the chance to read or talk to people about homosexual relationships as I was growing up in Ethiopia. It was (and I believe it still is) a total taboo, and worse.[12] I was the product of my society. But, as the proverb *'While in Roma, do as the Romans do',* goes, I had to learn to live as most Chicagoans did, i.e., accept individual rights and choices no matter what.

A few weeks after I arrived in Chicago, as one of my left wing tendencies, I had subscribed to The Guardian, a liberal

---

11   Tigrigna and Amharic word for 'meat.'
12   Homosexuality is still illegal in Ethiopia.

newspaper that I received on a weekly basis. In one of its articles about gays and lesbians, the Guardian had argued that if someone was so prejudiced or so insistently opposed to something, it either could mean that the person was not so confident of his/her own position or that the person had something of what he/she opposed in himself/herself in the first place.

At first, I did not understand what the Guardian was trying to tell; it was a bit too complicated for me. So, my immediate reaction was to cancel my subscription of the Guardian with a strong letter of disapproval of the arguments posed supporting the rights of gays and lesbians. Of course, no one responded; but the Guardian ceased coming.

Then, after reading the Guardian's arguments repeatedly, I started to ask myself why I should be bothered by the sexual choices or orientations of other people if I were confident of my own choice or orientation? I figured this question applied in other situations like in religious orientations: if people were sure of their own religious inclinations, why should they be so bothered by the inclinations of other people if they happened to be different?

Then I concluded that The Guardian, after all, was absolutely right: prejudiced people do not have confidence in their own inclinations or they secretly admire the inclinations that they oppose so profoundly in public. It took me some time, but I got it!

So, the more I thought about it, I simplified and extended the Guardian's argument and concluded that it was all a matter of choice. For instance, if I went to a café with a friend and he chose to have coffee and I chose to have tea, who was to say that he made the right choice and I made the wrong choice or vice versa? Similarly, as long as I am sure of my own sexual orientation whatever it may be, who am I to question, much less oppose, somebody else's orientation?

I also understood that supporting a position does not make one part of that position; conversely, not to be part of a position is not necessarily opposing it. Problems arise when one tries to force his or her position (choice or inclination) on others; and this is true in most aspects of life; gays and lesbians are no exceptions. I knew, such a position was something that would put me on a path of conflict with most, if not all, my friends when I return to Ethiopia. I knew exactly how they would react!

But still, in spite of my revised position, there was one lingering doubt in my mind on the issue. For instance, even if I believed that it was a matter of personal choice or orientation; wouldn't I still mind to hear that one of my beloved ones was gay? In other words, would I pretend to support gay rights only as long it did not directly affect me?

I know parents who have accepted their children's homosexuality by hook or by crook; but I do not know what they went through in the process. Honestly, I suspect they have gone through a lot, and I also believe such people are to be admired.

Hence, to my mind, the questions 'Do you support gay rights?' and 'Would you like to see one of your loved ones to be gay?' are two totally different questions that, if honestly answered, might produce two totally different answers.

But, nevertheless, I have learnt a lot, and come a long way. So, with some adaptation on this and similar issues on my part, I thought I owed an apology to my brother Miemen. So one day, I found him at the university's main cafeteria all by himself reading. And, using his nickname, Mimi, which I use when I want to be nice to him, I struck a conversation with him. I have, by now, learnt to apologize!

Aklilu: *Hey Mimi; I owe you an apology.*
Miemen: *What about?*
Aklilu: *You know I was hard on you on the deodorant and gay/lesbian issues; that was because I did not know.*
Miemen: *What do you know now?*
Aklilu: *Well, I now know it is a matter of choice and orientation; and it is live and let live. I am also sorry I blamed you for bringing me to Chicago. I did not mean it*
Miemen: *Good; one more thing, Aklilu.*
Aklilu: *What Mimi?*

Miemen: *You don't hold hands with men in this county unless….*

He said this with such a mischievous smile I almost quarreled with him again. Of course, he knew that we grew up in Gore not only holding hands with our boyhood friends but also putting our arms around each other's shoulders wherever we went. The good old days!

'It is too late for me to do that now, anyway', I told him. By now, I had learnt to control my temper, and I was also learning and adapting.

Also, unlike in Italia, and for the first time in my life at age 28, my race had become an issue in Chicago. It is not that I personally experienced overt racism, but I belonged to a racial group that was a victim of personal and institutionalized racism. I was repeatedly reminded about racism in the media, from my classmates, and from my Ethiopian friends who had lived in Chicago for some time. So, as a black man, regardless of my country of origin or whether I personally experienced it, by definition, I was a victim of racism too.

So, for a person who lived his entire life with no racial prejudice one way or another,[13] this came as a big cultural shock to me. First, I did not understand it. In fact, when my father visited a few years after I settled in Chicago, he could not understand two things no matter how hard I tried to explain to him: racism and the snow. I suspect, this would be true for a vast majority (if not all) of Ethiopians at the time.

In any case, instead of adapting to racism as I had to many other cultural shocks, I identified and sided with black and white people who attempted to mitigate the problem while, at the same time, I held no blanket hatred towards all white people. That became my strategy for the rest of my stay in the United States.

All the while, I was struggling with my graduate program in English literature.

---

13 Out of respect for my African brothers and sisters, I defer to overstate the fact that Ethiopia was never colonized and, hence, most Ethiopians never experienced white versus black racism in their history.

*****

Now that my problems with deodorants and people of alternative sexual orientation were mostly resolved, I was more than happy to engage in the several issues of social consciousness that the students exhibited in those days; the 1970's and early 80s. Such social consciousness, by the way, had faded in the 1990s and, I suspect, had totally disappeared from United States campuses in the 2000s.

So, for international students, three major issues dominated at the time: the Shah of Iran, Apartheid in South Africa, and occupation of Palestine by Israel. There were always student leaders, sometimes from the countries at stake, who organized and led demonstrations, public speeches and group discussions, which I was willing to attend more than the graduate classes that I had registered for.

My highly politicized student years at Haile Selassie I University in the early 1970s came in handy for these. So, I became friends with students from Iran, Palestine and South Africa. I learnt firsthand about the injustices in these countries inflicted upon them by corrupt leaders or outright racist political and religious groups and governments.

Unfortunately, the United States government was directly or indirectly behind these governments, a situation that highlighted to many others and myself that 'hypocrisy' was no concern to political establishments, especially those with the military power.

I remember in late 1978, just a few months after I enrolled at the university and with the leadership of active Iranian students, we repeatedly marched against the corrupt and brutal government of Mohammad Reza, the Shah of Iran. He was overthrown in January 1979, and not much that I remember happened on campus after that.

Then, apartheid, a brutally violent racial segregation system, in South Africa, was a target during much of my university years in the United States. I teamed up with students or refugees from South Africa to march against the classification of people into racial groups; and the use of forceful relocation of black people from their natural homes into artificially created segregated neighborhoods. We marched supporting the African National Congress (ANC) and condemning countries that invested in apartheid, including countries like the United States[14], Israel and most of the so-called free world.

It was becoming clear to me that there was no 'right' or 'wrong' in politics; there was only 'benefits' attained through 'might' or 'deceit.' But what hurt me the most was the brutal occupation of the Palestinian people by the Israeli government. It hurt me because, as a young boy in Ethiopia, I had witnessed my parents and all the people I knew, for that matter, believing in and swearing by the 'God of Israel'. I would hear my grandmother, a very pious woman who spent her last several years as a nun, mention the word 'Israel' every few minutes.

So, in my young mind, Israel must have been a blessed country with blessed people. I was never a religious person and personally did not care for all those biblical fictions - I had seen enough religious hypocrisies and double standards. But my family's religious feelings was something that I appreciated and cared for deeply. And, I felt they were betrayed or at least so blatantly misinformed. Was there something I could do?

*****

Fast forward to April 25, 1991, The New York Times, on Page A3 published an article entitled '*Odd Twist in West Bank Punishment.*'[15]

It was a true story, accompanied by a photograph of six Palestinian children standing near their demolished house. A few days earlier, their father had been killed by the Israeli Defense Force (IDF) for 'injuring' an Israeli soldier.

If nothing else, I thought I should write a letter of protest, against the advice of some of my friends who feared some kind of retribution. I did not care; I knew the brave ones had faced inhuman retributions all their lives for demanding dignity and

---

14   The United States and much of the western world had declared the
     ANC and Nelson Mandela 'terrorist' until 2008!
15   I still have a copy of the article.

freedom. I also knew that my letter of protest would pale in front of the bravery of such people.

'If that is how you feel', my wife said, *'go ahead.'*

So, as if I was doing it on behalf of my parents and grandmother, if not on behalf of the Palestinians suffering under vindictive and crippling occupation, I wrote a potent but polite letter of protest, dated on May 1, 1991, which read as follows.

Wednesday, May 1, 1991
Dear:
Last week the New York Times reported a moving story about six Palestinian children in the West Bank whose father was killed by an Israeli soldier (The New York Times Thursday April 25, 1991. p. A3). To punish the family of the dead Palestinian, the Israeli government evicted his widow and six children, sealed his house, and is getting ready to demolish it.

The children have already been punished: their father is dead, the scar and terror of their father's death will remain with them forever. How much more could they be punished? It hurts. It MUST hurt. The world is full of examples where similar actions in the past were ignored at the time they were being committed, only to haunt us at future times. We MUST protest. We owe at least this much to the past, present and future history of the human kind. We owe it to ourselves. Most of all, we owe it to our children.

Regardless of your religious or political persuasion, if you as an individual believe in the fundamental principle that innocent children MUST not be punished for actions that they have NOTHING to do with, and if you also believe that there is more to life than to make a career and a comfortable living, I challenge you to write a letter of protest to the Israeli government and to organizations that may have some influence on it (see list enclosed.)

We are ALL mortal. As Leo Rosten says, let us stand for something and see if we can make some difference that we lived at all.

Thank you.
Aklilu Kidanu
3009 Winterhaven
Newark, DE 19702

I sent copies of this letter to 48 organizations all over the world: 2 US government offices; 5 Israeli government offices all over the Unites States; 24 Jewish organization within the United States; 5 human rights organizations within the United States; 6 Jewish organizations outside the United States; and 6 international peace organizations outside the United States.[16]

I also put a copy in every mailbox of the staff of University of Delaware, where I was a student at the time.

My letter simply highlighted that innocent children MUST not be punished for 'crimes' that their father may have committed. I got responses from 8 organizations, 3 of them Jewish.[17]Some agreed with me, and some accused me of being one sided; and some both. I knew such responses were crocodile tears and did not mean much since it was clear to us all that the occupation had been going on for decades before I wrote my letter of protest, and probably will go on unabated for the foreseeable future.

There were also a couple of responses that suggested that I worry about the famine and starvation in my own country instead of pocking my nose in somebody else's business. In a way, even if they were blunt, at least they were more honest. Their argument, of course, missed the whole point, and was not worth responding to.

A few of my American friends told me that I was naïve and that I failed to understand the distribution of power and benefits in the United States and in the world. My graduate assistantship supervisor at the university, Edward (Ed) Ratledge, read my letter which he found in his campus mailbox, called me to his office and told me point blank: *'Aklilu, do not be stupid. What rules this world is not compassion; it is power.'*

---

16 I still have the list of the organizations.
17 They were: Jewish Peace Fellowship; Canadian Jewish Congress; and Tel Aviv University. I still have copies of their letters.

Ed, by the way, is a character I would never forget. Only a few years older than me, he is a blunt no-nonsense guy with no trace of formality. One day, in early 1989, I was struggling with my dissertation where I had to mount the homicide data-tape for the entire country from the NCHS (National Center for Health Statistics) Atlanta data-base onto our university's mainframe computer, and I had a hitch. It was about mid-night, and I could not interrupt the process or else I would have to start all over again some other time. So, I took a deep breath, and called Ed; he was the only one who could help me.

Ed: *Why are you calling me at this time?*
Aklilu: *Well Ed, I am having difficulties with copying data from the NCHS tapes.*
Ed: *So, what do you want me to do?*
Aklilu: *I need your help.*
Ed: *Do you know what time it is?*
Aklilu: *I know, and I am sorry. But, if I quit now, it will mean I have to start all over again which is like 6 hours of work; you know that.*
Ed: *Ok, tell me what is the problem?*

I was in the process of explaining the problem when the telephone hung-up without a warning; obviously he did not understand me. I sat on my chair wondering what to do. Then, within ten minutes, the door of the graduate students' office where I was working swung open, and it was Ed in his pajamas. He didn't even look at me much less talk to me. He pushed me from my chair and sat facing the terminal. Within minutes he had fixed the problem.

Before I got the chance to thank him, he looked at me and yelled, *'Why don't you use your block head!'* and stormed out of the room. He was also mad because he took a sip from my cup of coffee which had some sugar in it. Ed hated sugar in his coffee!

I wasn't offended, but kept on working till I finished at 3 am in the morning. I actually liked Ed a lot! If the proverb *'Barking dogs seldom bite'* holds some credence, it was true with Ed.

Besides, I learnt much of the skills that formed my livelihood for the coming three decades from Ed Ratledge.

*****

In any case, back to the Israel-Palestine issue, I continued sending similar letters, the last one being on February 23, 1992. So, a week later, I got a call from the Information Officer at Consulate General of Israel in Philadelphia, inviting me to his office to 'exchange views/information' regarding my letter. I obliged, in spite of strong warnings and advice to the contrary by my friends; I have then wondered why Americans were so afraid of Israel.

Anyway, I went to Philadelphia, which was only a one-hour drive from my office in Dover, Delaware. It was the morning of March 3, 1992. After security procedures that bothered me a lot even in those days, I was led to his office, took a seat, and our conversation ensued.

Officer: *Welcome Aklilu, can I offer you some juice.*
Aklilu: *No thank you, I have had my coffee.*
Officer: *I have read your February 23 letter, now tell me about yourself.*
Aklilu: *I am Ethiopian, and working in Delaware for the time being; there isn't really much interesting thing to know about me.*
Officer: *What do you mean 'for the time being'?*
Aklilu: *I will go back home soon.*
Officer: *Ok, in your letter you said your parents worshiped and swore by the God of Israel, and you were raised in that culture. Tell me more.*
Aklilu: *Yes that is true, that was before I knew what I know now.*
Officer: *What do you know now?*
Aklilu: *I know now that my parents were let down.*
Officer: *What do you mean?*
Aklilu: *I know now that Palestinians are under a brutal occupation by Israel and Israel, after all, was not as holy and as blessed as most Ethiopians, including my parents, believed.*
Officer: *Do you also know that there was violence coming from the Palestinians towards innocent Israelis?*

Aklilu: *I know and I am sorry innocent Israelis are dying. But, Palestinians have been under occupation for decades.*
Officer: *Does that give them the license to kill innocent people?*
Aklilu: *No, but it gives them the license to resist.*
Officer: *Through terrorism?*
Aklilu: *I am not sure what you mean by terrorism.*
Officer: *Don't you think killing innocent civilians is terrorism?*
Aklilu: *Well, it depends. When one is occupied one has the right to fight back. We have done it in Ethiopia during the Fascist Italian occupation, and the French have done it against Nazi German occupation. Without occupation, there will not be terrorism.*

This answer, which, in the eyes of the officer, compared Israeli occupation of Palestinians with the Fascist Italia's occupation of Ethiopia and Nazi Germany's occupation of France, did not settle well with him at all. I did not do it intentionally; it came in the course of our discussion, but he was clearly agitated by my answer.

He cut our conversation short, and asked the security guard to show me out. I drove back to my office and a few days later sent a letter of apology to the officer.

Here is a copy of the full letter.

Saturday, March 7, 1992

Dear Dr. Pollock:
I thank you for taking the time to share your views with me and to listen to my views. In spite of our differences on the surface, I can feel that, deep inside, we do have a lot of things in common.

I sincerely apologize if I have offended your sensitivities during the course of our discussion. It was not intentional. I also appreciate the difficult situation you are in. Nevertheless, I stand firm on my view that any occupation is fundamentally wrong because, by nature, it could only be violent and unjust. Its primary victims are always the children.

I very much hope that, for the sake of Israel itself and for the sake of the Palestinian people, particularly the children, your government will find a way of ending this occupation as soon as possible.

Sincerely,
Aklilu Kidanu

I did not get a response; neither did I expect one.

I sincerely believed and still believe that unless Israel ended Palestinian occupation, apartheid is the only other outcome; if it hasn't happened already.[18]

Such being the case, in my view, Israel cannot claim to be a democratic country and run an apartheid system. Israelis should be smart enough to know that they cannot have the cake and eat it too; history will tell as we have witnessed in South Africa.

I feel better when I think half of Israelis probably believe the way I do; I trust they do not want to be part of a system that occupies and denies millions of people their basic human rights. But unfortunately and sadly, a rigged political system in the country allows a minority religious zealots to rule the country and influence the United States and, by extension, much of the so-called free world in their favor.

So, right in front of our eyes, Israel's reputation as a high-tech science and medicine country is slowly being replaced by a pariah apartheid state. Where is the country heading? This is not a question for me to ask; it is for the Israelis themselves, and before it is too late!

Sadly, though, much more brutal things have happened to Palestinians since the 1991 New York Times article: walls that separated neighborhoods; brutal and dehumanizing searches and blockades; and blanket bombings of entire neighborhoods with thousands of civilian, including children, causalities have now become the norm. But for the early 1990s' this incident

---

18 But, later, to my dismay, I heard Noam Chomsky, a prominent American linguist and philosopher, say it is 'much worse than apartheid' suggesting a 'real' third outcome: systematically destroying Palestinians as a people. Noam, Jewish himself, said, 'The Israeli relationship to the Palestinians in the Occupied Territories is totally different [than South Africa's apartheid. They just don't want them. They want them out or at least in prison.'

reported by the New York Times of demolishing the house of a dead Palestinian father with six children was as bad as it could get; but little did I know.

I very much hope that Israelis would one day end the occupation and let Palestinians live in dignity and in freedom. I also very much hope that I will one day visit free Palestine - if not me, my children - and learn about their struggle - just like we did in free South Africa.

In shaa Allah!

Married Life and More Learning

Early married life

Rewinding back to Chicago, it was in 1979 that I first discovered the wrath of the cold in the winter and the heat in the summer. I had never seen snow or humidity before, and I may have regretted coming to the United States just on the basis of one of these two anomalies. For a change, my brother Miemen would have had nothing to do with it!

In any case, I had lived with my brother for about a year when he got married to a Haitian young lady, Jacqueline, with whom he had two children, Pascal and Henock. So, I moved out to my own studio apartment on Deming Street, just a couple of blocks away, until my wife joined me in April 1980.

In a combination of luck and an I-20 (admission letter) I sent her from one of the Chicago colleges, she had managed to get a student's visa to the United States. Then, we moved to a two-bedroom apartment in Oak Park, Illinois, a suburb just west of Chicago, to start married life, something overdue by almost two years!

Oak Park, with about 45 thousand residents at the time, was considered to be one of the most racially balanced suburbs in the United States. It was also once the home of a renowned architect, Frank Lloyd Wright, who was partially responsible in preserving the historical districts in the suburb.

Early married life, finally. Winter in the windy and cold Chicago, 1981

As a literature student, I was also happy to learn that Oak Park was the birthplace of Ernest Hemmingway, an American novelist who won the Nobel Prize for literature in 1954. I remember reading his books '*The Sun Also Rises*' and '*For Whom the Bell Tolls*' as a literature student at Addis Ababa University in the early 70s.

Oak Park is connected to downtown Chicago, where my wife and I went to school, with two city-train lines that were affordable. In addition to the relatively low cost of living and the tree-lined streets, Oak Park proved to be the most logical place for us to reside. It was a 'dry' suburb, but we managed to get our beers and wines from another suburb, River Forest, just across the street from where we lived in Oak Park.

A few weeks after my wife and I started living a married life in Oak Park, for some strange reason, I thought I needed to impress upon my wife, right from the outset, that I would go back home - no matter what. So, one day, I told my wife that I had something to tell her.

'What is it?' she asked with some astonishment.
I answered, *'I am going back home, no matter what, when I am done with my studies; I have made up my mind.'*

'So?' she asked with more astonishment.
'So', I replied, *'I want you to make up your mind too, if not...'*

'If not, what?', she asked.
'If not, it would be better if we did not continue to stay as husband and wife; it would be better if went our own ways.'

That was bad, very bad! It has been only a couple of weeks since we started to live together. I didn't even give her the chance to take her time and make her own decision. There was sometimes something in my upbringing that allowed me to say things without having to weigh the outcome; it was not out of spite, but it was just that I didn't know any better.

It was clear that I had yet to transform from a happy go lucky young bachelor to a responsible grown up married man!

Luckily for me, there was no question my wife was a much more mature person than me, despite the five year age difference between us. She responded that I was her husband, and she would follow me wherever I went. Her response solidified my resolve to go back home, and we stayed together happily. Both of us were the kind of people where, once a decision was made, it would be very difficult to follow another course.

We both hated hypocrisy equally, and tried our best to do what we said we would do.

But, for the record, if my wife had called my bluff and changed her mind, in spite of all my bravado and threatening, I might have succumbed to her wishes and stayed in the United States. Then, I suppose my life would have taken a totally different course that I could not or would not even want to try and imagine what it would have been like.

In any case, my life style and quality changed completely after April 1980 when my wife joined me, and we started living together for the first time - 22 months after we got married back in June 1978. I had to learn quite a few things, and one incident was particularly persuasive.

About a year after she arrived in Chicago, I had taken my wife to my bank to add her name to my savings account. An African American female bank employee was ready to help us.

Then, the following three-way conversation ensued.

Bank employee: *How can I help you?*
Aklilu: *My name is Aklilu Kidanu; and this is my wife, and I want to add her name to my savings account.*
Bank employee: *Sure, what is your name darling?*
Menby: *My name is Menbere Alemayehu Lidetu.*
Bank employee: *Ok, great; now we have to fill-out some personal information about you. What is your day of birth?*
Menby: *April, 22, 1956.*
Bank employee: *Today? Happy birthday!!*
Menby: *Thank you so much!*
Aklilu: *Whose birthday is it?*
Bank employee: *It is your wife's birthday today, and you mean to tell me you did not know your wife's birthday was today?*
Aklilu: *Is today your birthday?*
Menby. *Yes.*
Aklilu: *Why didn't you tell me?*
Bank employee: *You are supposed to know! Is she not your wife? Shame on you! Men, you are all the same no matter what country you come from!*

I never forgot my wife's birthday since then; well, maybe just a couple of times so far. One of them was much later in life, in Addis, and it was about 4 pm in the afternoon, and I was working in my office when Hasabie, our youngest daughter who was about thirteen years old at the time, called me.

Hasabie: *Hey dad, I hope you have not forgotten.*
Aklilu: *Forgotten what?*
Hasabie: *It is your wife's birthday today!*
Aklilu: *Yes, of course, I remember.*
Hasabie: *Did you get her a gift?*
Aklilu: *Not yet, I am thinking about it. By the way, what do you suggest I get her?*
Hasabie: *This is a special birthday and so you should get her something special.*
Aklilu: *Why do you say every one of your mom's birthday is a special one? I do not remember you saying the same thing about my birthday.*
Hasabie: *I will say that for your next birthday.*
Aklilu: *Thank you; I appreciate your fairness. Anyway, what should I get her for a gift?*
Hasabie: *You know dad, one day I heard mom say, 'I hope I will not die before I own a gold watch.'*
Aklilu: *A gold what?*
Hasabie: *I said a gold watch.*
Aklilu: *You are not suggesting I buy her one!*
Hasabie: *Yes, I am.*
Aklilu: *Are you serious?*
Hasabie: *I am serious; have you not lived together for more than 20 years now?*
Aklilu: *Yes, but do you know how much a gold watch costs?*
Hasabie: *She deserves it.*
Aklilu: *I know she does but…*
Hasabie: *Dad, this is a one-time thing; it is not like you were going to buy her a gold watch for every birthday!*
Aklilu: *You are crazy; no promise but let me just see first how much they cost.*

So, I borrowed all the petty-cash money at the office and headed to the gold shops in Piazza business district looking for a gold watch. Despite the fact that I had never bought any gold before, I confidently walked into one of the stores, hands in my pockets, and asked to see the gold watches they had. I was shown a few selections, and I focused on one of them almost randomly.

When I asked the price, it was three times the petty-cash money I had borrowed from work! Then, I made a big mistake: I called Hasabie! There was no stopping her because, by then, she had already concluded that I had decided to get the gold watch for her mom's birthday, and may have even spread the news.

So, the choice I had was to break Hasabie's heart or to get additional money from work. I just couldn't do the former; and got the watch.

But Hasabie never mentioned a gold watch come my next birthday! Daughters' mother preference was not lost upon me!

*****

Anyway, back in Chicago, there were other interesting encounters too. One summer day in 1980, soon after my wife arrived in Chicago, I was showing her around when we saw a commotion at the Daley Plaza in downtown Chicago. We walked closer to see what was going on. Then, we saw President Carter walking towards our direction to his car entourage. He was smiling and shaking hands with people as he passed by.

So, we happened to be on his way, and he first shook hands with my wife. Then, while still holding her hand, he shook hands with me and the next few people before he let go her hand. Apparently, he had just made a campaign appearance for his re-election bid; which he lost, and I hope our handshake was not the bad omen. In any case, that made our day and we talked about it for a long time, as a reminder of the good old days!

Living and learning together

It was clear that my wife's arrival in Chicago was changing me in many ways, even if it were after the late age of 30. And one major change was in my outlook towards women. As I was growing up in Gore, it was only natural for me, and all my friends for that matter, to follow the chauvinistic and paternalistic culture that dominated at the time.

For instance, I saw my mother as the nice lady who prepared good food for us, and nothing more. My entire attention was on my father; he was the authority, the breadwinner, and my role model.

Similarly, I never paid attention to my three sisters to the point where it was as if they never lived with me. When there were rare times I noticed their presence, I saw them as more of a nuisance than as my own siblings. I spent all my time and energy with my brothers and my male cousins and male friends; doing things those only boys would or should do, according to the norms of the time.

Even during my high school and early college years, this outlook did not change much. I saw our female friends and classmates either as our dance partners, at best, or as sex objects, at worst. There was no pressure coming from any direction to teach us to try and know and behave better, despite the fact that we were full-blown adults in our mid-20s.

All these changed gradually with my wife's influence beginning in the early 1980s. Through her, I saw that women were equal with, if not better than, men in many aspects; it was never too late to learn and change.

On my part, I tried to teach my wife what I had learnt about the norms, values and adjustments one had to make living in a city like Chicago. She was actually more versed than me on issues like deodorants, but she too struggled with the issues of racism and homosexuality. Compared to her, I now claimed some expertise on these subjects. She listened to me with wonder and the memory of her paternal grandmother, Kershi, who kept on saying that *the world is coming to its end* whenever she heard something unbecoming of God-loving peoples.

*****

In any case, as life went on in the Chicago suburb, Menby and I had a few more things to learn together.

It was Thanksgiving Day in November 1980, and the first one we were spending together. The few days earlier, all the talk was about turkey. We heard about it on TV and radio so much that we decided to go to a supermarket near our apartment, and get the all-too-important turkey to cook for dinner; just like everybody else. It was a beautiful cold Thanksgiving morning. But, the store was almost empty.

Once inside the supermarket, we were standing by the container where there were all sizes of frozen turkey in display. We would pick and drop a turkey, evaluating if it was big enough for two people or if it was fresh enough - as if we knew.

From a distance, an old white elderly lady was watching us. Then, she slowly approached us, and with a very inquisitive look, asked, *'Honey, is this turkey for today?'* Although she was looking at my wife, I responded that it was for today dinner. I thought, given her age, she may have forgotten it was Thanksgiving Day, and I wanted to remind her.

My wife was more polite and told the lady that we wanted to buy and cook it for dinner for today, just like most American households would. The lady's face turned even more curious. Then she said, *'But honey, this is frozen plenty hard. It would take three days to defreeze. It won't be ready for today. I am sorry.'* And she walked away, shaking her head, perhaps wondering what planet we had dropped from.

Craving for turkey for which I hadn't developed a taste yet, I wasn't sure if I should believe the lady. But, my wife knew better and agreed with the lady. Of course, we did not have turkey for dinner that day.

But over the years, though, my wife became an expert in cooking turkey, with an Ethiopian twist - meaning with a lot of *awaze*[19] to go along. Every thanksgiving day till we left Chicago in 1985, we would invite the small Ethiopian community to turkey dinner at our apartment. To this day, our friends talk

---

19   Specially prepared spiced pepper.

about the wonderful Thanksgiving dinner my wife would make available to them - free of charge!

*****

Then there was one other thing that surprised and amazed my wife the most: a wedding party that we attended soon after my wife arrived in Chicago. My colleague at my part-time job in Chicago, Larry, was getting married to his Mexican sweetheart, Maria. And he, of course, invited me and my wife, his only Ethiopian friends, to the wedding.

Now, weddings in Ethiopia are big, as we all know. Whether they can afford it, the parents of the bride and the bridegroom would each throw parties with a lot of food, drinks and music and dancing. In many instances, festivities begin a few days before and end a few days after the wedding day. Even if it meant bankruptcy, no self-respecting parents would miss the opportunity to pay-off the numerous wedding parties they had been invited to, by having a big one of theirs! It was with this background that my wife and I went to our first wedding party in the United States.

We drove the two-hour drive to the wedding reception in a small suburb outside Chicago. We had a nice colorful Ethiopian handmade basket made of straw as the wedding gift for the bride, so she could save her jewelries in it. When we got there, a small group of people had already assembled and the bride and groom were standing in the middle chatting happily. After some pleasantries, we eventually all went outside the house by the garden, to observe the open-door religious wedding ceremony on a small bridge.

Once that was over, we went inside a small hall where we helped ourselves with refreshments - just cold drinks; there was no beer or liquor. Some music was playing, but not the kind of wedding songs we were used to in Ethiopia. That was fine, but we started getting hungry. My wife would ask me where they had set up the buffet. And, if we in Ethiopia could provide that much food at a wedding, we could not wait to see the amount and quality of food we would be served in the United States; our anticipation reached its height.

For sure, we had some cake; but, there was no talk or smell of food. However, from a distance on a small table, we could see a disposable aluminum bowl covered with aluminum foil. There was also a jar next to it. It never occurred to us that it was our lunch until the groom announced that food was ready and invited us to serve ourselves, pointing at the table.

We walked to the table to find out that the pile covered with aluminum foil was actually boiled macaroni; the jar next to it contained readymade tomato sauce. After wondering for a few minutes as to what next to do, we took a paper plate, put some macaroni on it, added some tomato sauce on top, and called it the wedding lunch!

We laughed all the way back to our apartment in Oak Park; my wife was amazed beyond belief. We remembered the amount of food and drinks that would be available at a wedding, even a modest one, in Ethiopia. But we eventually agreed that Larry and Maria were being practical - why waste all that money for a day's festivities when they could use it for a much more productive cause?

Besides, even if it were cooked pasta and tomato sauce only, Larry and Maria had done much better than us when we got married back on June 13, 1978, and did not serve any food to anybody!

We agreed: *something was better than nothing!*

Early graduate school years

In the mean time, my graduate studies as English major, was not going well. It wasn't that I did not try hard enough or that I did not learn anything at all, but I was not able to compete with my classmates. While they could read a book in a couple of days and come back with their critique the next class, it would take me about a week just to finish a book.

I read and read and read, to the point where my fellow Ethiopian students at the university nick-named me '*Shemdaju*' an Amharic word which, when loosely translated into English means *'A person who studies all the time.'* Little did they know that, in spite of my nickname, I was lagging far behind in my studies.

My professors understood this and tried their best, but it was hard for them to help someone like me. I must have been the only non-English speaking student in the class, and they did not know how to handle me. So, at the end of a disastrous first year, I set out looking for a new major. With no advisor or vision of my own, I was desperate to find a department, any department, which would accept me to its master's program.

The catch was that I could only stay in the US legally if I continued my studies.

So, one bad day, I went to the MBA (Masters in Business Administration) office and took the application form the secretary who was a young African American lady. She first corrected a couple of my pronunciations, one of them being the word 'development', before she handed me the application form. I could not understand how or why we got into that; but I felt I was being unfairly teased by the young woman. I simply shrugged it off.

A couple of hours later, I came back to the department with a completed application form filled-out by hand. I had also written a cover letter. In those days, there were no desktop computers; and I didn't have access or even the knowledge to use word processing on the mainframe computer; only a handful of science students had access to the mainframe computer.

So, when I got to the department, it was about lunchtime and the secretary who teasingly gave me the application form earlier was gone for lunch. When I knocked at her desk real loud, one white man, dressed in a suit with suspenders, came out of the adjacent room and asked if he could help me. For some reason, he looked really irritated; I guess I interrupted his lunch; and I wasn't sure what position he had in the college.

So I said, '*I want to submit my application form to the MBA program.*'

Without even looking at me, he took the completed forms and started reading my cover letter, also written by hand. After a few minutes of reading my hand-written cover letter, he looked up at me and asked, *'You can't even spell the word "receive" correctly and you want to join our prestigious masters program?'*

I knew it! I never really liked the looks or attitude of this guy; and, I never liked the word 'receive' either, in spite of my degree in English literature. I never knew how to spell it correctly to this day! So, it was the combination effect of two dislikes at one time; and I started getting angry. But, I tried and ignored his question. Then he repeated his question with a voice that demanded an immediate answer. Now, the situation reminded me of my encounter with the Italian teacher colleague back in Addis at the Italian school.

I knew he was the redneck type whose linguistic capabilities did not go much beyond the English language, so I wanted to hit him at his weak point where it hurt.

'Mr., English is my third language. I speak two other local languages [Actually, I spoke only one well enough] *So, tell me, how many languages do you speak other than English?'*

This was enough to make him angry, and my plan had worked! His eyes fixed on mine; he stormed into his office without giving me an answer, and slammed his office door shut behind him. Of course, he was not about to consider my application after my unbecoming of an MBA student's response.

I knew I did wrong, and should have been more respectful. But with a smile of success on my face, I had by now forgotten about my application. I left the MBA department and randomly went across the street into the office of a certain Bob Meier, a young Jewish guy and a Berkeley Ph.D. who also happened to be the director of the College of the Graduate School of Urban Planning.

Dressed very informally in jeans and a t-shirt, which I liked, his hair balding but long, he looked at me and started asking me questions.

Professor: *Hey there, come in and grab a chair; how can I help you?*
Aklilu: *I just wanted to learn about your program - just in case I may be able to join.*
Professor: *What was your first degree in?*
Aklilu: *English literature.*

Professor: *Where did you go?*
Aklilu: *Addis Ababa University in Ethiopia.*
Professor: *Hmm, did you start the graduate in English program here?*
Aklilu: *Yes, I did.*
Professor: *What happened? Why do you want to change?*
Aklilu: *I failed in the courses.*
Professor: *So you think you will pass here?*
Aklilu: *I will try my best.*
Professor: *Have you taken any statistics courses before?*
Aklilu: *No.*
Professor: *Economics?*
Aklilu: *Yes, Economics 101 in 1970 at Addis Ababa university*[20].
Professor: *Hmm, I tell you what. Why don't you take a course in introduction to statistics and if you get a 'B', come back to me, and I will see what I can do.*

I had by now learnt that when Americans say *'I will see what I can do'*, most of the time there is something positive behind it. Besides, I had already liked this guy even if he had turned me down point- blank. He was the flip side of the professor at the MBA program, both in manners and looks.

He also reminded me of Ayalew who, more than 10 years earlier in 1969, had challenged me to just get a 'B' in one of those compulsory subjects in order to make it to Haile Selassie I University. If I had not let down Ayalew, I promised myself, I would not let Professor Bob Meier down.

In any event, for one semester, I worked so hard on introductory statistics and managed to get a 'B'. This was also about the time my wife had joined me, and I was energized. I went back to Professor Bob Meier, and proudly and happily presented my report cards; not only because I was going to be accepted but also for successfully meeting the challenge he had thrown at me.

In consultation with his colleges, Bob admitted me to the program with a two-year research assistantship, which covered

---

20 I actually remember the lecturer, Dr. Eshetu Chole, more than the subject matter.

my tuition and a decent living stipend. That was all I needed! Professor Art Lyons, barely older than me, was to be the professor I was to assist.

One day, Art assembled his graduate research assistants and issued instructions which each one of us would be responsible for. One Nigerian student among us asked that we needed supplies. This came as a surprise to Art and to me because I had thought the stipend we were paid would cover supplies too. Art argued the same way, but the Nigerian did not budge. So, Art gave up and got some cash money from the department and gave it to the Nigerian who had volunteered to go and buy the supplies from downtown Chicago.

Then, a three-way conversation ensued.

Nigerian: *What about transportation money?*
Art: *You need transportation money?*
Nigerian: *Am I supposed to walk there?*
Aklilu: *I actually have a train pass which you are welcome to use.*
Nigerian: *No, I want to play it safe.*
Aklilu: *It is a pass, not an ID. Anyone can use it; it is safe.*
Nigerian: *No, no, I do not want to take the risk; I want to play it safe.*

So, he follows Art to his office and gets the transportation money. Then he comes back to me and says, '*Aklilu, can I use your pass?*' A bit surprised at first but, out of the solidarity that I was expected to show to my classmates, I gave him my pass.

The incident reminded me of the Nigerian lady I met in Roma a couple of years earlier and who I thought was making her money the good old way; unlike this guy, she was earning it.

My Nigerian experience continued in later years.

*****

Fast forward to 1999, when I was working at a research center in Addis Ababa, I went to Nigeria to do a study with a group of researchers. One of them was Ethiopian-American scholar and public health consultant, Dr. Belkis Wolde Giorgis. There was also our team leader, a white gentleman in his mid 40s, whose name I forgot, on the team. We were to look at the efficacy of women-run NGOs all over Nigeria that worked on reproductive health issues and were funded by the USAID.

I flew to Lagos and met my partners in our hotel. During our first group meeting, I noticed our team leader was a bit nervous and scared of the city and the people. He repeatedly advised and warned us to watch our pockets, or to be alert at the market places, to avoid the streets or risk being robbed at gunpoint. In short, he had come to Nigeria with a lot of preconceived ideas that the country was a living hell.

Yes, of course, it was a difficult time for Nigerians in those days, and there was a lot of violence on the streets, especially at night. But, I also found out from Belkis, who had worked in Nigeria before and knew Nigerian culture very well, that what most Nigerians wanted, even those in the market places, was simple respect. Simply put: you respect them, they respect you; you mess with them and, as my good Nigerian friend Godfrey Okoye would say, *'Then, you are looking for trouble and you will soon get it.'*

I had also read *'Things Fall Apart'* by a renowned Nigerian writer, Chinua Achebe, in my literature student years back at Addis Ababa University, and I knew better than messing with a Nigerian. I remember the main character of the book, Okonkwo! So, during my entire stay in Nigeria, I used this simple gesture of respecting them, and I got respect in return.

So, one day I went to the market with our team leader who was bargaining so hard to avoid 'inevitable rip off.' So, he would offer about a tenth of the price of an item. Of course, the Nigerian shopkeeper, like any shopkeeper of any citizenship, would get mad; and all hell would break loose. On my part, I would offer about sixty to seventy five percent of the price tag, and got along well.

In fact, there was a time when I bargained to buy a wood-carved plaque of two bulls fighting for what I thought was a very small amount of money. It was clear that the shopkeeper was too desperate to refuse any money that he needed so badly. I took the plaque home and the more I looked at it, the more I could see how much work it required and how little I had paid in contrast. To this day, whenever I see the plaque, I shudder with guilt and shame. It wasn't something I was proud of.

In any case, as part of our fieldwork in Nigeria, one afternoon, we drove from Kano to Abuja, where we had hotel reservations. When we got to the hotel at about 6 pm, tired and dirty, our rooms were taken. Apparently there was an emergency meeting of all the governors of the states in Nigeria, and they had taken our rooms. They might have not been an exception, but that was when I learnt that Nigerian officials travelled with large entourages - many of them close relatives.

This is not something you can argue about in Nigeria, or in many other African countries for that matter, and the hotel clerks could not do much to help. But our team leader demanded to get his room and, when that did not work, demanded to speak to the manager of the hotel. The manager calmly explained the situation; but our team leader was not to be calmed down.

In the meantime, sensing that all hotel rooms in Abuja would be full, our Nigerian colleague offered to host us for the night at his house. Belkis and I gladly accepted the offer; our team leader refused. Instead, failing to get his room at the hotel where we had reserved rooms, he took the driver around town looking for a room in other hotels.

In the meantime, I hope I speak for Belkis too when I say, thanks to our Nigerian host, I had the most incredible time in a crowded large family which included a great authentic Nigerian dinner and plenty of African hospitality. In the morning, after Belkis and I were well rested and had wonderful Nigerian breakfast, we ran into our team leader who looked miserable, tired, sleepy and dirty. He had been looking for a hotel room most of the night and had eventually ended up in a shanty hotel where, he said, he did not sleep at all.

*****

Anyway, back in Chicago, after two years of struggle, and with a lot of support from my wife, my teachers and classmates,

I graduated with a master's degree on June 12, 1983.[21] My thesis was on zoning laws and housing discrimination in the Chicago metropolitan area. Well, the fun-loving kid from Gore has now become a sort of an 'expert' on housing segregation in the Chicago metropolitan area. *'What do you know?'*, as my friend Smithy would say!

In those days, the United States would allow a two-year practical training status (the H-1 visa) for those with student's visa, once they graduated with a master's degree. So, taking advantage of this, I managed to get a job at the Leadership Council for Metropolitan Open Communities (LCMOC), aka Leadership Council, an NGO that was founded following Dr. Martin Luther King's 1966 campaign for 'fair, affordable and open housing' to all.

The Leadership Council, located at 220 South State Street, in the heart of downtown Chicago, was right in the middle of one of the greatest shopping paradises of the country. As a relatively well-paid full-time employee after three years of graduate school, I was able to afford sneaking into some of the restaurants and stores once in a while.

In fact, there was a jewelry shop on the ground floor of the Leadership Councils' building where I used my first salary to buy my wife a small diamond ring and a watch; in installment payments. I told my wife that I was making up for our 2 Birr (40 cents USD) wedding expense back in 1978; and she accepted and she still wears them 40 years later.

In any case, the Chicago metropolitan area was one of the most, if not the most, segregated areas in the country. This was an opportunity for me to do something about one of the cultural shocks I faced in the city: racial discrimination. It was also a chance for me to practice what I learnt in college; exactly the objective of the H-1 visa.

---

21 My wife typed all my term papers using a manual typewriter that worked only if you put a quarter (25 cents) in it every half hour. There were no personal computers, and the mainframe was not accessible to non-science students in those days.

Our director was Mr. Kale Williams, a white middle-aged Quaker[22] and perhaps one of the most stable and genuinely kind persons I have ever met. My immediate boss was David Schucker, a white man in his mid 30s, with a passion for his job, for amateur wrestling, and for The Chicago Bulls, a professional Chicago basketball team.

But first, David was a dedicated employee of the Leadership Council, and firmly believed in its objectives which included eliminating, 'discrimination and segregation in the housing markets of Chicago and surrounding suburbs.' By so doing, the Leadership Council set out to encourage and support African Americans move to more economically and racially diverse communities; and I was game.

My role was to identify, using demographic profiles and color-coded maps, the racial distribution of housing in the suburbs of the Chicago metropolitan area; and I was more than happy to be part of the whole process. I remember a suburb, Cicero, Illinois, where the only black person who lived there was a stable attendant for a wealthy white household. Even then, his son was not allowed to go to the Cicero public schools.

My favorite part of the Leadership Council's activities was the Legal Action Program, run by a very sharp Italian lawyer, Bill Caruso, against those who violated the Fair Housing Law. The way it worked was simple but effective. First, Bill's staff would identify 'For Rent' signs in one of those segregated suburbs of Chicago. Then, he would pick one address and send a white couple and have them collect all the necessary requirements to rent the apartment or house.

Then, he would send a black couple to the same place. If the information collected by the black couple were different from those collected by the white couple, Bill would be ready to take a legal action. But, first, he would warn and advise the landlords to amend their ways. If that did not work, Bill would

---

22 As much as I disliked religion, because of Kale, there were times when I
    secretly longed to know more about the Quakers and their philosophy
    of life, just in case.

usually win the case in courts, with additional damages collected. I remember the pleasure Bill took when he won such cases at courts; which he did with the effectiveness of a mafia hit man.

David succeeded in making me a devoted employee of the Leadership Council, but not a fan of the Chicago Bulls or of amateur wrestling. I had watched English soccer and professional wrestling way too long to change now. David once took me to a live Bulls' game in Chicago, a big treat at the time, and all I was interested in was the size of the arena and the enthusiasm of the supporters. Of course, David was too involved in the game to notice my total lack of interest in the game itself. As stubborn as a camel, I would not accept anything that would potentially erode my childhood love for soccer.

David was also the first person to tell me that the professional wrestling that I have been watching on TV since my boyhood years in Addis, usually with my father, were all fake exercises. I knew my father, who was also a big fan, would not like this kind of talk.

So, no matter how hard I argued otherwise, he would still insist that professional wrestling was a hoax, and he invited me to watch amateur wrestling when there was a tournament. That did not happen. But later, I began to see what David was talking about and, eventually, was convinced that professional wrestling was indeed a fake sport, and people watched them since they either did not know any better or just to feel good about the hoopla that surrounded the matches. This is not to say, though, the wrestlers were not excellent athletes.

All said, my two-year stint at the Leadership Council was an excellent opportunity for me to practice what I studied at school and, in the process, serve the people whose tax money sent me to school.

*****

In 1985, after the two years at the Leadership Council, which I enjoyed immensely, I had three options in front of me.

The first one was to go back to Ethiopia. But, when I thought about it, I just wasn't ready. My wife had started school, and the situation in Ethiopia was getting from bad to worse, and we just had to wait.

The second option was to apply for a political asylum. I had witnessed every Ethiopian around me, including my own brothers and friends, had already applied for political asylum and been granted or were waiting for a response. Given the political situation in Ethiopia in those days, it was a relatively easy status to obtain.

The advice I was getting from left and right was that I should do the same. But, I did not want to apply for political asylum because I had always wanted to return to Ethiopia without compromising my student's visa and my Ethiopian passport and, of course, my 'identity', for whatever it's worth.

Besides, I wasn't prepared to go through the implications of applying for a political asylum. I also did not like what I saw in the application forms either. One day in the early 80's, an Eritrean gentleman I met in Chicago came to me and asked me if I could help him fill out the forms for a political asylum. Since he understood very little English, he needed help. It was the first time I saw the forms; it was also the last time.

I did try to help my friend, but I also noticed the kind of questions one would be answering and the commitments one would be making in the process; they would have been unacceptable to me - a kid who grew up in Gore.

With all humility, and at the risk of offending some of my closest relatives and friends, and also sounding a bit too nationalist, I could say I was just too proud to agree with the terms and conditions implied in the asylum process. This was not to suggest that my upbringing was different from those who willingly filled out the forms; in fact, to the contrary.

Now, if I didn't have a choice at all, I do not know if I would have considered it. But, luckily, I had one other choice left.

The third and last option I had was to apply for yet another graduate program and extend my student's visa for a few more years - till I was ready to go back home. I opted for this option and applied to as many universities as I could. To my surprise, a few schools accepted me but none with a four-year scholarship offered to me by the College of Urban Planning and Public Policy at the University of Delaware at Newark, Delaware. Besides, I was told, the school had one of the best programs in the country in the field.

My wife had just completed a two-year college in Chicago and was ready for a transfer to a four-year program, and the University of Delaware offered a possibility.

Once again, I was ready to go to school, not by choice but by default.

More graduate school

Founded in 1694, Newark, Delaware, is a small university town at about 800 kilometers east of Chicago or 240 kilometers west of New York City, with a population of about 25,000 at the time. Most were students, but there was also a significant work force at the Chrysler Newark Automobile Assembly plant where Bob Marley once worked as an assembly-line worker in the 60s. The school first started as Delaware College in 1834, one of the earliest colleges in the country, and later became the University of Delaware in 1921.

So, one summer day in 1985, my wife and I packed our entire belongings in a tiny Datsun B 210 and headed to Newark, Delaware. We were ready to try out a small historical town after having lived in Chicago and its suburb for seven years. The drive was long, about 12 hours, but enjoyable as we took turns singing our favorite Amharic songs to each other. When we got to Newark our first task was to find an apartment, and some cheap furniture.

Given our budget, we could only afford used furniture that sold at an auction place in one corner of the town. The most expensive furniture for which we bid and won was an old but sturdy couch that served as a sofa and a bed - for just two dollars and fifty cents, and we were content. But we still remember the sarcastic *'Don't the two of you sit on it at the same time!'*

comment which an elderly gentleman made as we carried the couch out of the store. [23]

We were also pleased to meet a small group of Ethiopians and Eritreans studying and/or teaching at the university. They showed us around and made us feel comfortable. We became so close to one Eritrean family, the Debessays,[24] in particular, that we now consider each other as family members; and there were also a few more Ethiopians.[25]

This way, for the third time, I started my life as a reluctant university student. I was now a Ph.D. candidate and my wife had transferred to a B.Sc. program in apparel design; a program that she had been dreaming about since childhood. Ever since she was a child, my wife had been a useful assistant to her mother who was sewing dresses to supplement her husband's income. So, with this background, she pursued her studies with passion, and excelled in her grades. And, she began collecting awards, which partially contributed to her tuition fees.

In any case, the late Professor Robert Warren, a liberal thinker from California, was to be my advisor; and I was to assist Mr. Edward Ratledge, Director of the Center for Applied Demography and Survey research - which later became my area of specialization. With more renowned professors like Dan Rich, Robert Wilson and Francis Tannian at the helm, I pursued my education with the benefits of older age and the work experience at the Leadership Council in Chicago.

I also had wonderful classmates[26] who, through continuous dialogues and exchange of ideas during class seminars and over beer sessions, made life as a doctoral candidate both productive and pleasurable. The days and months went by quickly while my wife and I enjoyed the tranquil life in Newark with

---

23 By the way, we used this couch till we left the country for good in 1992.

24 Professor Araya Debessay and his wife Semret Asfaha; brother Dr. Mengisteab Debessay and sister Ms. Alganesh Debessay; Tecle Woldekidan.

25 Notably Dr. Kalayu Belay.

26 Including Audrey Helfman, Steve Groff, Lamia Al Fatal, Subisiso Nkomo and Kim Ik Sik.

occasional drives to major close by cities, like Atlantic City and Philadelphia; and of course to New York.

One major event during this time was when Genet, my wife's younger sister, showed up with her 'fiancée' who we have heard about through the grapevine, but not seen before. His name is Melesse Maru, and it was the beginning of the closest family-to-family relationship that lasted for over 30 years, and counting.

*****

So, I was done with my course work and still working on my dissertation in 1988,[27] when I was offered a job at the state's health statistics bureau. The state would sponsor me for a four-year H-I visa, which allowed me to take a professional job, just like in Chicago after my master's degree. I would join a team of three young people whose job would be to analyze the vital statistics of the state in comparison to the national data. My immediate boss was to be Don Berry, a closet revolutionary, who later became a good friend of mine. Our third colleague was a young man called Dr. Ted Jarrel, a family man with enviable skills in statistical analysis of health data.

The place of work was Dover, a small town founded in 1683 as the historical capital of the State of Delaware, which is also known as The First State.[28] Dover is an hour's drive from where I lived in Newark, Delaware, so I had to commute.

A group of four gentlemen, including me, teamed up to carpool from Newark, where we all lived, to Dover where we all worked: Michael, David, Fred and I. Every morning at 7 am, from Monday to Thursday, we would meet at a designated location, from where we would take turns to drive to Dover; on Fridays we were free to drive alone in our respective cars.

---

27 My dissertation topic was: Effects of social, economic, and demographic factors on homicide mortality rates in the United States; public health policy implications (1990).

28 Delaware was the first state to ratify the United States Constitution in 1787.

All four of us were completely different from each other in terms of our tastes, driving habits, and even looks. But, whoever was driving had the say as to what radio station to listen to or what subject to talk about. The rest of us would accept the choice - whether we liked it or not.

Mike in his early 30s, married and with two kids, loved golf and all he would listen to, when it was his turn to drive, was the golf section of radio sports programs. In a rare occasion when he talked, he would be telling us about the upcoming golf tournament he was going to attend; this was how his annual leave was spent with his golf-loving friends. For the most part, the rest of us, disinterested in golf news, would be reading books or newspapers quietly as the golf news bored us to death. Mike didn't care.

Fred, in his mid-50s, was the oldest of the group and lived with his mother; he did not have his own family. All he was interested in was the stock market. Throughout the one-hour drive, especially back to Newark at 4:30 pm, he would listen to live radio reports on how the day's stock market fared. Perhaps, privately in his mind, he was calculating how much money he lost or won. Since nobody would really be interested in what he had to say, he would mumble either approval or disapproval of what had happened at the stock market; the rest of us would keep on reading with boring stock market news at the background. I had sometimes feared if he would be too preoccupied to get us home safely; but he was a good driver.

David in his mid 30s, married with two kids, was the odd one but also the nicest of us all. He did not have any particular interests, but he was always late to show up at the 7am meeting time. So, he would spend the whole one-hour journey talking about and apologizing for being late. One day he told us he was late because he looked everywhere but couldn't find his car keys. Finally, after a lot of exasperation, he was able to find his car keys in his wife's purse. The last place, he said, he would look for his car keys.

So, that day David must have asked, *'How could she do this to me?'* about a hundred times. On another day, it would be his kids who refused to wake up early enough, and on and on and on. Probably, I was the only one who listened and partially believed his stories. Fred, once in a while would say *'Whatever'* in his usual sarcastic way; and Michael would be snoring.

Interestingly enough, these three gentlemen respected each other's boundary and never intervened, however painful it was to listen to some of the stories and excuses; I learnt to do the same too.

So now, it was my turn to drive. I had listened to golf news, stock market news, and excuses for being late; none of which really interested me but I listened to them quietly and patiently. So the first morning when it was my turn to drive, I knew it was my decision as to what to put on the car radio. I took out a tape and played Tilahun Gessese, a famous Ethiopian singer.

Of course, none of the three gentlemen in my car had ever heard the songs before, but they kept their boundaries and kept quiet. Fred was sitting next to me in the passenger's seat and I could see him pretending to be reading a newspaper, but he was also sneaking a look at the tape player once in a while wondering what the heck he was listening to. Of course, I didn't do it out of spite; I was only exercising my rights - the same way they did theirs.

In any case, after a few months, poor David could not catch up with us; he was late too many times. So, we decided to replace him with a young woman, Mary, who had just obtained her graduate degree and been employed by the state. Mary, unfortunately for her, was a very social person. That meant, regardless whose turn it was to drive, she talked a little bit too much for the rest of us. She kept on talking and no one would listen, much less respond; but once in a while I would hear a long *'Whatever'* from Fred; it was clear he preferred Dave to Mary.

Fridays were freedom days, which we all very fondly looked forward to. Those were the days when, driving to and from Dover alone, I would struggle with myself as to what in the heck I was doing in Dover, Delaware, over ten thousand kilometers away from where I really should be, and want to be!

Yes, of course, I liked my work and colleagues in Dover, and I liked what I was producing at work as well as what I was learning in the meantime. And, needless to say, I was very grateful to the people of Delaware, the taxpayers who paid for my education.

But, I wondered how long I would stay in Delaware, and when I would go back home. In my mind, in spite of my long stay in the country, I was still the 'guest' of the United States, and I dreaded to overstay!

Of Family and Country

The children

The year 1988 on September 18 was also when our first child Mizan was born. There are no words to describe, and I wouldn't even try, how we felt about her arrival to this world; although she started out her life with a long cry as soon as she came to this world.

Within weeks of Mizan's birth, her maternal grandmother, Amanelwa, was at our disposal. She had come to the United States all the way from Ethiopia to babysit Mizan - as long as we needed her. She ended up staying for one-year; and she even cooked for us! The sacrifice one her part, leaving her husband and children back in Ethiopia, to provide crucial support to us was simply unbelievable.

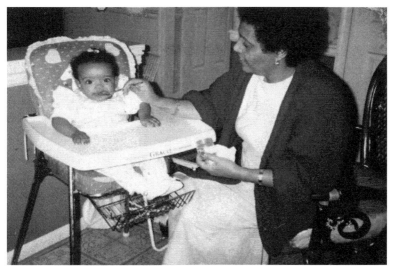

My mother-in-law, Amanelwa, babysitted Mizan for one year while we finished our studies!
Newark, Delaware, 1989

One day I told one of my American classmates that my mother in-law was with us babysitting our daughter Mizan. So, every few days or so, he would ask me if my mother-in-law was still with us. And, I would answer positively. I would also add how selfless she was for committing herself to such a difficult task on our behalf.

My friend, who also had a couple of young children himself, kept on asking me the same question whenever he saw me. Finally, I asked him why he was so eager to know if my mother-in-law was still with us. He told me it was because he could not stand his own mother-in-law and, if she happened to come to his house for a weekend, he would go to another nearby town and stay in a hotel till she left. He may have had his own reasons, which I wasn't so eager to know. By then, I had already gone through so many other cultural shocks, and I wasn't surprised!

In any case, with a new addition to the family and Amanelwa on our side, my wife and I kept on pushing on our studies. I did defend my all-important dissertation successfully, and so did my wife the requirements for her B.Sc. degree in apparel design.

We graduated on the same day, May 27, 1990, with tiny and talkative Mizan toddling every each way at the background.

My wife and I graduated on the same day. My younger brother, Yemane, posing next to me, and little Mizan struggling to escape. University of Delaware, Newark, Delaware. May, 1990

Our second child Hasabie was born on November 26, 1990, multiplying our joy. Mizan was happy to have a living toy. This time, my mother, Asegedetch, came to Ethiopia to babysit both Mizan and Hasabie, and stayed for one year. Again, it was the same sacrifice that my mother-in-law, Amanelwa, made when Mizan was born.

We were just lucky and eternally grateful to both fine ladies!

The decision

I continued to work for the state for two more years till the end of my four-year work-permit, i.e., my first round of H-1 visa, in May of 1992. And, once again I was faced with yet another major decision. The choice this time was between extending my H-1 visa for another four years, which my bosses were more than willing to do; and to go back to Ethiopia. By then, my wife was working for a small designer company; Mizan was almost four, and Hasabie was one and half years old.

Not that it would have made a difference regarding our return, but it so happened that, one year earlier in 1991, the Dergue in Ethiopia had been replaced with another government - a coalition of rebel forces known as the *Ethiopian People's Revolutionary Democratic Front* (EPRDF).

To the surprise and disapproval of many, we chose to go to return home.

Interestingly enough, Americans at least in those days, admired and even respected people who left the United States after accomplishing what they had come to the Unites States for. This was not because they did not want them to stay; it was because people who willingly leave the richest country on earth, the USA, intrigued them. After all, all they knew was people came from all over the world to the United States - to stay.

So, during my fourteen years in the United States, I have had discussions on this issue with several American friends and colleagues. I had always told them, loud and clear, that I would go back home when I was ready. Many thought I was bluffing; and many others were confused. *'Why would you leave the richest country to go to one of the poorest countries on earth?'*, they would ask with astonishment. Little did they know!

One day, I remember a discussion I had with my former boss at my part-time job, Dan Angeles, at the University of Illinois, Chicago campus. When I was almost done with the masters program at the university, Dan struck a conversation with me.

Dan: *Hey Ak, are you straightening up your papers?*
Aklilu: *What papers?*
Dan: *Your green card or whatever it is called?*
Aklilu: *No, all my papers are in order; I do not need a green card.*
Dan: *Are you not staying once you finished your studies?*
Aklilu: *No, I will go back to my country.*
Dan: *Are you crazy? No one leaves the United States!*
Aklilu: *What would I do here?*

Dan: *Live the American dream, get a job, buy a house; and raise children like everybody else...this is the land of opportunity.*

Aklilu: *I have my own Ethiopian dream. I will try and do all those in Ethiopia.*

Dan: *You mean you do not like it here?*

Aklilu: *Yes, I do. But I would be lying to you if I told you that I like the United States more than my own country.*

Dan: *Yes, but that shouldn't keep you from living in the United States; this is where the opportunity is.*

Aklilu: *That may be true, but I am not after opportunities; I am after happiness. And, no matter how you define it, I will be happier in my own country.*

At first Dan thought I was crazy. For him Ethiopia of the 1970s and early 80s represented famine and wars; nobody in his right mind would go there - especially not from the United States! His parents had come from Lithuania decades ago running away from something, and settled in the United States looking for a better life. That was all what he knew to be the norm.

But, after a long pause, he continued his conversation with a slightly different tone.

Dan: *You know Ak, I really admire that.*

Aklilu: *What do you admire?*

Dan: *That you want to go back home. The country needs you, and I can see you will be happier in your country.*

Aklilu: *Thank you Dan. But let me just say I was not going back home because the country needed me; it is because that is where I am happy.*

Dan: *I wish you all the best, Ak!*

Aklilu: *Thank you so much, Dan!*

I haven't heard from Dan Angeles since I left Chicago for Delaware in 1985. But I remember him to this date, with his face clearly imprinted in my mind, as one of the calmest, nicest and solidly humane human beings I ever met in my life.

Later on, it was at times when I remember people like Dan Angeles that I start missing the United States.

*****

A similar discussion took place later in May 1992 with Robert Welch, Director of the Delaware Bureau of Health Planning and Resources Management, where I worked my last four years in the United States - between 1988 and 1992.

In a letter written on April 29, 1992, I submitted my resignation letter to Robert, and here is an excerpt.

> It is with a great deal of mixed feelings that I hereby submit my resignation as the Administrator of the Delaware Health Statistics Center as of June 4, 1992. My feelings are mixed because, on one hand, I feel sorry to leave an excellent working environment and a dedicated group of people working towards a worthy goal. On the other hand, I feel happy to return to my home country where my modest skills maybe most useful.

Robert was intrigued that I would willingly leave a well-paid secure state job and the chance of getting the Green Card - and eventually American Citizenship. Time and again, he told me that he would do his best to have my H-1 visa extended for another four years, and then an automatic Green Card, should I decide to stay in the United States.

> Robert: *Aklilu, are you sure you want to leave?*
> Aklilu: *Yes, Robert.*
> Robert: *Nobody leaves once they get to the United States, especially with a good job and the possibility of getting a permanent work permit.*
> Aklilu: *Sadly, that is true.*
> Robert: *Your Ghanaian colleague is doing everything in his power to stay.*
> Aklilu: *That is his prerogative.*

Eventually he gave up too, but not before he sent me a letter, dated May 1, 1992, in response to my resignation letter, in which he wrote the following excerpt.

While your presence here will be sorely missed, I admire your commitment to Ethiopia and your determination to improve the lot of its people. I know I speak for the entire Bureau and numerous other colleagues in wishing you well in this next phase of your life. You leave with the respect and admiration of all of us, not only on a professional level but as importantly, on a personal level.

Robert's sendoff letter was very touching, and he was absolutely right that I was moving to my *'next phase of life.'* However, he may have exaggerated my commitment to my country. Yes, after my family, I will be delighted if I could *'improve the lot'* of my fellow Ethiopians in the process. That remained to be seen.

*****

My immediate boss and friend, Don Berry, was a totally different breed; an ultra-liberal fellow if there was one. He would actually encourage me to leave and, if he could, he had told me several times that he would have left the United States too; he had his own reasons which I think I know.

Anyway, Don was committed to his work and, when it came to making his position heard, he was merciless. Many times I would be sitting in a meeting with him trying to convince the state's health planners to pay attention to our vital statistics reports. First, he would patiently listen to all kinds of arguments or excuses until he would be the only one left who had not yet spoken.

Then, he would take his turn and, in cool and deliberate persuasive skills, would destroy any potential view against using our reports. I would watch and take notes.

Don, by the way, had two personalities, which not too many people knew about. On weekdays, from Monday to Friday, he was the typical bureaucrat: he would put on a suit with a tie, carried a briefcase and drove his small non-American car. On weekends, which for him would start on Friday after work, he would change into his motorcycle gear, which included a helmet, black leather jacket and pants, high boots and dark goggles.

Sometimes, his girlfriend Betsy would be seating at the back of his expensive Harley-Davidson[29] with a similar outfit. Then they rode for hours in every which way in and outside the state. My extended experience, way back during my childhood in Gore, riding bicycles without tires was a joke compared to what Don and Betsy were experiencing with their Harley-Davidson!

He once gave me a ride and, knowing it was a first time for me on a motorcycle, took it easy with some teasing. He also told me that, unlike the popular myth, not all people who rode motorcycles in dark leatherjackets and pants were members of criminal gangs; and I believed him.

In any case, one day over lunch at our favorite Amish Thursday open market, Don came up with what I thought at the time was a crazy idea.

Don: *Aklilu, do you still teach night classes at Delaware State University?*

Aklilu: *Yes, I enjoy teaching, plus it is useful extra money.*

Don: *What subject do you teach?*

Aklilu: *Economics; it is not exactly my field but I manage.*

Don: *I have an idea.*

Aklilu: *What?*

Don: *How about giving a couple of lectures to inmates at correctional centers in Dover.*

Aklilu: *Are you kidding; aren't those prisons?*

Don: *So what? They are still humans. It would be a great service to the inmates as it would be a great experience for you. And, I have done it.*

Aklilu: *Really, what about safety issues?*

Don: *Don't worry about that; these are not hard-core criminals; it is a community correctional center. They are already taking other classes and you will go in for a couple of lectures.*

Aklilu: *What subject would I speak about?*

Don: *General knowledge; talk about Africa, Ethiopia; something that would interest them.*

---

29   The most popular American-made motorcycle.

Aklilu: *How would I know that? But, I will think about it.*

I talked to my wife and we decided that I would give it a try; besides, Don won't leave you alone until he convinced you. So one weekday afternoon, I went to the correctional center and introduced myself. I was led to a classroom where about twenty inmates were waiting; most of them were male African Americans of all age groups.

I introduced myself, and started my talk on Apartheid system in South Africa, and the liberation struggle by the African National Congress (ANC). They were interested and listened attentively and asked a few general questions. At the end, I drove home with a new sense of adventure and satisfaction I never felt before.

On another day, I talked about my own country, Ethiopia. I talked about our religions; Coptic Christianity and Islam being the main ones. I talked about our languages with Amharic being the most spoken and the only language in Africa, other than Arabic, that had its own unique alphabet and numbers.

I talked about our two main seasons and a calendar, which not only had 13 months but also was 7 or 8 years behind the Gregorian calendar depending on what time of the year one was doing the conversion. I talked about the weather; that it was pleasantly temperate and that we had no snow or humidity to talk about. They listened with a lot of attention.

The first question I had at this class was from one inmate who asked to know how the heck I knew all these; I did not have a satisfactory answer. This was followed by a series of questions from one other inmate.

Inmate: *Do people speak English in your country?*
Aklilu: *Yes, a small minority of us do. But we have our several local languages; and one of the main ones is Amharic, which I speak.*
Inmate: *What kind of language is that?*
Aklilu: *Well, Amharic is an old language with Semitic roots; and has its own alphabet with about 230 letters or characters. One feature in Amharic is that, if you know the language and can write it too, you cannot make spelling mistakes.*
Inmate: *What do you mean?*

Aklilu: *You see, in Amharic we do not as such have words like you do in English language. Instead, what we have is a collection of letters or characters that make up words when they are pronounced individually. So as long as you know the alphabet, you do not make spelling mistakes.*

Inmate: *It is not clear.*

Aklilu: *It may be hard to explain, but let me try. For instance, in English, you have the word 'table' which is a word with its own distinct pronunciation. So, you may know the word but you could still make spelling mistakes when you write it out. Not so in Amharic.*

Inmate: *Still not clear.*

Aklilu: *So, in Amharic, we write the Amharic letter or character equivalents of 't', 'a', 'b', 'l' and 'e' individually and we pronounce them individually to form the word 'table'. You have to do it real fast, as if you were pronouncing the letters altogether as one. That way, so long as you know the alphabet and the word equivalent for table in Amharic, you do not make mistakes writing them down.*

I was not sure if I made myself clear; it was a tough thing to explain. But Don Berry was right; the experience was a big learning curve for me. I had never been, save one[30], inside a correction center or a prison before, and my views of prisoners were very much influenced by the dominating social biases and stigmas. What I saw at this center was a group of people, human beings, who perhaps were at the wrong place at the wrong time, made mistakes and, perhaps, were not given a second chance.

I could not but think that I may have done a similar offense more than once in my life but was lucky enough to get a second chance, and escaped prison. I remembered the incident that involved a revolver back in my high school years, about 25 years earlier, and how lucky I was to get away with it or, perhaps, to be given a second chance!

In any case, all in all, I worked for the state's Health Planning Bureau for four years, and it was a win/win situation.

---

30 I have once been to a high-security prison near Wilmington, Delaware, to visit a friend who was convicted of a crime.

On one hand I learnt so much and was gainfully employed; on the other hand, I served the state's population that carried the burden of sending me to school. It was time to go!

The preparations

A few months before we left the United States, I had written a letter to my dear old friend in Ethiopia, Mrs. Innes Marshall, asking if she knew if there was a teaching position at Addis Ababa University (AAU) that I could apply for. This lady, who was responsible for the action that triggered a chain of events that happened to me since 1977, responded with a copy of an AAU advertisement that came out on Ethiopian Herald on August 20, 1991.

The university was looking for a person to hire as an assistant professor with a research base at the Institute of Development Research (IDR) and a teaching base in the masters' program at the Demographic Teaching and Research Center (DTRC).

I contacted the Director of IDR at the time, Dr. Andargachew Tesfaye, immediately. After a number of letters back and forth, he informed me that I had been offered the rank of Assistant Professor Grade II, with a research base at the Institute of Development Research (IDR) and a teaching base at the Demographic Teaching and Research Center (DTRC); I was to report to work on June 8, 1992. The salary was to be 970 Birr a month – gross!

It was the first sign of hope for me that there was at least one person in Ethiopia who was indeed professional, honest and genuinely helpful in the name of Dr. Andargachew Tesfaye. I accepted his offer happily and with a lot of gratitude. Mrs. Marshall had delivered once again!

*****

There was one final matter that I had to attend to in preparation to return home, however.

A few months before we left the United States, my wife and I made sure that our Ethiopian passports were valid, and we had not in any way violated our students' visas. All was in order as far as my wife and I were concerned. It was a different scenario with our daughters. Legally, they could be issued American passports by virtue of being born in the United States; so they would be American citizens. That did not settle well with me; and I did not make any attempts to get them American passports. I wanted them to move to Ethiopia - as Ethiopians with Ethiopian passports.

So, I convinced my wife that we would get them Ethiopian passports from the Ethiopian Embassy at Washington D.C. when we were ready to leave. My wife was a bit reluctant at first, but she went along.

So, one morning in late March of 1992, I went to the Ethiopian Embassy in Washington D.C., and the following discussion ensued between me and an officer at the embassy.

Officer: *How can I help you?*
Aklilu: *I want to get Ethiopian passports for my two daughters.*
Officer: *How old are they?*
Aklilu*: They are four and one and half.*
Officer: *Where were they born?*
Aklilu*: In Delaware, United States.*
Officer: *So they are citizens; don't they have American passports?*
Aklilu: *No, they do not.*
Officer: *What do you mean?*
Aklilu: *Well, since we wanted them to return to Ethiopia as Ethiopians, we have not obtained American passports for them.*
Officer: *Are you telling me that you did not want your children to have American passports and you have come here to get Ethiopian passports for them.*
Aklilu: *Exactly.*
Officer: *I have never had such a request before.*
Aklilu: *Well, there is always a first time.*
Officer: *You do not like it here?*
Aklilu: *That is not the issue.*
Officer: *Ok, I cannot issue passports to your children now. As you may know, we have just had a change of government in Ethiopia, and we do not have passports to issue.*

Aklilu: *We are returning to Ethiopia and, obviously, I cannot leave without my children.*
Officer: *Ok, I understand; we can issue them laissez-passer instead.*
Aklilu: *What is that?*
Officer: *It is a travel document that will allow your daughters to travel to Ethiopia. It is as good as a passport.*
Aklilu: *That would be great, thank you!*
Officer: *Give me passport size photos of your children.*

I got the laissez-passers[31] for our daughters on March 30, 1992, and we were ready to say *'Ethiopia, here we come - back!'*

A decision has been made!

*****

Fast forward to 1997, five years after we settled in Ethiopia and our children were nine and seven, we were ready to travel outside the country as a family for the first time. As a student in the United Sates I had vowed to myself that I would visit South Africa and Palestine when they inevitably became free. South Africa was the first to become free in 1994, and we planned to go and visit three years later.

My wife and I, both with our valid Ethiopian passports, got our visas to South Africa without much problem. Then it occurred to me that our children had the laissez-passes, and needed to apply for Ethiopian passports, which in those days, was a long difficult process.

As I was wondering what to do, my wife went to her closet and came back holding some envelops in her hand, and handed them to me.

Aklilu: *What are these?*
Menby: *Our daughters' American passports.*
Aklilu: *I thought we did not obtain them while we were in the United States.*
Menby: *Well, I actually did without telling you; just in case.*
Aklilu: *Just in case what?*
Menby: *Just in case the children needed them.*

---

31   I still have copies of the laissez-passers as souvenir.

Aklilu: *Are they valid?*
Menby: *Yes, they need to be renewed here at the American Embassy, and the children can use them to travel.*

Without my knowledge, my wife had obtained and kept our children's American passports with her all the time. She never told me and I suspect our children were her accomplices on this issue as they may have been in almost every other issue regarding the family matters.

My in-laws Genet and Melesse Maru and their children Selam, Aman and Mikias joined us for a fun time in South Africa. Cape Town, 1997

By then, I was not so gang-ho about our children holding Ethiopian passports. After all, I figured, in a few years when they come of age, they would decide what nationality to become and choose what passports to hold.

Of course, they travelled to South Africa without a visa. With my in-laws and their children from the United States joining us, we had a wonderful time in apartheid-free South Africa!

In any case, back to the United States in early June 1992, our flight itinerary took us from Washington D.C. to New York, to Frankfurt, and to Addis; and we were ready.

But a few days before we departed, we went to the house of Menby's younger sister, Genet and her husband, Melesse Maru, in Maryland, to spend our last weekend with them and their children, Selam, Aman and Mikias. This was the one big family in the United States, which also included my wife's other sisters (Yewubdar and Bethlehem, and their spouses and children; and Surafel their brother) with whom we spent a lot of memorable times in the United States over the previous several years.

On June 5, 1992, they accompanied us to Dulles Airport in Washington D.C. and we said good-bye to each other with tearful eyes.

It was a very difficult occasion for all of us.

Chapter 3.

COMPLETING THE CIRCLE

Having spent 14 years abroad, almost exclusively in the United States, one would be expected to go through many emotional and cultural reorientation and adaptation upon returning home. However, one would know about them only if one had actually returned home; and I had that chance. There would always be some cultural counter shocks when coming back home, but the identity formed during childhood and boyhood, family support and a number of traditional festivities would have major mitigating effects.

'I would not lie by telling you that I love my country more than I love my family'

The Return

Homeward bound

Our long journey home began with a flight from Dulles Air Port, Washington DC, to John F Kennedy Airport, New York, in a tiny plane. The ride was not that long but the weather was bad, it was bumpy and it felt like it took forever to get there. The four of us were sitting at the end of the plane, which made things even much worse. After circling New York City a couple of times, and even detouring to places as far as Atlantic City because of bad weather, we finally landed and breathed a sigh of relief.

The second leg of our journey was a Lufthansa flight from New York, to Frankfurt, Germany. The flight was long, smooth and very comfortable, especially compared to the last one we had. The kids and I slept much of the way while my wife Menby was struggling; she finds it difficult to sleep on a plane even today.

When we landed in Frankfurt, we had only a couple of hours to scramble to get our luggage and find the gate where another Lufthansa, this time a day flight, would take us to our final destination: Addis Ababa.

Once we boarded the Addis bound plane, Mizan was asking all kinds questions about Ethiopia, mostly about food and playgrounds, neighborhood kids etc etc. Whatever I told her, she would, in turn, explain to her sister in her own way about what to expect in Ethiopia. Hasabie was a little too young to comprehend what was going on. Instead, she was preoccupied with the clouds she was looking at through the airplane window. Once in a while she would poke her tiny finger at the window hoping to touch the clouds. Mizan would laugh at her and add a sisterly advice, *'Do not be silly Hasu, you cannot touch the clouds because you are inside, and the clouds are outside the airplane.'* Hasabie would look at me, and I would nod a nod of approval.

Looking at my children interact that way, I did not even for a second second-guess the decision to come back home. Even if the jury was still out and in spite of all the arguments against it, I never doubted to return home was the right decision for me, for my wife, for our children, for our families and for whoever wished us well.

I knew I had made the most important and correct decision in my life.

*****

A few hours into the flight, after some food and refreshments, the lights went off and the widow shutters closed; and everybody around me, including even Menby, was asleep. I was awake, and all by myself.

So, I started thinking about what happened in my life in the previous fifteen years that separated me from most of the kids I grew up with and put me on unexpected life path which, for a reckless kid who grew up in Gore riding horses without saddles and bikes without tires, was a big deal indeed. Not that comparable thing did not happen to other kids with similar backgrounds, but when I thought about it, I had really come a long way in spite of my weak scholarly vitae; and I wanted to know who I owed it to.

So, somewhere over the skies of Northern Sahara Deseret, this time moving southward, I started a process of elimination to find out what really happened in my life that changed me so much.

It was not 'prayer', since I never prayed, not knowingly at least; nor did I believe in praying.

It was not that I was a 'bright' person, since I knew I just barely made it to college, and neither was I the scholarly type while in college.

It was not 'hard work', since the only time I ever worked hard was in graduate school, which was much later in life and because it was an absolute necessity.

Then, I thought maybe I was a bit 'lucky' in being at the right place at the right time. One may call this 'coincidence' but it probably is the same thing. So, there must also have been a little bit of 'hard work', a little bit of 'luck' and, I might add, a little bit of 'personal charm' which, even then, may explain only some of it.

What else?

I thought a little bit harder and realized that, by far, the most important factor for my 'success' was 'people.' When I thought about it, I was like the 'baton' in a relay race in a track-and-field contest.

First, my parents raised me, the 'baton', and put me in high school; Ayalew took over and, with his invaluable advice, set the baton up in college. Richard took over from there, used his incredible good will, and hand off the baton to Innes.

Then, Innes used her vast network and passed the baton over to Steganini, who sent the baton off to Italia. From Italia, my brother Miemen used all his persuasion power to put the baton on a flight to the United States. Andargachew picked up the baton from there, and delivered it to its final destination: Addis Ababa University.

The baton has come a full circle - the track-and-field was run successfully!

If that was what happened and using Leo Rosten's words, at least as far as I was concerned, these mortal people *'have made some difference that they have lived at all.'* The track, the life circle, has been completed for me with the help of these people.

Of course, there were many other people in between each step who have contributed immensely, but it was very clear to me that, without these people, I would have been a high school dropout by now; not that I have anything against them, though.

So, unable to return what I owed these people for various reasons, the question now in my mind was: would I be able to do the same, i.e., carry the baton for others?

Then, tired from all the thinking, I dozed off and joined the rest of my family in the obscure world of slumber.

Home sweet home

After about eight hours in the sky, the Lufthansa flight landed at Bole International Airport in Addis Ababa on June 6, 1992 - almost exactly to the day I left 14 years earlier. I was 42, Menby was 37, Mizan was 4 and Hasabie was one and half years old. I looked around me and noticed, not to my surprise, that we were the only Ethiopian family aboard the plane that has come to return home, and for good.

As the plane taxied to its stop, I couldn't help but wipe out a few teardrops with no one noticing. In spite of the heavy responsibility, they were tears of joy and satisfaction that I had made a bold and correct decision, regardless of what awaited us.

When the airplane door finally opened and we were asked to disembark, I had one quick look at my family, sighed deeply and said, *'Here we are guys!'* My wife, a normally very strong willed person, was a bit apprehensive; but our kids were tired but excited.

We literally rushed to the exit door as soon as we got the chance.

Once we got out of the plane and into the terminal, it was very clear that we had come from the richest country in the world to one of the poorest; one could see it everywhere. Since I was doing it with my free will, I was not even paying attention to that. After all, it was the same condition in which I lived for my first twenty-eight years and, as such, I was part of it. No big deal!

We cleared the passport control with our Ethiopian passports; and the Ethiopian laissez-passers for the children. We then collected our luggage and got out of the old terminal building to breathe the fresh Addis air by night; and it was drizzling.

Looking across the road from the terminal, I could see many people at the dimly lit parking lot, waiting for relatives to show up. There were no shed or light; just a swarm of wet people eagerly and patiently waiting in the dark for their loved ones to come out of the terminal building.

Among them were my entire family members, most eager to see us after a long time; and the kids, for the first time. We too were excited to see them and ready to accept whatever they and the country had to offer. After all, we have returned home.

In a convoy of small cars, we drove to my parent's house where even many more relatives, old and new, have braved the rainy night to greet us. For many it was the first time that they saw a family coming back home from the Unites States; it did not happen that often in those days.

They wondered what we dressed and looked like, what and how we spoke and ate. Some asked if we remembered them or if the children spoke Amharic or ate *injera*,[1] the curiosity to know was boundless. I tried to answer all questions with as much detail as possible. After having been away from them for so long, I thought, I owed them at least that much.

None, at the time, asked if coming back home was the right decision. In fact, for the older family members like my outspoken paternal aunt Abaye, we have done a courageous thing: we had come back for our families. She was once overhead saying, *'Kidanu has given birth to a real man who had returned to his country to take care of his parents at old age'.*

That may or may not be the case, but I was touched by the true love they exerted on us; it had been a while since so many people poured so much of their true affection on me and my family.

Anyway, after a lot of food, drinks and family interaction we retired to our bedroom at about mid-night. At some point before that, I was told that Mizan had gathered everybody and, in fluent Amharic which surprised and fascinated all,

---

1   A spongy sour flatbread made of 'teff' flour used to scoop meat or vegetable sauces that comprise one of the traditional dishes of Ethiopia.

announced that she had dropped from the sky, she was tired, and all she wanted to do now was go to sleep; and we all obliged.

*****

One of my most memorable days was the first morning after we arrived in Addis. All four of us were sleeping in one big bed in one of the bedrooms at my parent's house when, at about 6 am, I heard two things simultaneously: the crow of a rooster and the opening music for Ethiopia Radio morning program. They were both very familiar and it was as though I never left the country.

I was listening to them for a long time while still lying in bed, again with some tears sneaking out my eyes, when I heard a familiar knock at the door. It was the same knock that I was used to as a high school student reminding me that it was time to wake up and go to school.

Of course, it was my father, an early riser, who was announcing that it was time to get up and have breakfast. Actually, he just could not wait to see us again. In any case, I promptly woke up and after peeking through the window at the eucalyptus trees that I haven't seen for a long while, I was at the coffee table with a cup of pure Ethiopian coffee in my hands and chatting with my father. This was something I had waited for, for fourteen long years. We did not know where to start, but we had the entire world to talk about.

I remember, among other things, I kept on telling him that I was just happy that I have come back to where I belonged; and my father listened quietly. Although he had initially opposed to our return for mostly safety reasons, once I had made up my mind, he went along and never questioned my decision.

That was the kind of father he was.

Counter shocks

Although I was excited and happy beyond description, I was not totally naïve about what would await us when we returned to Ethiopia - with two little girls in tow.

To begin with, there was a government in place where it was not clear if it would be any better than the government it replaced.

Day to day necessities that we took for granted in the United States like tissue papers, diapers or aspirins were nowhere to be found in Addis. Strange as it sounds, most of the shelves at the government groceries were either empty or carried non-food items, like shoe polish, that one also had to buy in order to buy essential items like sugar. If those were the rules, no problem; we went along.

There were no private pharmacies, much less clinics or hospitals. Most of the city roads were in shambles; garbage was everywhere and no building seemed to have been painted, much less repaired, for decades.

I remember a few years later, while things were still very much the same, my three-year old niece, Gracie Flynn, arrived from the United States with her parents, Rod and Betty, for a short visit. Looking around her in confusion she asked, *'Uncle Aklilu, what happened to these houses? Has there been a tornado around here lately?'*

'No, Gracie, it is called poverty!' I replied.

Moreover, fuel was still rationed at the rate of fifteen liters per week, and that was if you were lucky to know or tip the clerk at the gas station. There was curfew at midnight, and random searches were common. The economic decay, albeit a carryover from the Dergue years, was apparent for all to see. The political uneasiness and bureaucratic quagmire were everywhere.

One incident was particularly telling. We had waited for a long time for our old car, a Subaru sedan which we used in the United States, to arrive in Addis. It took even longer for the customs office to figure out how much tax we needed to pay.

When we finally cleared all the paper work and paid the taxes, including storage fees, I was driving the car through the gate of the customs office when the guard stopped me.

Guard: *Can I see the receipts of your payments?*
Aklilu: *Yes, of course, here they are.*
Guard: *What do you have on the back seat?*
Aklilu: *It is a car seat for children.*
Guard: *Is that part of the car?*
Aklilu: *Maybe not, but it is a safety seat for one of our daughters who is less than two years old.*
Guard: *Did you pay taxes on the car seat?*
Aklilu: *I do not believe so.*
Guard: *You can take the car, but not the car seat. It stays here.*

There was no point in arguing further. I left the car seat behind and left with the car. When I enquired about the car seat later, I was told it was stored in the customs' warehouse - until it would be sold at an auction six months later. And, if I wanted to, I was told I could come and bid for it.

Although it sounded ridiculous that I would bid for my own property, but given that there were no car seats to buy in Addis, I first considered bidding for the car seat six months later.

But, by then, Hasabie had learnt to sit at the back seat with a seat belt; the car seat was not required. The traffic police in Addis at the time had no idea about using car seats for the safety of children. Perhaps, they had never seen one before!

I wonder now, unless somebody bought it, if the car seat is still at the customs' warehouse!

*****

In any case, I was also aware that I had returned to Ethiopia when everybody else seemed to be eager to leave the country, usually at tremendous social and economic costs. Many people I knew had left the country for one reason or another, and opted not to return.

The Voluntary Departure Visa (aka DV), a lottery based program that opened the chance for one to become a permanent resident of the United States, accelerated the out-flow of Ethiopians to the United States.

Young and old, poor and rich, students and professionals equally scrambled to win this lottery. Many left the country, perhaps not to return, at least not in the short and medium terms.

The brain drain for a poor country like Ethiopia was criminal!

Still, many more filled out the DV forms year after year, in anticipation of winning the lottery and, in the process, putting their lives and livelihoods on hold for years. I know a young nephew who had applied for seven consecutive years and basically had quit planning his life in any other direction for that long. He finally managed to go (not through the DV program though) but paid in seven years of his productive life for it.

I was intrigued, if not shocked, by what I learnt. I wondered what it was that people knew which I didn't know about, that they were ready to pay so much to go to the United States, and not necessarily for a secure or a better livelihood. I also wondered what the effect of the DV program was on both the participants (those who won and those who lost), in particular, and on the country, in general.[2]

*****

Most of my old friends who were still in Ethiopia when I returned were no exceptions. They were dying to leave Ethiopia, and I had willingly returned to Ethiopia. Right there, there was a mismatch between my friends and me.

So, our interaction and relationship, unfortunately, was evaluated on the basis of this mismatch, and I was in awe of the task ahead of me to minimize the inevitably negative effects it had on our friendship.

---

2   It might be interesting to study this issue.

I had thought it was going to be a simple matter of re-adapting to my own culture upon returning home; I was wrong. My fourteen years in the United States had actually exposed me to new values and ways of life.

Not that I practiced them all the time or believed there were no other choices, but I had learnt a few life-skills which, unfortunately, had separated me from my friends in some ways.

For instance, I had learnt to try and give one the benefit of the doubt; in other words, unless I saw enough evidence I would try not to judge a person, or a government for that matter.

I had also learnt to try and not be defensive; in other words, I try not to be in a position of always declaring myself correct.

I had learnt to try and keep my boundary; in other words, I refrain from providing unsolicited opinions or poke my nose in somebody else's personal business.

I had learnt to try and call a spade a spade; in other words, 'to speak frankly about something even if it is unpleasant.'

I had learnt to try and agree to disagree; in other words, to tolerate views even if they were different from mine.

I had also learnt to try and listen before I talked, to admit mistakes, and apologize when necessary.

This was mostly in contrast to my behavior at the time I left Ethiopia as young man in the late 1970s! Again, it wasn't like I practiced them all the time but, yes, these were some changes that I went through. Changes that, perhaps, I would never have known about had I not returned to my country. Changes, perhaps, I would have taken them for granted if I had stayed in the United States.

I didn't think these were necessarily bad life lessons or that they changed my identity as an Ethiopian in any significant way. Nevertheless, it was a struggle to maintain my relationship with my close friends. So, by separating our differences in opinions from our friendship, no matter how much we differed on issues, I tried to value our friendship even more.

For instance, if there was something that they strongly believed in, usually on political matters, I would simply defer to them; and this strategy worked to some extent.

Interestingly enough, I found out that it was much easier to deal with my twin friends. In terms of their behavior, I have found them exactly where I left them. To begin with, in spite of the fact that they were the typical urbanites, kids from the Merkato area, they still were unassuming, honest and predictable. Just like during our boyhood years, I could read them like an open book, which made it easier for me to handle them and maintain our close friendship – even after the long separation.

On their part, and to my pleasant surprise, they were totally oblivious to the changes that I may have gone through. As far as they were concerned, it was as if I had never left. They were, in their own way, too confident about themselves to be threatened by a friend who had been away, in the United States, for such a long time. They did not seem to notice or care how long I stayed away or what I have come back with. They never asked me, and I never offered to explain; and, hence, I was totally free with them. And, I never was expected to apologize for anything; neither did I expect one from them – like the good old days!

Hence, we accepted each other 'as is', and that was the basis of our 'true' friendship.

50 years later, I still have difficulties telling who is who. Banjaw and Bezuayehu (or the other way round) Addis Ababa, 2017

*****

Regarding my close relatives and from those who were living in the county at the time[3], I was lucky enough to get most appreciated support in dealing with the counter shocks of returning home. I also actively tried to create opportunities where as many relatives as possible would meet at different venues and know and spend time with each other.

One afternoon in early July provided a perfect opportunity to share some quality time with close relatives when some 'Diaspora' and many locals got together to watch the finals of the South Africa 2010 World Cup.

The venue, the Millennium Hall in Addis Ababa, with huge screens, sound system and food/beer stands, was temporarily transformed into a kind of mini-stadium with a capacity of about eight thousand people; but, typical Ethiopian style, ended up accommodating over twelve thousand. The 'Giros',[4] two

---

3   Most notably, my brother in-laws Hiruy and Tadesse.
4   The first name of my maternal great grandfather.

generations in all, ranging from below puberty to well above the reproductive years, were well represented. It was as much to see real good football as it was to just being in a family get-together.

South Africa, in the name of Africa, put on a fantastic show, of organizing the games which made us all proud; a rare experience for us Africans. And, I had also thought the *'vuvuzela'*[5] was limited to South Africa. But, despite the lot of noise they made, it was heartening to see that some resourceful Ethiopians had many of them imported into Ethiopia, which appropriately found their way to the Millennium Hall. If they only put the same resilience into more productive things, I thought the country would have become a middle-income country long before the projected year!

So there I was, at age 60, in the middle of the closest people to me watching football and socializing with the likes of Senay and Aman (at the time, about 14 and 12, respectively), my two die-hard Arsenal football fan Diaspora second nephews, with strange Scottish accent which I tolerated. I could not have asked for a more 'quality' time to spend with my relatives.

In any event, the final game was between Spain and The Netherlands and most of us, with the exception of my nephew/niece Andy/Mati and a few late convert nephews like Paul, Babi and Mickey, were rooting for Spain. In earlier games, most of the teams that we rooted for had lost; notably United States and Brazil. But nothing was as bad as watching Ghana losing the game to Uruguay. If Ghana had won, it would have propelled an African team to the semi-finals for the first time in the history of the World Cup. We all agreed it was the result of bad officiating.

In the end, Spain got the 'gold cup', South Africa got the 'respect' and Ethiopia got the *'vuvuzela'*! But what was most significant for me was the gathering that attracted so many of

---

5   An elongated plastic instrument that football fans in South Africa blow to make a loud noise in support of their teams.

the *Giro* family members at one place, and eyes focused on one screen.

'People' were the unit of happiness.

And then, by pure instinctive impulse, I turned around to look across the aisle from where we were sitting and saw a bunch of familiar looking people, much like our group, having a good time. I looked hard, and discovered that they were my cousins and second cousins from my father's side of my family.[6] Hmm, I told myself, maybe I can bring these two groups together one day; I also knew such gatherings could only be possible in Ethiopia!

Sadly, many of the family members who I watched the games with went back to their adopted motherlands soon after this gathering - to be swallowed by the 'Diaspora' monster. But, at least, it was with the satisfaction that the Millennium Hall family gatherings were by far the highlights of their visit to their motherland; I was happy I was part of it.

My Saturday events

My Saturday events with my father, which started in Gore when I was barely a child and had continued till I left the country in 1978, took off immediately upon my return from the United States in 1992, albeit in different ways.

This time, every Saturday noon, I would leave my office and go to a bakery called *Dewale* where some Somali refugees, for some reason, would make the best bread of the time in Addis. Then I would go to a butchery called *Mulushewa* where I would buy the most select beef in Addis. Then I drive to my parents' house.

I know my father, who by now was in his late 70s, would be waiting for me sitting on his favorite chair at his favorite corner on the verandah of his house. He would always receive me with the same words, '*What have you brought today, my son?*', while he knew exactly what. I would always answer with the same words,

---

6 I have always been proud and happy to say I have 56 first cousins on both my parents' sides. I won't even try to count their children d grandchildren.

'Not much, dad.' My father actually had the capacity to buy what I buy, and much more; but when I am the one who is buying, he took a particular pleasure in it; and that, in return, pleased me immensely.

Then, I would walk to the kitchen where I would find my mother preparing in her own way. *'Just like last week, son?'*, she would ask, referring to the meal she had prepared for us a week earlier. I would node with a quick kiss on her cheeks. My view of my mother from my boyhood years as the kindest lady I knew who made sure that we ate properly was forever encrypted in me. Even today in her late 80s, she cooks for us. We could be eating the entire food at the house and she would still not be satisfied that we had eaten enough.

That is the kind of mother she is.

In any event, what will follow would be a small feast, which included my father's favorite dish: raw meat. Needless to say anybody who happened to be around would be invited to join in. So, nothing pleased me more than watching my father eat his meal with deliberate dignity and with the highest respect for every tiny particle of food item on his plate.

After lunch, we would retire to his favorite spot on the verandah with his favorite bottle of whisky, the White Horse, in tow. A couple of drinks, which my father needed to 'help digest' the raw meat he had just eaten, would conclude the weekly feast with a high note; and we would be ready to venture out. At about 4pm, my father and I would be ready for our much enjoyable drive around the city; my mother would stay behind and, *'play with my beautiful grandchildren'*, as she always liked to say.

My father, a very development oriented person, loved to see new buildings and roads. So every Saturday before I went to my parent's house, I would plan where to drive him, in search of new roads or buildings or new hotels.

My father and I always ready for one of our social events. Addis Ababa, 1996

My father had been to the United States a couple of times while I was there, and I knew how fascinated he was with the highways. So I would take him to the completed sections of the Addis Ababa ring road, and he would be excited just like a small boy. As we drove around, we would talk about everything under the sun, mostly about our kids' education, my wife's work or the house that, one day, we were hoped to build.

This would last for a couple of hours and, as a finale, we would go to *Parisiene*, a café in an area known as *Olympia*, where they sell *keshir* - hot ginger tea that my father loved. He believed *keshir* cured people from all kinds of malaises, including excess cholesterol and high blood pressure, which he had.

Routinely, he would ask me how much I paid for the *keshir*, and I would respond 'not much.' I remember a day when I told him the real price of tea at a café, and he thought we were throwing our money away for nothing.

At about 6 pm, we would go back to his house where I would watch him put his pajamas on, and get ready to listen to the evening news on the radio. My father did not like eating dinner, one of the many habits that I copied from him. Then, he would ask me to go home before it got too dark. *'Don't forget to call me when you get home'*, he would instruct; and I never did.

Unless either of us was outside the country, my Saturday affairs with my father, although slightly modified over the years, continued till I was in my mid-fifties and till he died at the age of ninety. We missed the two Saturdays he was at the hospital. But, nothing that I remember in my life gave me more satisfaction and pleasure than my Saturday events with my father. Following the advice he once gave me, I tried to celebrate the happy times we had more than to dwell on the grief of his death.

I really never felt I lost him when he passed away, since there was so much in me that reminded me of my father. I was simply grateful that I was able to be close to him for most of his life, particularly during his last 12 years.

I would never have traded that for the world, or the heavens.

*****

On my wife's side, re-adaptation to the values and ways of life in Ethiopia resumed too. Her mother, W/o Amanelwa Mulatu, had married her husband, Ato Alemayheu Lidetu when she was only fifteen. By the time she was 21, she had had five of her six children.

My in-laws were constant hosts to a number of family gatherings at their house.

Growing and enjoying grandparental stories, food and love with grandmother Amanelwa (far right), Addis Ababa, 1994

Our children enjoyed their maternal grandparents and one surviving great grandparent as much as they enjoyed their paternal counterparts, not to speak of the multitude number of cousins and second cousins on both sides who were more than happy to play with them or tell them Ethiopian folk stories.

In the process our daughters learnt and grew with a lot of love and attention; in a way, it was the opposite of the lonely times during their first few years in the United States. This is not to even speak of the following several years of their lives if they had stayed in the United States.

To and from Addis Ababa University

My colleagues and students

There were also some other encouraging normal things going on in Ethiopia, despite the talk to the contrary. There were many close relatives and non-relatives, with all kinds of backgrounds, who were working and living in Ethiopia. The Institute of Development Research (IDR) at Addis Ababa University (AAU) where I took a job was filled with scholars who could easily have gone anywhere in the world, and stayed away if they had wanted to.

In subsequent years, I also realized that there were people who would go abroad for a short visit or work, and promptly returned. I was encouraged. My decision to return to Ethiopia, after all, was not a reckless one! Not that I needed to, but I sometimes rationalized, if they could work and live in Ethiopia, why could not I?

So, I set out determined to start my new life in Addis, and take on whatever faced me. I was re-adapting reasonably well; and there were no regrets whatsoever. Besides, I might add, with no Green Card or American passport in my hands, I did not have much choice; perhaps a blessing in disguise?

Anyway, after I spent a couple of days with family members, I went to Addis Ababa University to report to work. The university's Sidist-Kilo campus is a place where I spent eight years of my youth as a student in the 1970s. Needless to say, I was familiar with every curve and corner to the point where, even if I were blindfolded, I would still find my way.

It was also here that I became friends with wonderful people[7] many of whom, by now, were gone and have already been consumed by the monstrous 'Diaspora', a word that makes me shriek with anger and pain, because it took away the people I cared for so dearly.

I realized it was naïve of me to have expected those individuals to still be around. Instead, I focused on and enjoyed the memories and the locations and landmarks on campus, which we enjoyed together. I frequented these places by myself. I have often sat alone in one of these locations and hoped, against hope, that my dear old friends and classmates would somehow show up from some corner of the vast green campus as they used to; of course, it never happened.

---

7   They included Tsegaye Beru, Asfaw Goitom, Zewditu Tesfaye, Tadesse Berhanu, Tewodros Gebre Michael, Girma Araya, Daniel Yifru, Tesfu Zewdu, Tadesse Gosheme, Berhane Habte Mariam, Yoahnnes Gebre Michael, Segewkale Asrat, Anteneh Belay, Moges Kassa, Asrat Gamo, Mulat Amde.

In any case, it was on the first Monday, and two days after I arrived in Addis, that I reported to the Director of the Institute of Development Research (IDR) at Addis Ababa University. I was to have a research base at the Institute with a teaching base at the Demographic Training and Research Center (DTRC) housed within the Institute.

The Director of the Institute, Professor Andargachew Tesfaye, was very happy to see me and told me about the Institute and the staff at the Institute, most of whom I have known during my student years as elegant and dynamic young professors; many of them were my idols. I could not believe that I was going to have an office amongst them and attend the same staff meetings.

My salary was to be a gross payment of 970 Birr per month, which amounted to a net payment of 835 Birr per month; a far cry from the salary I had during the previous four years of full time employment in the United States. But, I did not complain; it would be a detail I would worry about later in life.

The Director then took me to my office already labeled 'Aklilu Kidanu (Dr.)' on the outside door. And, I settled on my wooden chair and table in my office on the third floor of the then-new Social Science Building.

The first thing I did was get a razor and cut out the (Dr.) from the label on my office door. I was later told that, whether I liked or not, I would always be called 'Doctor' as long as I lived in Ethiopia; and that ended up being true. In fact, kids in my neighborhood would send me a new-year's card, of course to solicit money, and would address me as 'Dear Mr. Doctor'; they did not even know my name; and that was fine by me.

Later in life, an incident on the same issue rattled me a little bit. I was about to enter the gate of my house in Addis when an elderly gentleman approached me with extended polite greetings. I did not know him, but I responded as much as I could to match his greetings while I was still seating in my car waiting for the gate to open.

Gentleman: *Greetings doctor, how are you and family?*
Aklilu: *We are fine sir, how are you?*

Gentleman: *I am not feeling well.*

Aklilu: *Really, how do you feel?*

Gentleman: *I am hurting all over my body and I do not know what is causing it.*

Aklilu: *Why don't you go and see a doctor?*

Gentleman: *I did, and have also taken some medication. But I am still not feeling any better.*

Aklilu: *Maybe you should go and see another doctor.*

Gentleman: *I am a poor old man, and I was wondering if you could help me with the cure.*

Aklilu: *But, I cannot help you. It is not my job to help people who are not feeling well.*

Gentleman: *Then why do they say you are doctor? Isn't that true?*

Aklilu: *Yes, but I am not a medical doctor who helps people when they are not feeling well.*

Gentleman: *What kind of doctor are you then?*

Aklilu: *You see, there is another type of doctor who doesn't treat people…..*

Gentleman: *So, you are not a doctor?*

Aklilu: *No, not exactly…..*

Gentleman: *So, all what I hear about you is a lie? A damn lie!*

The gentleman walked away in disgust, swearing that he would never believe people like me again. And, I sat in my car for a few minutes regretting the day I got a Ph.D.!

*****

Anyway, back to my first day at Addis Ababa University, I was sitting in my IDR office wondering what to do next when I heard a light knock at the door. When I answered to please enter, an elderly slim lady walked in with a bunch of tissue papers, small soaps, and a big welcome smile. She introduced herself as the cleaner, handed me a tissue paper and a small soap, and asked me to sign against my name on a piece of paper.

I asked what it was all about, and she told me that I could use them should I want to go to the washroom; those were the rules. I fully concurred, put my signature against my name, thanked the lady, put my tissue paper and tiny soap in my drawer, and waited until she left - to laugh aloud alone.

'Welcome to Ethiopia!', I told myself, with a little bit of astonishment!

Then, I ventured out of my office and walked around the corridor just to see who else was at IDR. So, I began reading the names on the office doors: Mekonnen Bishaw (Dr.), Befekadu Degefe (Dr.), Dessalegn Rahmato, Almaz Eshete, and Solomon Gebre! I could not believe that these scholars of their time will be my colleagues! I was honored to be among them, but I also knew my job was cut out for me to catch up with them. I am eternally indebted for the support and encouragement that I got from these scholars during my tenure at IDR.

I also found out that there were much younger scholars who had just graduated from the university and, because of their good grades, have been kept by IDR as junior lecturers. These included Markos Ezra, Gebre Egziabher Kiros, Emebet Mulugeta, and Yeshi Habte Mariam. I correctly concluded that they were happy to see me, as much as I was pleased to be their colleague.

*****

One of my first tasks while on campus was to visit my dear old friend, Mrs. Innes Marshall. She was instrumental in my leaving the country 14 years earlier, and now she helped me get this job at IDR. So, a few minutes after I settled in my office, I went to the building where she had an office. At the entrance I met a lady, W/o Aster Maru, who was related to me through marriage.

W/o Aster: *Welcome to Ethiopia, Aklilu, I heard you had come.*
Aklilu: *Thank you W/o Aster, how are you, and the family?*
W/o Aster: *We are all fine. Have you also come to see Mrs. Marshall?*
Aklilu: *Yes, she helped me find the job at the university, I just wanted to say thank you.*

W/o Aster: *Yes, I know she always talked about you and Menby.*[8]
Aklilu: *Is she in? I want to greet her.*
W/o: Aster: *Come in to her office, and please sit down.*

I sat and waited alone for some time looking at some photos on the wall, but Mrs. Marshall did not show up. After a while, W/o Aster came back by herself, and sat in front of me quietly; I felt something strange.

Aklilu: *Where is Mrs. Marshall?*
W/o Aster: *I know you did not hear.*
Aklilu: *Did not hear what?*
W/o Aster: *She passed away a few weeks ago; she had been ill for some time.*

The person who counted in my life so significantly had passed away just a few weeks before I got back to Ethiopia to thank her. I felt so sad; I really had wanted to see her, tell her about my studies and thank her for what she did for me. But, that was not to happen. Instead, I went to see her husband, Mr. Marshall, at his house, and pay my respect. He was gracious enough to tell me the circumstances of her death, and where she was buried.

A lady who had abandoned her job at the Royal British Air Force and followed her love all the way to Ethiopia, served the country for decades, died and was buried in Addis Ababa; it was a great touching story.

*****

I settled at IDR, and the days, weeks and months went by quickly. My main task was to co-ordinate social development research within the Institute, and I also had a couple of classes to teach at DTRC. As a researcher, I had the opportunity and the privilege of partnering on several social science research

---

8   Mrs. Marshall had once employed Menby during a summer recess at AAU Printing Press.

projects with established IDR scholars; notably with Dessalegn Rahmato, a renowned researcher on peasant livelihood and production in Ethiopia.

I travelled to various corners of the country with my colleagues and students, and learnt about the country first-hand. We collected data and wrote reports and shared them with stakeholders both within and outside Ethiopia.[9]

I did not do much research, especially compared to my colleagues, during my three-year stay at IDR because, for the most part, I was still learning. Some of the topics that I was beginning to research with the help of students and colleagues, however, included coping strategies regarding rapid population growth; the use of local social systems for development; and integration of population and development in DTRC curriculum.

At my teaching base at DTRC,[10] I enjoyed my students immensely, very much like I did during my Shire Inda Selassie and Italian School years in Tigray and Addis Ababa, respectively. But this time it was a graduate school, and the students were older and more mature, which meant that I could have beer, equivalent of Shire Inda Selassie *tella*, with them once in a while.

My teaching approach was that no student should fail unless it was the weakness of the teacher. This approach, added to my informal beer drinking episodes with my students, which I inherited from my professors in the United States, was not appreciated among some of my DTRC colleagues.

That did not bother me much; since I did not care for teachers who still maintained a master-servant relationship with their own students. Through my teaching approach, not only did I put the burden on me as to the performance of the students, but also many of the students who graduated, albeit much younger than me, ended up being my friends. To this

---

9   Just as a foot-note, within three years of my return to Ethiopia I had already been to over a dozen countries in the world. In contrast, in the 14 years I was in the Unites States, the only country I went to was Canada.

10   My assigned subjects were migration, urban poverty and vital statistics.

day, I run into them or they deliberately look for me when in town, just to talk about the good old days -over beer.[11]

I also used new and daring approaches in my lectures. In a way, I saw a little bit of my Peace Corps teacher Ash Hartwell in me! I had also thought it was my chance to carry the 'baton', for one or more of my students as well as the junior lecturers.

That, I knew, would not be possible with the kind of attitude most senior teachers at the time had with their students or with the younger and junior staff members. I knew I had to be close and informal with them so they have the trust for open and frank discussion not only about school but also about life in general.

In our beer sessions, in order to know each other well and break the ice that existed between a teacher and a student, I deliberately teased them with personal issues like marriages or filling out the DV forms; or my decision to return to Ethiopia, which confused them.

One evening, again over a glass of beer, I cornered three of my most favorite students, Melaku Eshetu, Tadesse Alemu, and Dilnesaw Asrat.

Although, they were talking in unison as if they had exactly the same issues, Melaku was the most vocal.

Aklilu: *You guys seem to be in your late 20s or early 30s; why don't you get married?*
Melaku: *Why?*
Aklilu: *Well, for one thing, you will find a partner in life.*
Melaku: *I can't even survive by myself, let alone with a wife.*
Aklilu: *Exactly, that is the point. You help each other and make life tolerable and enjoyable for each other. As I see you now, you are wasted.*
Melaku: *What do you mean?*
Aklilu: *You eat outside all the time, which is not only expensive but also unhealthy. You must also be very lonesome since you sleep in one room alone all the time.*

---

11 It was not like we drank a lot of beer; we were using such occasions to establish that we were discussing on equal footing; and it worked.

Melaku: *We have our girlfriends.*
Aklilu: *Then, if you love them, get married!*
Melaku: *No, no, you do not understand.*
Aklilu: *What do I not understand?*
Melaku: *Ok, let me explain to you. I come from outside Addis. When I was an undergraduate student, I was living in a small room I rented in the service quarters of a house; sharing a toilet with six other families. Then I got a job at the university as an assistant lecturer with the option of continuing my maters degree; I am still living in the same room. I will tell you, even with my master's degree, I would still be living in the same room. There is no possibility for me to live in a decent place, let alone have my own house and a car.*
Aklilu: *Don't you think there would be a better chance of living in a decent house with two incomes, if you had a partner?*
Melaku: *I don't want to marry just because I want to live in a decent house.*
Aklilu: *I agree, you should marry for love. But, I can tell you one of the outcomes of marriage is improving one's standard of living because two is better than one.*
Melaku: *I know what would improve my standard of living.*
Aklilu: *What is it?*
Melaku: *Leaving the country.*
Aklilu: *What makes you sure that would improve your life?*
Melaku: *At least I will go there and try my chance; here it is a dead end.*
Aklilu: *You will abandon your career in the hope that you will try your chance in the United States?*
Melaku: *What do I have to lose?*

There was no point, I gave up. These guys would leave the country if they got the chance - no matter what.[12]

---

12 Both Melaku and Dilnesaw later went to Brown for a short training/seminar and stayed in the United States after their program ended. Tadesse also somehow ended up in the United States; they all live there as far as I know.

Fellowship at Brown University

One day in the morning in late 1994, I was walking to my IDR office on campus when I saw a lady in front of me who looked lost. I caught up with her and asked if I could help her. She told me she was looking for the Dean of the College of Social Sciences, Professor Seyoum Gebre Selassie. I told her that my office was on the same floor, and I would be happy to take her to his office. She thanked and followed me to Professor Seyoum's office. I knocked at the dean's office, opened the door, and let the lady in. Then, I went to my office.

A few minutes later, there was a knock at my office door, and I said to please come in. The same lady who I took to Professor Seyoum's office walked in.

Lady: *So it is you again!*
Aklilu: *Yes, it is me; and it is you again.*
Lady: *Yes. Professor Seyoum sent me here.*
Aklilu: *You are most welcome, please sit down; how can I help you?*
Lady: *Let me introduce myself. My name is Lina Fruzzetti, I am a professor of anthropology at Brown University.*
Aklilu: *I am Aklilu Kidanu, assistant professor here at IDR, AAU.*
Lady: *I have come to Ethiopia looking for collaboration for a study that I want to conduct in this country; Professor Seyoum sent me to you.*
Aklilu: *I am honored he did so. What is the study about?*
Lady: *It is about social migration of diseases, focusing on HIV/AIDS. If you agree you can be on the team; I have already found a medical person to work with us.*
Aklilu: *Who is that?*
Lady: *Professor Redda Teklehaimanot; do you know him?*
Aklilu: *Everyone knows Professor Redda, but I have yet to meet him in person.*
Lady: *Good, but would you be interested?*
Aklilu: *Yes, could you please tell me more?*

I found out that Lina, probably in her mid-30s at the time, is half Eritrean and half Italian. She grew up in Khartoum, and studied at the University of Chicago, United Sates, and eventually ended up as a professor at Brown University, one of the Ivy League universities in the United States. I also met Redda in due course and found him to be very knowledgeable, genuinely helpful and with plenty of humor.

The study itself was about social migration of diseases, focusing on HIV/AIDS, in the Butajira area of Southern Ethiopia. For the next year or so Lina, Redda and I worked together on the study, and came to know each other very well. Lina would travel several times to Ethiopia, and we would all go to the field to collect data, which we entered in SPSS, a statistical package, and had the preliminary frequency tables printed.

In September 1995, I got a one-year Population Council[13] Post-Doctoral Fellowship to spend on analyzing the tables and writing the report on our Butajira social migration of diseases study. When I was looking for a university to give me the base and facilities that I needed, Lina managed to get me one at Brown University located in Providence, Rhode Island, United States.

I was to stay at Brown for one academic year as a Visiting Scholar, mainly working on the report on our study, and appearing in seminars and classes as a guest lecturer. I would be working with the staff members of the Department of Anthropology and the Population Studies and Teaching Center (PSTC) at this famous university.

Hence, back to the United States! I left my wife and my two small children and set out to Providence for the one-year fellowship. It was not easy on my wife and my children, but the opportunity opened up a whole set of future possibilities for me.

To begin with, at Brown, I came to know very closely people like Professor Sidney Goldstein, world-renowned migration specialist, and his wife Alice. Aside from their academic guidance, this couple was indeed like parents to me.

---

13   The Population Council is a non-profit non-governmental organization that conducts research to address critical health and development issues.

They fed me at their house frequently, a situation that one would appreciate a lot when one was living alone in a university guesthouse. They showed me around the state of Rhode Island on several weekends, and introduced me to historical places in the state including the first synagogue built in the United States.

I was grateful they made my stay in Providence productive and enjoyable. Later, in the coming years, when Sid and Alice travelled to Ethiopia, I tried to reciprocate their hospitality, but it paled compared to what they have done for me while at Brown.

Professor and Mrs. Goldstein from Brown University with my family during their visit to Addis Ababa, mid-1990s

Still at Brown, younger but renowned scholars like Professors Dennis Hogan and David Lindstorm later came to IDR/Addis Ababa University to conduct collaborative public health research in Ethiopia. Some IDR junior staff also went to Brown University for further studies through this collaboration.

All in all, here I was, a former rural tree-climbing kid from Gore, interacting with the likes of Lina, Sidney, Denis and David from one of the Ivy League universities in the Unites States!

Goodbye Addis Ababa University

Back at Addis Ababa University in June 1996, I was in trouble. In a complex set of misunderstandings and tendencies to go by the book, I had to resign from an institution I was so much attached to. When I first left for Brown University in September 1995, the then-Vice President of Academic Affairs had given me permission for a one semester stay at Brown, with the possibility of extending it for the second semester of the academic year.

By the time I came back to Ethiopia in December at the end of the first semester for the Ethiopian Christmas break, there was a new Academic Vice President who was not willing to or could not give me the extension for the second semester. Since I still had permission to stay at Brown till mid February 1996, I went back to Brown defying his decision denying me an extension.

Once at Brown, in a letter dated February 15, 1996, I argued very strongly as to why I should stay at Brown till the end of the academic year.

February 15, 1996
Dr. Hailu Ayele
Academic Vice President
Addis Ababa University
Addis Ababa, Ethiopia

Dear Dr. Hailu:
This is a request for extension of my fellowship at Brown University by three months as of the end of February 1996. My request for extension is based on the following concrete reasons.

First, three senior Brown University staff would come and visit IDR and AAU to see the possibilities of beginning a working relationship between PSTC and DTRC. Their visit might also result in the recruitment of IDR staff for further studies at Brown University.[14]

Second, I have been talking with the staffs of World Hunger Program, who have shown interest in helping start a sustainable research project on food security at our institution. This may begin with a workshop on food security in Ethiopia -which may take place at IDR as early as this summer. I will push towards that end during my stay here.

Third, The Population Council, the agency that gave me the scholarship, is very much interested in demographic issues and research in Ethiopia. My successful completion of the fellowship will open opportunities not only for other similar fellowships to AAU staff but also create a very useful contact with a respected and influential agency in the academic world.

Fourth, during my stay at Brown University, I have learnt a great deal about the role of anthropology in helping understand demographic events. There is much more to learn. As a result, my teaching and research activities at IDR, will improve a great deal from this experience.

Finally, while I am here I have easy access to universities and other research institutions which eventually could help our institution. Similarly, I communicate regularly with those institutions with whom we have already established a working relationship.

In light of these, I very much hope you will consider my request kindly and grant me the extension I am asking. As you can see, although the fellowship was meant to advance my personal career, I am trying to use the opportunity to forge major working relationships and contacts which would provide institutional benefits over the long-term.

I hope to hear from you soon.

My best regards,
Aklilu Kidanu
Population Council Fellow at Brown
    CC: Johannes Kinfu, Professor
    Director, IDR

---

14   In subsequent years at least four DTRC staff went to Brown for short-term seminars, and one completed a doctoral program in demography.

On March 18, 1996 (Ref. No. AC.202.01/88/281) I received a reply from the Academic Vice President; the following was the full content of the letter.

Dr. Aklilu Kidanu
Brown University
Department of Anthropology
Box 1921
Providence, Rhode Island 02912, USA

Dear Dr. Aklilu:
This has reference to your letter of 15 February 1996 regarding the extension of your research leave at Brown University. I understand your short-term leave was earlier approved until 17 February 1996 (Yekatit 7, 1988 E.C) and you were briefly back at the Institute of Development Research from late December to mid January during which time you were urged by the Director of IDR to submit a report on your activities and plans. As far as I know these were not received by the institute.

Your efforts towards professional advancement and the attempts you are making to develop contacts that will be useful to our institution might have some merits. However, these must be accompanied within the framework of established rules and procedures of Addis Ababa University. I am sure you know and were, in fact, fully informed about the rules governing the extension of leaves and you have neither sought nor obtained a formal support for the extension of your leave from the Institute of Development Research. Under the circumstances, I find it difficult to grant the extension of your leave beyond the specified time when your leave was approved earlier.

By copy of this letter, the Institute of Development Research is advised to take the necessary action by taking into account that the extension of your leave has no official support and approval.

Sincerely Yours,
Hailu Ayele (Dr.-Ing.)
Academic Vice President

Cc: President's Office
Prof. Johannes Kinfu
Director, IDR
Addis Ababa University

Fair enough, I thought to myself, the academic vice president has made his decision, and I will make mine and face the consequences - I stayed. When I came back to Addis Ababa University in June 1996, the 'necessary action' for over-staying my leave turned out to be some kind of administrative rebuke and forfeiting my salary for the following six months.

Since I was well compensated by the fellowship program, I was able to withstand the salary blockade, for the lack of a better word, without much difficulty. By then, our kids had started school, and my wife was gainfully running her business, Menby's Design.

But, for the first time since I returned to Ethiopia four years earlier, I felt like Addis Ababa University, as much as I was attached to it, was not the place for me to stay. I found the bureaucracy at the university to be stifling, to say the least. So, I was waiting for the last straw that broke the camel's back to leave the university. And sure enough, in the next couple of months, the last straw came in two forms.

First, the university came up with what I thought was a rigged system of evaluating staff. In fact, for the academic year that I was at Brown, I was evaluated poorly - in absentia! As a result, I was informed that I would not have any salary increment for the following academic year.

Second, the university got into a system where staff members could not even elect their department heads, let alone their deans and president. This, I remembered, was even worse than the Dergue's era when I was a student; and I did not like it at all.

So, I submitted my resignation in November 1996. However, I felt sad I was leaving my colleagues at IDR and, in particular, the junior staff and graduate students who, as they told me later, were beginning to see a role model and a fresh persona which they liked in me.

In any case, some of my colleagues indicated, some openly, that I was selling out, and was looking for better income opportunities outside the university. Yes, it was partially true that I needed better income than what the university paid me in order to support my family. But 'selling out' was a bit too harsh for a person who left a decent work and income in the United States only to be employed at Addis Ababa University with a 95% income reduction.

Nevertheless, some followed my example and left the university for similar reasons; our contacts and friendships, however, continued long after I left the university.

Hello Miz-Hasab Research Center

I left Addis Ababa University with a sad, if not broken, heart since it was the place where I had a lot of attachment both as a student and a faculty member. My student days were fun and, in some instances, challenging and dangerous; but I endured. As a staff member, I teamed up with scholars who not only accepted me as one of them, but also taught me a lot by example, and I am very grateful.

Needless to say, though, it was not easy to leave the institution for good. But, it was also the beginning of a brand new career for me that stretched for the following twenty years. It was a career that helped me learn a lot of things, including about myself; things that I probably would not have known had I not left the university.

I had been toying with the idea of having a research center that I called my own where I made the decisions and took the responsibilities - whether the outcomes were good or bad. I wanted to try, for the first time, if I could start something small and build it up; all with my own responsibility should it fail or succeed. I guess, at age 46, I also felt that I was too old to be told what to do, and what not to do. In short, I wanted to be my own boss, and see what happened.

But first, I had to rule out working for government at any level. I remember a brief telephone conversation I had with Daniel, one of my close friends from our Addis Ababa university student years, at a time when I was pondering my future after Addis Ababa University. At the time Daniel was a high level official at one government ministry.

Aklilu: *Hey Danny, how are you?*

Daniel: *I am fine, what about you?*
Aklilu: *Fine, how is work?*
Daniel: *You know how work is at government offices?*
Aklilu: *I do not know, how is it?*
Daniel: *You see, we pretend to work and they pretend to pay us.*

I was careful not to find myself in such a situation; a government job was not for me, with all due respect to my friends who are government employees! Not just because of the pay, but because I could already imagine a stifling situation. In my view, the dilemma of working for the government may be that if you got a good job, it probably was not because you qualified but because you were loyal to party politics. For instance, successive mayors of Addis Ababa.[15]

If, on the other hand, you were qualified and got a government job, you probably would not be able to use most of your qualifications. It would be a sort of lose/lose situation, and I decided to steer away in spite of a couple of good possibilities.

So, one day in early September 1996, a few weeks after I left Addis Ababa University, I was driving with my wife past a brand new building, Zerihun Building, on what was known at the time as Asmara Road.[16] My wife suggested that we might want to walk in and ask if they had vacant office space for the research center I was thinking about opening.

Sure enough, if we paid one year's worth of advance payment, a nice fifty-square meter office space would be available to us. We did, and all of a sudden, I had an office. In the next few weeks, we furnished the office, hired some help, bought a couple of computers, got our licenses, and declared ourselves open. We were to be called the Miz-Hasab Research Center, after the name of our two daughters Mizan and

---

15 By the way, Mr. Mayor, if you want to reduce the huge transportation problem in Addis by about 30%, build pavements and maintain them! About a third of Addis Ababans who take mini buses to work would walk if there was a well kept pavement network for pedestrians!

16 It is now called Haile Gebre Selassie Road.

Hasabie. It was also to be the first private research center, not a consulting firm, to be opened in the country.

*****

At first, we declared that we would do population and development research and training locally and internationally. But that turned out to be a bit too ambitious for our capacity, and we narrowed it down to public health research, focusing on HIV AIDS and family planning in Ethiopia.

The specific objectives were to undertake quantitative surveys and qualitative studies to analyze critical issues of reproductive health, particularly family planning and HIV/AIDS; evaluate programs on family planning and other reproductive health activities; and assist individuals and/or institutions in the country that were engaged in social science and public health research.

It also happened to be the best time to conduct such research in Ethiopia due to the tremendous amount funding that was available through various donor organizations, and local as well as international NGOs in the country. It was also true that not many studies were conducted on public health issues, especially on contemporary reproductive health issues like HIV/AIDS, in Ethiopia at the time.

Also, during my three-year stay at AAU and one-year stay at Brown University, I had made contacts with fellow researchers, mostly in the United States and Europe, who were more than happy to work with us. Soon, Dr. Hailom Banteyerga, one the most exhaustive and meticulous social science researcher I ever knew, joined us. Our staff grew to include capable data collectors and data entry personnel. We established Internet connections and installed demographic and statistical software in our computers, and we were game.

Universities in the United States and Europe were looking for local partners to study an array of public health issues in Ethiopia, and we were capable and available. Later on, even private research centers in the United States joined in, and our Center became one to be reckoned with in Ethiopia.

What happened in the next 20 years amazed me, a person who is not usually easily amazed by himself. I never thought I had the capacity in me, albeit with the help of my colleagues at the Center, to accomplish as much. The responsibilities and the need to deliver forced me to dig deep into my capacity and my potentials, which I never knew I had.

All of a sudden, weekends and holidays became working days; the nine to five working hours extended to 6am and 10pm; there were no tea and coffee breaks; lunch hours were often forgotten; the occasional after-work beer sessions disappeared.

We travelled to all corners of the country, usually under very difficult conditions, looking for evidence. We ate whatever was available, and slept for weeks in so called hotel rooms that made our dormitories at Addis Ababa University look like five-star hotel rooms.

A research project took me (far right) to my old school in Gore (late 1990s) for the first time since I left in 1965 when I was 15 years old.

More importantly, we reported what we found as honestly as we possibly could; that gained us a lot of respect among partners who valued evidence-based reporting; some regretted them for their own reasons. Many of our study findings, in collaboration with our research partners, were published in reputable international public health and/or demographic journals.[17] Some, of course, may have just been left on shelves to dust.

In addition, our Center hosted and shared knowledge with several interns and graduate students and scholars from various institutions within the country and internationally.[18] Many used our raw data to write their theses, and our reports as references.

In return, we learnt and increased our capacity by working with renowned scholars like Professors Amy Tsui and Duff Gillespie of the Bill and Melinda Gates Institute for Population and Reproductive Health at Johns Hopkins Bloomberg School of Public Health; Professor Coen Beeker of the University of Amsterdam, Department of Urban Planning and Demography; Dr. Susan Howard of Howard Delafield, Washington D.C.; and Dr. Ross Kidd, my friend from Gaborone, Botswana.

I am grateful not only for their scholarly contributions but also for their good will, social skills and, most of all, their friendship.

All in all, in the two decades between 1996 and 2015, our Center conducted 45 major public health studies/evaluations in Ethiopia. Many produced results that were valid and useful to scale- up health interventions or take corrective measure in real-time.

If I ever contributed to my country's well-being, it must be through the findings of these studies.

In 2006, we celebrated our 10th anniversary. We invited most of the local and international organizations and individuals as well as government agencies working on reproductive health issues in the country. We displayed the methodologies and findings of most of the major studies that we conducted in the previous ten years.

---

17 Please see the Center's website Miz-Hasab.org for details including copies of the reports and published articles.
18 Most notably, Heather Bradley and Sabrina Karklins, from Johns Hopkins University, School of Public Health, Baltimore; Katie Callahan from Columbia University, School of Public Health, New York.

Our motto for the anniversary was *'Knowledge Shared was Knowledge Multiplied'*, something that we 'stole' from Johns Hopkins University Center for Communication Programs. My daughter Mizan introduced the Center, while my friend Amy Tsui gave the key-note speech.

Our Center's 10th anniversary. Key-note speech by my good friend Professor Amy Tsui, Director, the Gates Institute for Population and Reproductive Health; Johns Hopkins University, Baltimore, United States. Addis Ababa Hilton, 2006.

Not too bad for somebody who barely made it to college and struggled throughout, to be able to work with distinguished scholars at distinguished universities and institutions and be able to produce important public health findings that may have contributed to *'improve the lot'* of the people in my country.

Sadly, in December 2015, a few months before its 20th birthday, Miz-Hasab Research Center closed its doors. It was necessary to leave the stage to a younger more energetic generation of researchers.

In any case, among the many things that I learnt from the experience was that, one would not know his/her potential until he/she starts working for himself/herself. In other words, the burden of being personally responsible, for good or bad outcomes, brings the best out of a person.

So, now, I am on a two-year gap as of December 2015 to reflect on my past and plan for something else to do for the rest of my productive life. If they allowed me, in addition to running a small young-girls focused NGO, I would like to teach English or Civics or both, in the 6th or 9th grade at any one of the public schools in Addis Ababa - just like my time in Shire Inda Selassie in the 1973/1974 academic year!

In shaa Allah!

Our Center's 10th anniversary. Honored by the presence of distinguished participants. From left to right: Prof. Seyoum Gebreselassie, Menby, Aklilu, Prof. Redda Teklehaimanot, Drs. Hailom Banteyerga and Ayalew Gebre.

Where there is a Will...

My wife Menby

In the meantime, for the first two years after we returned to Ethiopia, my wife Menby was taking care of our children. She was also planning how to make use of her degree in apparel design. She had worked at a small clothing factory in the United States where she accumulated enough knowledge and experience in all aspects of dressmaking - from the fabric stage to marketing.

So, when our youngest daughter Hasabie was four years old and joined Cathedral preparatory school in 1994, Menby launched her first shop, 'Menby's Design', making custom-made dresses (suits, occasion dresses, bride and wedding gowns etc.) for women. It started out with only two employees but, in the next five years and a lot of hard work, Menby's Design had thirty employees; gainfully employed and supporting their respective families.

However, custom-made dresses took a lot of time to make; and the competition with the ready-made cloth coming from countries like China made dress making a difficult business endeavor in Ethiopia. So, after making dresses for women for ten years, Menby moved to producing handmade textiles for home furnishing and fashion accessories.

In 2002, Ellen Dorsch, an American businesswoman, proposed to Menby the idea of making handmade crafts for the United States' market. For the following ten years, Menby's Design partnered with Creative Women, Ellen's Vermont-based company, and taking advantage provided by AGOA,[19] supplied handmade Ethiopian gift products to about ninety stores in the United Sates. During these years, Menby also participated in several international trade shows, learnt new skills and ideas and found ways of combining them with the long tradition of weaving in Ethiopia.

Unfortunately, after ten years in the export business, Menby got frustrated by the bureaucratic bottlenecks related to exporting goods from Ethiopia, and had to stop exporting. Instead, she focused on the local market, catering for those who needed readymade traditional hand-woven fabrics for human décor (such as pillow cases, table runners, wall hangings) and personal accessories (such as hand and shoulder bags, shawls and scarves).[20]

---

19 The African Growth and Opportunity Act (AGOA) with the purpose of assisting the economies of sub-Saharan Africa and to improve economic relations between the United States and the region.
20 For more information, please see Menbys.com

Menby now employs over fifty weavers to make the hand-woven fabrics locally and, in her public speeches, routinely speaks highly of them:[21]

> *When you have a section with a design, each line has to be picked by hand. It takes two days to make one wall hanging. You can't imagine how smart the weavers are. Many of them don't know how to read and write, but if you give them just a picture, they can copy and weave it.*

Menby's success originates not only from her trainings but also from her strong will and childhood love for sewing. Incidentally, Menby made her own pocket money since age 12, making dresses for her sisters, relatives and friends.

Also, Menby does not regret her return to Ethiopia in 1992 at all; and she explains why.

> *Going back home [in 1992] was the best decision we made. The government was in transition and the country was emerging from socialism, so talking about fashion was a shame; it was the last thing you talked about. It was a big risk, but that was the time to go.*

And go, she did.

Our children Mizan and Hasabie

In the meantime, over the years, our two daughters Mizan and Hasabie, were growing deep in the culture of the country with frequent visits to their paternal and maternal grandparents and extended relatives. They learnt to love and respect them and benefit from their vast wisdom. In return, the extended family members showered love and affection on the children that, I hope, would last for a long time to come.

---

21 'The Challenges and Opportunities of Running a Socially Responsible Design Business in Ethiopia.' A public speech at The Department of Fashion and Apparel Studies, University of Delaware, USA. 2006.

Hasabie and Mizan (third and fifth from left) with cousins Mikias, Dagem, Nardos, Mahelet and Endrias. Ready to perform at their grandparents' 50ᵗʰ wedding anniversary. Grandma (far right) watching. Addis Ababa, 1996

On my part, I made sure they missed few family gatherings or cultural festivities as they were growing up. One such event was their grandparents' 50ᵗʰ wedding anniversary. Our daughters and their cousins entertained us with plays which they produced and directed!

I also wanted my children to know and celebrate social and religious holidays not so much for their religious significance but for their useful service as venues for family gatherings and interactions. Luckily, Ethiopia was never short of such holidays, both Christian and Muslim; sometimes, I might add, to the country's detriment.

The Christian ones included the popular *Fasika* [Orthodox Easter] celebrations in April or May each year, following a 55-day fasting period where no meat and dairy products were consumed. On this day, we would be the first to reach my parents house where a major feast of Ethiopian traditional food would be prepared for all who would gather for the festivities. As part of the celebrations, my daughters and their cousins would dress in traditional attire, would 'produce' short plays and show them to the gathering after dinner; and we applauded enthusiastically.

The *Enqutatash*, the celebration of the new Ethiopian year, is another popular and colorful non-religious holiday, which is celebrated on September 11 of each year[22] (September 12 in the leap year). This holiday, which follows the rainy season and indicates the approach of harvest, is the time when the countryside would be covered with bright yellow flowers known locally as *Meskel Flowers*. I remember many trips to the countryside just outside Addis Ababa with the children to hand-pick these flowers and take them home for the celebrations; the children would just get wild running up and down the yellow flower covered fields.

There were also the *Adis Amet* [New Year's Day] celebrations where very young girls, dressed in their newest dresses, would go door to door singing songs of the New Year, soliciting gifts in the form of traditional homemade bread, or some coins. I would invite these girls into our house so my daughters joined them and learn the songs and dances involved in the process.

My favorite festivity, however, was the night before *Meskel* when a bonfire with a wooden makeshift cross on top and decorated with *Meskel* flowers, would be erected just outside the house to involve as many neighborhood kids as possible. The children would sing and dance around the bonfire while adults, which included me, once in a while would jump over the bonfires. My daughters would watch me with mixed feelings of worry and admiration.

Whenever invited, we also enjoyed eating with our Muslim friends and relatives after the communal prayers, especially during *Eid al Fitr*'s celebrations of the breaking of the Ramadan fast. We particularly liked the informality and warm hospitality that accompanied the roasted lamb dishes; not to speak of the

---

22   Ethiopia follows the Julian calendar, which consists of 13 months - 12 months each with 30 days and a final month with 5 days (6 days in the leap year). The Julian calendar is 7 years and 8 months behind the Gregorian calendar, which is used throughout most of the Western world.

sweet dishes including the dates and raisins - all eaten in Islamic style on a blanket spread on the floor.

Sergs [weddings] are among the many cultural events in Ethiopia that, for some reason, had special effects on girls, no matter their age. My daughters were no exception; they were just happy to attend several weddings as flower girls, when young, as bridesmaids when teenagers, and as invited guests, when adults.

In the process they learnt and enjoyed the traditional wedding songs and dances; and a few tips on how to behave among boys and young men.

Hasabie and Mizan (center) with cousins as flower girls at a wedding. Addis Ababa, 1995

As often as we enjoyed the holidays and festivities, we also visited sick people in hospitals or at homes; and attended the funerals of beloved family members, relatives and close friends. For Coptic Christians, funerals in Ethiopia usually take place in church compounds attended by hundreds of people in mostly black attire. Men and women cry loud, beating their chests continuously for a long period of time, indicating the closeness of the deceased person and the severity of the loss.

A funeral is a big affair in Ethiopia that involves entire community members. Neighbors voluntarily organize in community associations such as *Idir* to support the bereaving families by raising money to cover the funeral costs, and to support the healing process. They erect tents nearby the house of the deceased that would stay for about three days after the funeral, also indicating the launch of a 40-day intense mourning period. Relatives and friends, who have not seen each other for years, come from far-off areas to pay their respects. Food and drinks, supplied either by *Idirs* or by neighbors and relatives, are served throughout the mourning period to all people in attendance.

We took part in several such mourning and healing processes and met new and old relatives who we have not seen or known before. We shared their grief, and they shared ours. In a strange way, funeral ceremonies and the following rituals in the Ethiopian cultures are effective venues not only to mitigate the pain of death and loss but also to bring people closer to each other, thereby underscoring the importance of 'people' in one's life - both during happiness and sadness.

Also during school breaks, I encouraged our daughters to visit the historical and tourist sites in the country including Harar, Lalibella, and Gondar; the Rift Valley lakes like Hawassa, Langano and Ziway; the parks like Awash Park - sometimes with us and sometimes by themselves or with friends, so they could have a good understanding of the historical, cultural and physical roots of the country. Roots that I hoped would buttress their identity as Ethiopians, in spite of their American passports that I had come to gingerly accept by now.

In a few years, our daughters had mastered the Amharic language both in reading and writing, and had forgotten whatever they knew about the United States.[23] So, more than anything else, I enjoyed and gave tremendous amount of value

---

23 When we left the United States, Hasabie was too young to remember anything; the only thing Mizan remembered about the United States, until she started going there for summer vacations during her teenage years, was Mc Donald's.

to talking to our children face-to-face about all kinds of issues at length. In my view, this could not have been possible if we did not use Amharic as the means of communication. This is because I believe talking to one's own children requires the culture, history and the identity to back it up. It would also require the knowledge to pick the right words and phrases, especially if the issues were sensitive and personal. There was no way that I could have communicated with our children clearly and honestly if I had not used my own language, Amharic.

Our daughters also took time to take piano, chess and swimming lessons and, over the years, acquired enough skills to be reckoned with in their age groups. Mizan now plays the piano and sings as her chosen profession. And the last time I played chess with Hasabie, I lost real badly; I had thought I was good in chess. Swimming is still a passion for both, as it was for me most of my boyhood and adult life.

I am not saying it was the best way or the only way, but that was how our daughters were raised. I know I speak for my wife too when I say I just could not have asked for a more disciplined, well mannered, thoughtful and talented children than our daughters Mizan and Hasabie.

They are also two beautiful girls, like all girls in Ethiopia.

*****

School wise, they both went to the same elementary school (Nativity Girls' School; aka Cathedral) where their mother had completed her elementary education, and I had a run with the Amharic alphabet for the first time a very long time ago.

Nativity Girls' School, a 65-year old Catholic School in the center of Addis Ababa, was the first time where our daughters interacted with a large number of Ethiopian girls of their respected ages. Average class size was about 85, and they came from all kinds of familial backgrounds: poor and rich; Muslim and Christian; educated and not so educated; government workers and merchants.

First day of school for Hasabie, posing with her sister Mizan. Nativity Girls' School. Addis Ababa, 1994

In my view, the sheer size and diversity of the students' backgrounds, in themselves, provided opportunities for the students to learn acceptance and tolerance. I had told to whoever would listen to me that if young children tolerated 85 students in one class for ten years (including two years of preparatory), nothing in life henceforth would be difficult. Because, by then, they had developed the skills and the demeanor to live and let live.

Our daughters were growing and learning not only how to think, write and speak in their native language but also what it meant to be poor, needy and different. They made friends indiscriminately, but once in a while they needed some parental help, and I was ready and always available.

A few years after we returned to Ethiopia, one Saturday morning I dropped my daughters, who were by then about 10 and 8 years old, at their friend's house who happened to be a Muslim. When I picked them later at about 4pm, we engaged in a small conversation as we drove home.

Aklilu: *So, did you have a good time?*

Daughters: *Yes we did; they are very nice people.*

Aklilu: *Why do you say so?*

Daughters: *Because they gave us a lot of cookies and other sweet things we have never eaten before.*

Aklilu: *Great, did you have lunch too?*

Daughters: *No, they are Muslims.*

Aklilu: *So, what is the problem?*

Daughters: *We are Christians, and we are not supposed to eat Muslim food.*

Aklilu: *Says who?*

Daughters: *That is what everybody says; don't you know?*

Aklilu: *That may be true, but it does not mean they are right.*

Daughters: *Would you eat Muslim food?*

Aklilu: *Yes, of course. And if I got the chance, I would also eat Buddhist or Hindu food too. Besides, all my Muslim friends eat Christian food.*

Daughters: *Well, we didn't eat any food but should we have eaten?*

Aklilu: *Yes, of course. I do not see any harm to you or anybody else. I understand some people raise religious and cultural issues, but you need not follow them; and, besides, they could be harmful.*

Daughters: *How are they harmful?*

Aklilu: *Well, for one thing, you missed your lunch and you probably are hungry now. For another, you created a gap in your relationship with your Muslim friends by refusing to eat what they eat which is not a good sign of friendship.*

I realized that things were getting a bit complicated for my young daughters. So, to make my point, I told them about the incident when, years earlier, I had watched my Coptic Christian father eat Muslim food with his friends at Eid al Fitr celebrations. I also told them I had eaten Muslim food on many occasions without hesitation and nothing had happened to me - so far.

My daughters listened attentively; albeit with some confusion. I took advantage of this and added my advice that it was important to reduce the tension among people that religion created artificially. Ever since, when my daughters want to eat outside the house, one of their favorite places was a Muslim restaurant on Bole road in Addis. My intervention has succeeded and they still eat there and, in the process, now have one and half billion less people to be threatened by.

With 85 children in one class, Cathedral provided the perfect scenario for tolerance. But, according to Mizan, it was also a bit too stifling. Students, my daughters somewhere in the middle, ready to celebrate Christmas. Cathedral school compound. Addis Ababa, 1997

*****

Just a few weeks before Mizan was to complete her 8th grade at Cathedral, I was driving her home when she asked if she could suggest something. Usually our conversations in the car, if we were not singing together which happened most of the time, would not start in that formal way; we would just be talking about whatever came to our minds without warnings. This time she looked serious, and I had to pay attention.

> Mizan: *Dad, as you know, I am about to finish elementary school here at Cathedral.*
> Aklilu: *Great, move on to high school!*
> Mizan: *I do not want to go to high school here; I want to change schools.*
> Aklilu: *Why? I thought you liked this school.*
> Mizan: *Yes, I like it but I have also been here for ten years; including my two-year preparatory classes.*

Aklilu: *If you like it, why change? Remember the saying; 'Don't fix it if it ain't broken?'*

Mizan: *Yes, I know. But this school is a bit stifling.*

Aklilu: *What do you mean?*

Mizan: *It is a good school for disciplining students, and I like my friends; and that is Ok up to a certain age. Do you understand what I am saying?*

Aklilu: *I am listening; go ahead.*

Mizan: *In a stifling environment, you cannot think for or be yourself; you cannot experiment and discover yourself; it is not healthy.*

Aklilu: *Is that what you found at Cathedral?*

Mizan: *Yes, but do not get me wrong. I love the school, I have learnt so much. But, I am growing up now and going to high school; I like to be in an environment where I am a little bit freer to express my views and my tastes.*

Aklilu: *I agree, so what do you want to do?*

Mizan: *Let us look for another high school.*

Aklilu: *Ok, where shall we start?*

Not that it was going to be easy, we decided to try out Nazareth School, a 60-year old girls' school in central Addis Ababa. It was considered to be one of the best schools in the country and we knew some people who graduated from the school and made it to universities and to successful professional careers.

As we were driving towards the school, however, we had to pass by another good school, Sandford International School; founded in the 1940s by an English woman, Mrs. Christine Sandford, for her children. I knew it was a very good school with international standards and with qualified professional staff, but I also knew it was a very difficult school to get in.

Since I was also a bit worried about Mizan going to another all-girls school, Nazareth School, I suggested that we went to Sandford and see, against all odds, if there was a chance for her to be admitted. We knew it was going to be a tough one, but we figured we could always try. So I parked my car nearby, and walked straight to the high school director's office, with Mizan in tow.

We found the high school British director in his office, and we started talking. The director was a college professor before he came to Ethiopia, and I was a college professor just a few years earlier; we clicked and talked for a while. Eventually, the director interviewed and then asked Mizan to take school-entrance exams in a couple of subjects. And the rest, as they say, is history. It was not necessary to go to Nazareth School; and two years later, Hasabie joined her sister at Sandford.

Mizan liked and talked a lot about her high school with affection. She met her closest friends at this school, proving my point about when a 'true' friendship would start. More importantly for her, there were no uniforms to begin with and she liked the approach where the school provided students with the opportunities and the resources, and it was up to the students to use them; or peril at their own choice. She felt free and liberated from all the stifling rules at Cathedral; not that she disapproved of it, but that she felt a little bit too old for that at the high school age.

*****

Sensing and agreeing with Mizan's search for 'independence', I wanted to do something that would facilitate it when she was 18 years old. She had one more year (the fifth year[24]) of high school; and I wanted to buy her a used but good and reliable car.

Luckily, we got a good two-door 2000 Suzuki Grande, which turned out to be the perfect car for a teenager. She got her driving license and started driving to school, with her younger sister in the passenger seat -for now.

I actually missed driving my children to school; we had made such a pleasurable habit of singing all the way to school. But, they grew up and had slightly different ideas than my usual fatherly pampering; and I had no choice but to oblige, though sadly and reluctantly.

---

24 At Sandford, there was the option of a two-year IB after the 11th grade; which we encouraged her to take. That meant one more year that she would spend with us in Ethiopia.

Now, this idea of buying Mizan a car did not settle well with some of my close relatives who meant well but also had crossed their boundaries just a bit.

Relative: *Do you think it is a good idea to have a kid drive to school?*
Aklilu: *Why is it not a good idea?*
Relative: *She is only a kid and besides she is a girl.*
Aklilu: *Well she is 18, a driving age; and I am not sure if being a girl would make a difference, whatever you want to talk about.*
Relative: *Ok, driving in Addis is very dangerous. Are you not worried about her safety?*
Aklilu: *I have trained her how to drive; and she has also taken formal classes and passed her driving license exams. She is good.*
Relative: *But, can't you see you are taking a big risk?*
Aklilu: *No; actually I am avoiding risks.*
Relative: *How?*
Aklilu: *Well, she is 18 and she may want to go out to parties and night clubs, and I cannot tell her not to.*
Relative: *You see you are already putting her at risk by making a car available for her to go to these places.*
Aklilu: *Well, if I cannot tell her not to go and she doesn't have a car, who is going to bring her home when the party is over at mid-night or 3 am in the morning?*
Relative: *If she must go out, you bring her back home.*
Aklilu: *I do not want to do that at 3am every time she goes out; and besides, she may not want me to do that.*
Relative: *Then, she doesn't go!*
Aklilu: *Of course she has to go! It is quite normal; and we have done it at that age or even at earlier ages.*
Relative: *I do not understand your logic.*
Aklilu: *Ok, let me explain. If she goes out and she doesn't have a car, she will have to depend on somebody else to bring her home. Right? Which means, I am putting all my trust on this 'somebody' who I may not even know. Who knows, he may have had a few drinks too. Then, she will be totally dependent on that 'somebody'; so I am putting her at risk. So, I would rather trust my own daughter and give her the means and the option to decide where to go and what time to come back home, than trust a person I may not even know. So, I am avoiding risks.*
Relative: *I do not understand you Aklilu.*

It was clear I did not convince my relative; but Mizan completed her high school successfully, no damaged car, and headed to college - to the University of Delaware at Newark, Delaware, in the United States in August 2007. She completed her bachelor's degree in English literature as major and legal studies, as a minor.

Mizan is now a musician with a part-time job at a legal office, living and working in New York City, with a bright future. She already produced her first EP,[25] which was successful enough for a debut, and she is now working on her second one.

*****

And, at the risk of sounding like a braggart, let me say just a few words only to make a point for those who argued back in 1992, when we chose to return to Ethiopia, that our children would not get good education in Ethiopia and, tragically, I was deciding on their fate.

Hasabie finished her elementary school at Cathedral and her high school at Sandford International School in Addis Ababa; with distinction. In August 2009, off she went to the University of North Carolina, Chapel Hill, to study Art History as her major and French as her minor.

During her four-year stay at Chapel Hill, she first won The National Society of Collegiate Scholars (NSCS) 2011 Merit Award Recipient; and pocketed a thousand dollars in prize money, a lot of money for a college student! Then, while still at Chapel Hill, she won two major scholarships to study at two different countries in Europe.[26] Then, she came back to Chapel Hill and completed her bachelor's degree - with honors.

---

25 For more information please see Mizank.com
26 One was at Université Paris Sorbonne (Paris IV) to study French Language and Literature, in 2011; and the other one was to the Honors Program, Sotheby's, London, England, in 2012.

Then in June 2015, after a two-year gap when she worked for two renowned art studios in New York [27]and also as a freelance writer, she was admitted to the only program she applied for: Master of Fine Arts (MFA) program at Yale University in New Haven, Connecticut. During her first year at Yale, she won yet another scholarship to study Ethiopian scrolls in Paris.[28]

Finally, during her second year at Yale, she was offered the 'exceptionally competitive'[29] and prestigious summer 2017 Session at Skowhegan, Madison, Maine.

Interestingly enough, Hasabie's admission letter to Skowhegan included the following excerpt:

And fundamental to our pedagogy is an understanding that diversity of voice, making, experience, ethnicity, gender, physicality, and class is critical in opening our eyes, vocabularies, and practices to those outside our own. We believe that through this exposure, we become better artists. Inherent to being able to see and hear each other, respect, patience, non-judgment, education, and understanding -even in the most challenging of circumstances- is our shared responsibility.

Interesting! Back in 1992, I had argued as follows as to why I thought it was critically important and useful to send our children to an elementary school in Addis with a class size of 85!

All 85 of them come from various backgrounds; there are Muslims and Christians; poor and rich; they come from liberal and conservative families; from well educated and poorly educated. It is a great mix of students. It is a great learning experience to have to deal with all kinds of backgrounds. Imagine, if you can handle such a large and diverse group at an early age, nothing in future life would be difficult.

---

27 Mickalene Thomas Studio and The Robert Blackburn Printmaking Studio.

28 The Kimball Fellowship to spend the summer at the Bibliothèque nationale de France, Paris, studying Ethiopian scrolls.

29 For the 2017 summer session at Skowhegan, only 65 out of nearly 2,000 applicants (about 3%) were offered admission.

If nothing else, I have been vindicated.

In any case, Hasabie graduated with the MFA degree from Yale University on May 22, 2017 and headed to Skowhegan.[30]

Hasabie with her sister and mother celebrating her MFA from Yale University. New Haven, USA. May 22, 2017

So, not bad for children who started their education in Ethiopia with 84 other children in a class! Needless to say, those who accused me of robbing the opportunity for my children to get good education by taking them with me to Ethiopia were wrong. I understand that not all students in Ethiopia get the same chance as my daughters; but I would also like to know where in the world the same thing was not true.

I do not know what would have been the fate of my daughters if we had not returned to Ethiopia. But then, I am not the kind of person who broods on such things, neither was there the need for me to do so.

All I know is, where there is a will, there is a way.

---

30   For details please see Hasabiekidanu.com

The empty nest syndrome

In the meantime, the children kept on growing as we aged, and once our youngest daughter Hasabie left 'home' in August 2009, my wife and I remained behind with an empty nest - perhaps the last significant change or adaptation that I had to make to a new life style. My wife did much better on this, or pretended to, but I was lost, unable to adjust for a long time.

I have often thought about what my relationship with my daughters should be as they move along from one age group to the next, and especially in their 20s. The challenge for me was to balance between the hands-on parenting I exercised during their early years and the hands-off approach I had to adapt during their teenage years, and beyond. I knew from my own experience as a son that things would come around and find their balance at a later age. But the question was: how to deal with the transition to that stage.

Yes, like any parent would, I was attached to our daughters; but I also worried a lot in their absence. I worried about their well being; if they ate or slept well; or whether they would return 'home' when they finished their studies; or when they would get married so I have grandchildren to play with.

Hence, unbeknownst to me, I had become possessive and protective. So much so that when Mizan first went to college in the United States, not only did I follow her to the university but also left her only after I made sure that she found the classroom for her very first class. Mizan bravely tolerated all this and many other similar episodes until, one day, she breathed-in deeply and pleaded in a very respectful way, *'Dad, please let go.'*

I have been in a situation where I was the student outside Ethiopia and my parents in Ethiopia worried about me. Now, I am in a situation where I am the parent in Ethiopia and worrying about my children studying outside Ethiopia. I suppose my generation is the first generation in our country's history that had to grapple with the dilemma posed by the two scenarios.

The gloomy faces of the empty nest syndrome; my wife did better. Addis Ababa, starting from 2009 when Hasabie left for Chapel Hill.

Taking the first scenario, when I was the student abroad in my late 20s, I never really knew or understood why my parents worried so much about my brother and me. As far as I was concerned, I was for the most part excited and happy, learning new things and making new friends, and felt very safe in the process. That my parents would be worried about me was the last thing in my mind.

Hence, without my knowledge, there was this mismatch between my parents' concerns in Ethiopia and my new and mostly exciting life in the United States.

In the second scenario, where I am the parent in Ethiopia, one would think that I would learn some lessons from the first scenario: that I should have known, just like my student's days in the United States, our children were excited and happy and making new friends and learning new things.

Our daughters, needless to say, appreciated that we worried about them but, as far as they were concerned, there was no reason for us to be worried. For them, they were simply living a normal student's life and it was hard to understand our worries; and they were right!

*****

This empty nest syndrome may be true for most parents in similar situations, regardless of citizenship or social and political status. With older age, most parents just could not handle that their children were going away, and it becomes painful. This actually is exasperated by the fact that the children do not always appreciate or understand this and sometimes may engage in or say things that would put fuel on the fire, so to speak.

I have also wondered if parents, including myself, were actually worried more about themselves than their children. I have often asked myself if I felt sorry for myself because I did not have my children next to me to play, talk and sing with; or because the house felt empty and lonely without them; or because I did not have them nearby to order them around and to pamper them -all for my own pleasure.

Once I read in the news that President Barak Obama was worried about his daughters growing and the prospect of leaving them.

So, as a parent who had experienced the same feelings, I sent him the following letter of advice, of course, with all due respect.

(June 24, 2015)
Greetings President Barak Hussein Obama

I am Ethiopian, 65 years old, married, and father of two daughters (in their mid-20s) who have gone through college. Lately, I have seen the kind of comments you have been making about your daughters. I have read you say, 'But there is something about your daughters that just breaks your heart. And that's not really even an issue of dating. It is just watching them grow up. You want them to be with you as long as you can.' I have gone through those kinds of feelings myself - painfully. So, with all due respect, please allow me to share my thoughts with you.

First, I think it is not only an entirely natural process for the children to grow, but also the right thing for parents to let them go. Difficult, I understand. But, willingly or not, it has happened to millions of families throughout the world -albeit in different forms and with different outcomes. Most parents have felt exactly the same way you are feeling now. But, hang on, things will change.

Second, as much as we parents think we are close and know our children well, there is so much that we do not know about them. For instance, we may not know how little, if at all, they know about how we feel to see them grow and, eventually, go. I think this is because, in their own world, that is not a priority - not yet. Their young minds are preoccupied with what they consider to be challenging and exciting things now, and those in the future. But, we worry about them; they are experiencing, perhaps enjoying, a new life. This is the first mismatch.

Third, with age, when the children get to be in their mid and late 20s, things, believe me, would change. The children would grow, leave home and, surprise, are OK! Parents would, naturally, have adjusted to situations and would be worrying about their children less and less. It would now be the turn for the children to start thinking, even worrying, about their parents. But, by then, parents have adjusted, and are pretty much OK; and do not see why the children are so worried about them. This is the second mismatch; we have come a full circle.

I am struggling with the second mismatch now, and I will see what will happen when the children get to be in their 30s!

With all due respect.
Aklilu Kidanu Wolde Giorgis
Addis Ababa, Ethiopia (June 24, 2015)

I did get a 'Thank You' note from the Office of Presidential Correspondence at the White House; but not from President Obama himself and, given all the important things he had to do, I did not really expect one. One of the few persons who I told about this letter, however, suggested as a consolation that the president might respond to my letter once he had finished his term and became an ordinary citizen; I will wait and see.

*****

But, Mizan was absolutely right when she advised me '*to let go.*' My love for her and her sister was stifling, very much like her elementary school at Cathedral back in the early 1990s. She knew I loved her, but I may have said it so many times within a short period of time that it was stifling, or it had become meaningless and, in the process of all this, I may have run the risk of being taken for granted.

I remembered my own father who never told me, or any one for that matter, that he loved me in so many words; but it was clear to me beyond doubt that he had the utmost love for me and the rest of his children. So, maybe, what I needed to come up with was something in between: express my love to my children but do not overdo it; worry about them but not to the point where it suffocated them.

If, indeed, all the worry and stifling was for my own selfish reasons, then I must learn to accept that I may be their father and intensively loved them as such, but I did not own them like property. They have their own lives to live and I must learn to respect that and, as Mizan politely but firmly told me, I needed to learn '*to let go.*'

So, the term 'let go' has been ringing in my ears frequently ever since Mizan told me to do so. It was a phrase I dreaded, but it was also an awakening call, a reality check, that I remembered every time I thought about our children.

I say it was the most pleasurable thing on earth, but who says it was easy to be a parent!

*****

In any case, all in all, in the twenty four years that I have come back to Ethiopia after fourteen years abroad, I had tried and taken care of my parents at old age; attended to the needs of my elderly relatives as much as possible; educated our children in their ancestors' culture and language and propelled them to good colleges along with a stable identity; helped my wife engage in something she loved doing which also created jobs for many women in the process; taught at a university where I was once a student; provided volunteer services at non-government organizations;[31]and started a research center that produced evidence based useful reports, and created gainful employment opportunities for myself and many others.

With my siblings soon after the loss of our father: Standing left to right: Aklilu, Yemane, and Miemen. Sitting left to right: Misrak, Meheret, our mother, and Hamelmal. Addis Ababa, 2007

---

31 Most notably, the Donkey for Development Organization (DDO) where, spearheaded by our friends Coen Beeker and Gulilat Aberra, we provided close to 900 donkeys free of charge to women whose livelihood was collecting and selling tree branches and leaves; Forum for Social Studies (FSS) a think tank group credited with several researches and publications on Ethiopia.

Friendship for over 70 years helps mitigate the pain of the loss of a loved one. My paternal aunt Abaye Beleyu (102) and my mother (91) were more than welcoming when we returned home. Addis Ababa, 2017

So, after all, what my by-now 100-year old aunt Abaye Beleyu said when we returned home, that my father Kidanu *'had given birth to a real man',* may actually have been correct - just kidding!

I very much hope that, somewhere in the process, I was also able to carry the baton for one stretch of the run for a few people. Then, again citing Leo Rosten, I would have been satisfied that I *'made a difference that I lived at all.'*

Chapter 4.

REFLECTIONS AND LIFE LESSONS

The United States has been very kind to me, and to my wife. We went to college, mostly through the support of the American taxpayers' money, and we got very useful work experience through which we hope we also served the people who taught us. We met and knew wonderful people from whom we learnt about, if not necessarily practiced, honesty and hard work. Wonderful family members and friends we loved so much lived in the United States. Our kids were born in the United States, leaving behind a lot of attachment and affection to the country. So, why did we leave the United States? Over the years, I have been reflecting on this major issue: why I have done something that most Ethiopians, including many with similar backgrounds like mine, would not do yet: return to Ethiopia for good.

'If I take care of the family (the penny), the country (the pound) will take care of itself.'[1]

Choosing to Stay

Some caveats

The question here is not why Ethiopians leave the country in the first place; although I have some ideas, it is not the focus here. So, before I tread into these uncharted waters of why or whether to return home, let me mention some very important caveats.

First, I know I am now treading in a very sensitive area, and I have to be very careful. I am hoping that most people who read this book will have enough confidence in themselves or in their positions that they would not be threatened by a different position if they found mine to be so. I also hope that such people can handle opinions different from theirs as long as they were not enforced upon them, which I would never do.

Second, let me very clearly say that I would never claim that I love or care for my country more than the 'average' Ethiopian. I say 'average' on purpose to indicate that, if there ever was a way of measuring one's love for his/her country, there could be Ethiopians, wherever they may be, who love and care for the country more than I do; I admit as much.

Third, no matter why an Ethiopian decides to stay in the United States or in any other country, I very strongly believe that the person is exercising his or her human right to choose where he/she would like to live; period. There is no wrong or

---

1   Rephrased from the popular English proverb 'Take care of the penny and the pound will take care of itself'

right answer; there are only differences in choice or opinions; in which case, as I mentioned above, I hope my reader would be mature and confident enough to accept each other's choices.

Finally, I realize we live in a world that is interconnected not only economically but also socially, even though there are countries that benefit more from this interconnection than others. I understand some of my views go contrary to this global trend, but I believe the jury is still out as to the effects of globalization on poor countries like mine. Hence, I am not yet ready to accept the social trends that globalization may unleash.

Some crosscutting issues

It is clear that I do not speak for them, but during my frequent short visits to the United States, I asked a few Ethiopians (not those who were born and raised in the United States) informally over drinks or family events as to why they opted to stay as opposed to returning to Ethiopia – for good. From the outset, a few crosscutting issues appeared for most, if not all, of them.

First, when they first arrived, not many of them imagined or thought they would stay in the United States as long as they did. Time flew by as they were engaged in day-to-day activities, mostly for survival.

Second, many of them did not think much about future life in old age in the United States. For many, old age caught up with them like a wild fire, and unprepared; and, eventually, they felt stranded.

Third, almost all wanted to send money back home to help their families. It was a source of some comfort or a coping mechanism if there ever was any guilt of being away; as well as a major rationale to stay where they were.

Fourth, many indicated that they would go back to Ethiopia at some point for good; they just did not know when.

In my view, these were the main crosscutting issues that applied to most Ethiopians in the United States who I spoke to. What I wanted to know, however, was why they did not return to Ethiopia for good once they had accomplished what they had come to the United States for; it could be a meeting, a visit, short-term-training or long-term education.

I also reflected in this chapter, even in instances where the childhood experiences were more or less the same as mine, on why I returned to Ethiopia when almost everybody else I know did not.

Some reasons

Without making any judgment, I state below what I found out to be the main reasons for Ethiopians to stay in the United States. In many instances, there may be a combination of reasons.

First, there were those who were concerned about their safety or the risk of being persecuted by the government in power in Ethiopia if they returned. This group may be divided into two. On one hand, there were those who had belonged to the previous government and argued that they had legitimate and tangible concerns if they returned. They point out that some who dared to return have been arrested or been exposed to persecution already. On the other hand, there were those who perceived, with really no tangible evidence, that they would be persecuted if they returned. So, they opted to stay till things changed to their satisfaction.

Second, there were those who believed that the United States provided them with the opportunity to excel in their education and/or professions. Such people were career-oriented and had tremendous ambition to get to the highest level of knowledge and skills in their respected fields; they valued their careers more than anything else. This was something Ethiopia would never be able to provide, and so why return?

Third, some felt that the United States was the bastion of freedom, real or imagined, where they could write, speak and express their ideas without fearing government reprisals. Since these were not possible in Ethiopia, many Ethiopians valued this freedom, notwithstanding whether they actually practiced them or not, and it was enough to decide to stay in the United States.

Fourth, there were those who had come to the United States and were not lucky enough to acquire skills or wealth, partially because they had come to the country with few, if any, skills to begin with. Such people would argue that they were ashamed to go back home empty handed; and, if you believed them, they say they would never return home.

Fifth, there were those who felt they were 'sacrificing' for the sake of making good education and, later, employment available for their children or dependent family members in the United States. Without this responsibility, they would have returned to Ethiopia as soon as they were done in the United States. Such people would very strongly argue that their children would be lost if they were brought up and attended schools in Ethiopia.

Sixth, there were those who argued that they lived a relatively better life in the United States; pure and simple. Such people would usually come from relatively poor families in Ethiopia and, the United States, no matter what they did for a living and how much they hustled for the money they made, would provide them with a much better life standard compared to what they had to cope with at home.

One Ethiopian actually explained this with an example and, with all due respect, this is how he put it: *'It is like a poor man who goes to the house of a rich man and refusing to leave.'* I did not necessarily entirely agree with him, but I thought it was an interesting analogy.

Seventh, another group of people argued that their health conditions required them to stay in the United States, since the treatments were available only in the United States, usually free of charge. For this group of people, Ethiopia was only a place to visit briefly whenever they get the green light to do so from their doctors.

Eighth, there were the very young ones who, as long as they got any jobs, their own apartments with hot showers and used cars to transport them around, they did not care where they lived. Not at least till they were old enough to question such a life style or till they think of a country across the Atlantic.

Ninth, and a very important reason, was when either the male or female spouse, if he or she happened to be Ethiopian, was not so eager about returning home. This was mostly true with female spouses who, for reasons of their own, would prefer periodic visits to returning home for good. It is not uncommon to run into an Ethiopian male who would lament his wife's refusal to return while he was more than ready to do so.

And finally, talking about marital reasons, for many Ethiopians who got married to non-Ethiopians, it would be very difficult to pack-up and return to Ethiopia for good. This was particularly true if children were involved.

'Diaspora'?

Regardless of the reasons to stay, the prominence of the word or concept of 'Diaspora' in the Ethiopian context was looming in the mid 1990's. Quite a few Ethiopians, albeit with different acquired nationalities, do have that label now. But, I am not sure I understand what it means; I am not even sure as to who is a Diaspora and who is not!

For instance, I lived abroad for fourteen years and came back to live in my country; am I a 'Diaspora?' Even if I had kept my student's visa all the time? If I am, would the identity that I already established before I left Ethiopia just be wiped out and be replaced by one vague identity in the form of the word 'Diaspora?'

I certainly do not consider myself a Diaspora because I do not even know what it means, nor do I know anyone who could explain to me what it was. Well, the Merriam-Webster dictionary defines 'Diaspora' as, *'A group of people who live outside the area in which they had lived for a long time or in which their ancestors lived.'* I have never come across a more vague definition of a term in my life; even the Webster dictionary could not help!

However it may be defined, my take is that the word 'Diaspora' represents a vague concept that takes away real thing from someone and assigns him/her something that no one seems to understand. I am not saying this in any mean-spirited way nor do I have any hard feelings toward those who are considered or consider themselves 'Diaspora.' After all, many of my closest relatives and friends, including my two brothers and a sister, not to mention quite a few cousins and second cousins, are 'Diaspora', whatever it meant!

But, it just does not settle well with me to have my older brother, for instance, referred to by a word that I could not even begin to comprehend!

Or, to see some Ethiopian 'Diasporas' treated differently than the non-Diaspora Ethiopians when it comes to business opportunities or other benefits or incentives to start life in Ethiopia!

Or, to see some former Ethiopians playing the 'Diaspora card' to show that they were more equal than others when they come to Ethiopia.

Or, to see Diaspora Ethiopians act as if they know better than the non-Diaspora Ethiopians when it comes to what is good for the county!

Also, nothing makes more distraught than to see 'former' Ethiopians show off their 'Diaspora' status, as if it were something to brag about.

I understand and appreciate that there are about three million Ethiopian 'Diaspora', and many among them may want to contribute to their country's economic growth one way or another. Remittance, for instance, hard-earned money for many, is one thing to consider favorably, although that might end, or significantly be reduced, with the second generation 'Diaspora.'[2]

I also have nothing against Ethiopian 'Diasporas' who know better than igniting fire in Ethiopia from the safety of a Mc Donald's in Atlanta, Georgia.

---

2   The second and third generation 'Diaspora' may not have anybody in Ethiopia to send money to.

I believe all people have the right to choose where they want to live. But, I just do not like the name or concept, if there ever was one, behind the word 'Diaspora.' In my view, it sadly reduces people, including those I love, to an ambiguous status that confuses their identity even further.

And, while we are at it, I suggest that the *'Diaspora Square'* in Addis Ababa be renamed to *'Engineer Simegnew Bekele Square'* to honor the Chief Engineer of the Grand Ethiopian Renaissance Dam (GERD). I very strongly believe that he has done much more for the country than hundreds of Diaspora or non-Diaspora Ethiopians, including myself, put together; and I am very appreciative of what he did.

Choosing to Return

Why I did not stay

No matter what their reasons were, let me just say that I accept why Ethiopians, including my own brothers and sister and some very close relatives and friends, would opt to stay with or without the option of visiting their country every so many years. I also understand that, no matter how closely they have grown up together, two people could have entirely different orientation as to where they feel comfortable to live in. I respect that and would never argue against their wishes or decisions, whatever they may be.

So, if anyone thinks that I judge those who wish not to return negatively, they have sadly misunderstood me. As a matter of fact, the strength of my resolve to return has a lot to do with the respect I have for the decisions other people make, whether they are similar to mine or not.

As indicated earlier, I accept the rights of people to live in the countries of their choices. So, on this issue, there is no right or wrong in making a decision as to where to live; there is no litmus test. Again, I invoke the choice argument: if I go to a café and order coffee, who is to tell me I should drink tea? The problem arises when the person who chooses to drink tea forces me to follow his/her choice.

Whether it was political or religious choices and decisions, I believe this is the simple but crucial logic that people fail to understand and cause so much hurt around the world.

So, why didn't I stay? Especially when practically everybody in those days did? I will speak for myself but, once in a while, I bring in my wife; our children were way too young at the time to know.

But, first, let me see if I fit in any one of those scenarios that I explained above as to why most Ethiopians choose not to return.

Now, I recognize I was not one of the many Ethiopians who could not come back to Ethiopia for safety reasons because they legitimately believed or somehow imagined that they would definitely be arrested or even worse, if they did. In my case, nobody really had noticed my return home except my friends and family members. As far as the government was concerned, I probably had set a good example for others to do the same. So, no problem on that account.

Neither was I in the category of highly trained professionals who believed that they could excel only in the Unites States. I never really had an ambition or a highly specialized profession that would necessitate my stay in the Unites States; I respect and admire those who do. However, unlike some Ethiopians in the United States, I had acquired some skills, which would help me forge a decent livelihood in my own country. So there was no reason for me to stay in the United States on account of excelling in my profession.

Regarding the freedom to speak and write without fear of governmental reprisal, I agree the United States is a better country than Ethiopia. But, more often than not, for most Ethiopians living in the United States, that is true more in theory than in practice. In my 14-year stay in the United States, the only political freedom I exercised were those demonstrations on campus against broad international government policies. But then, I was able to do that much when I was a student at Addis Ababa University. I have no illusions as to what would happen - in both countries - if things went beyond that!

Neither did I believe that my children would necessarily get better education in the United States than in Ethiopia. In fact, if you had asked me, I would actually argue the other way for at least elementary and high school education. So, why stay in the United States on that account?

The definition of 'better life' for me was dependent on how much one felt he or she 'belonged' where he or she lived. After having lived my first 28 years in Ethiopia, I would be lying if I said I belonged in any other country than Ethiopia. While I say this, it did not escape me that I was returning from the richest country to one of the poorest countries in the world. But, alas, that had nothing to do with my choice to return to where I felt I belonged: that is, to my poor mother from my rich stepmother - with gratitude.

Also, when I decided to return, I did not belong in the category of young Ethiopians in the United States who were satisfied that they had an apartment, a car etc which, in that age category, would be understandably exciting. But, by the time I was ready to return, I had also grown out of such sentiments.

Also, at age 42, luckily I did not have any health reasons to keep me away from Ethiopia. In fact, I had more energy and good will, which I could ever utilize if I had stayed in the United States. I know because by the time it was time to return, I had worked in the United States for four full years. At each additional day of work in the United States, I had wondered more and more if I could not have done much better and felt more fulfilled in my own country.

Finally, it so happened that I am married to an Ethiopian. And my wife's full-hearted agreement was perhaps the most critical factor for our decision to return to Ethiopia. I have known far too many Ethiopians whose desire to return to their country did not materialize because one of the spouses, usually wives, decided otherwise.

I am eternally grateful to my wife in this regard.

Defying gravity

I was fully aware at the time, as I am now, that the attractions and the temptations to stay in the United States once you set foot in that richest country in the world could be immense. After all, millions of people from every corner of the world would kill to live in the United States. So, in a way, it seems only natural to resist any rationale or argument to leave affluence and comfort, real or imagined, behind.

Abraham, one of the Ethiopians in the United States who at the time was a doctoral candidate in quantum physics, whatever it meant, once explained to me his view on this subject as follows.

> Abraham: *Aklilu, you know it is like what we call in physics, 'the gravitational pull of the sun.'*
>
> Aklilu: *What do you mean? I know nothing about physics.*
>
> Abraham: *You see, the gravity pulls the earth around an orbit that circles the sun.*
>
> Aklilu: *So?*
>
> Abraham: *So, the gravity constantly pulls the earth towards the sun and the earth keeps on circling the sun. Without this pull the earth would have flown off. Since it has not so far, it means the pull is there!*
>
> Aklilu: *Are you saying then that as long as the pull is there, the earth will keep on circling the sun forever?*
>
> Abraham: *Exactly!*
>
> Aklilu: *So how is this related to what we are talking about which is returning home?*
>
> Abraham: *It is related to what we are talking about! It is because of this pull that people who come to the United States could not leave.*
>
> Aklilu: *So, are you also saying that as long as there is this pull from the United States, people who come to the country would not leave.*
>
> Abraham: *Exactly because they would be in the orbit. And, once in the orbit and as long as the pull is still there, these people could not break away! They will be in the country forever!*
>
> Aklilu: *Ok, but the pull from the United States, say wealth, could end unlike the pull from the sun.*
>
> Abraham: *That actually ended sometime ago!*
>
> Aklilu: *So, what pulls people to the United States?*
>
> Abraham: *The perceived pull; you know, the imagined pull.*

Aklilu: *So, what if that ends?*
Abraham: *You see that is it! Imagined things never end!*

That may be true; but maybe I never found myself in the orbit that Abraham was talking about. Or, perhaps, when it came to the issue of retuning to my country, I had maintained such strong position that not even the gravitational pull of the United States Abraham was talking about could keep me in its orbit.

On the contrary, whether I liked it or not, my childhood, boyhood and adult years in Ethiopia were perhaps the 'gravity' that pulled me to the country and, hence, my orbit ran around Ethiopia - not around the United States. So the pull was not strong enough for me; and I was able to escape the orbit that went around the United States.

Abraham, with all due respect, was wrong in my case!

This should not be misconstrued to mean that I did not like the United States, though! My decision to return had nothing to do with whether I liked the United States or not. As a matter of fact, I may have had some issues with some government policies but I liked and respected the ordinary American citizens who I believe are hard working and honest. I was treated with respect, and in most cases with affection, throughout my stay in the United States.

In a similar way, my decision to return had nothing to do with the type of government that awaited us in Ethiopia. Regardless of who had the power of government, I would have returned when I was ready to return to my country. More importantly for me, no matter how much politicians try otherwise, there is a big difference between a 'government' and a 'country.' In my view, a 'government' basically is a group of people with a mission, while a 'country' is much more, especially if the stake was returning home.

Like in Alfred Tennyson's poem, The Brook Poem, *'Men may come and men may go; but I go on forever.'* I might add, *'Governments may come and governments may go; but a country goes on forever.'* Put in another way, I have always had a country that I called my own. Sadly, I have yet to say the same for a government.

In the end, my decision to return to Ethiopia was based on a number of selfish reasons that put my family first.

The power of the 'self'

So, why did I decide to return to Ethiopia?

First, I was and still am a selfish man when it came to making big decisions. I would be lying if I said that I had returned to Ethiopia mainly to help Ethiopia and its people achieve some vaguely defined developmental goals. I know that would not be true in my case. And, with all due respect, I suspect it would not be true when other people argue that they had returned to Ethiopia primarily to help change or develop the country in one way or another. I have seen too many who did return to Ethiopia, declaring why they had returned in a grand way, only to leave citing the weakest possible excuses.

So, honestly speaking, I had returned to Ethiopia to help myself and my immediate family live in a way I wanted to live: in my 'comfort' zone, with or without a government I liked. One may ask if there was a comfort zone without a government one liked. I say yes; but, if one were to argue otherwise, then I would argue that that would be true everywhere - in Ethiopia or in the United Sates!

In any event, for me, my family always came first, even compared to my country. A country is too big for me to take care of. So, if I can take care of my family (the penny), then perhaps the country (the pound) will take care of itself, as the British like to say and I agree with them.

If in the process, however, I happened to be helping my fellow Ethiopians, so much the better. And, we did eventually.[3] But I would be lying if I said the primary reason for me to return was to help my country, even before I took care of my own family.

---

3   By 2005, at the height of our respective activities, my wife and I had created employment opportunities for over 60 people, most of them head of households.

Complementing my selfish desire, I also wanted to live in a country where I had naturally developed an identity, and a belonging. I never saw it as an option to live in a place where I did not belong, no matter how rich and attractive the country might be.

Besides, I took my first-class citizenship, even in a poor country without the rights that should go along with it, very personally. That is not to say I was deliberately made to feel a second class citizen in the United States, but it was only natural for me to feel that way because I was one, whether I liked it or not.

Fortunately or otherwise, it so happened that there was a government change about a year before we returned to Ethiopia. And, some people concluded for us that we had returned because of the change in government.[4] Some even went as far as saying that I was either an Eritrean or Tigrayan to have the confidence to decide to return to Ethiopia in 1992. Or that I was somehow sponsored by the government to return.

Not that I cared about such allegations or what ethnic group I belonged to, but it was all unfounded, of course.

In truth, there was no government involvement in any way except that I was offered a job at Addis Ababa University, a government institution, through the normal and rigorous application and vetting process.

The time of my return was a coincident that, by the time we were ready to return, the Dergue government had changed. Besides, at the time we returned, there was no clear evidence that the new government would be better than the Dergue.

Second, I wanted to be close to my parents during their old age - also for my own selfish reasons. I would rejoice their unconditional love from a vantage point of being physically close to them; learn more from their example and wisdom;

---

4   The Dergue was replaced by a rebel group in 1991, just over a year before we returned to Ethiopia.

listen to the same stories they told me, as they told them to their grandchildren; and touch them and feel them at will.

In return, I would try and comfort them from a touching distance when they needed me in good times and hard times. There were numerous examples when that was the case and my presence may have made a difference for them. And, inversely, they definitely made a difference for my family and me.

Besides, again for selfish motives, I would not have excused myself forever if my parents passed away without me being close to them when they needed me. I didn't see anything in the United States that would have me change my mind on that issue. In other words, what was it that I would get in return if I traded all the above for living in the United States, and as a second-class citizen for that matter! By my calculation, no matter what it was that I would get, it probably would not have been worthwhile compared to what I would lose.

Yes, during my last four years in the United States, I had a nice and secure state-government job with an excellent working environment and a salary that would have allowed me to live a middle class life. My wife also worked for a small design company, and made a decent salary; which meant we could have bought a house in the suburbs, buy two cars and send our kids to a good public school.

So what?

So, looking ahead at such a life, we would be working our entire life, pay-off our mortgages, see our kids move out, sell our house and end up in a nursing home, and then die - after paying all the money we saved to the nursing home! I have seen this cycle in the United States repeatedly in people older than me, and I knew our fate would not have been much different if we had stayed. Hence, in my calculation, the opportunity cost of not returning home would have been too high to justify such a life in the United States.

Third, I wanted our two daughters to grow in the same traditional context that my wife and I grew up in; again, for whatever it's worth. I wanted them to enjoy and appreciate the love of their great grandparent,[5] four grandparents, many grand uncles and aunts, several uncles and aunts, numerous cousins and second cousins; and, above all, a multitude of Ethiopian classmates.

Again, this is not to say that the United States was not a place to raise children. But I believed that Ethiopia, despite all its material poverty, was a much better place for my children to grow and establish an identity which resembled their parents'.

One day, while still in the United States, one of my cousins lectured me that I did not have the right to subjugate my children to hardship by taking them to Ethiopia, and that I was deciding on their fate. I replied I wasn't necessarily subjugating them to hardship; but, yes, I was deciding on their fate. Wouldn't that be true if I had decided to stay in the United States?

Did I have the right to decide where my kids should be raised? Absolutely! Not only since they were minors at the time, but also since it was only where I was happy that I could provide them with a happy life, at least until they were of age. It is true there could be a multitude of things in Ethiopia that might affect a happy and productive life, but I would also like to know where in the world that that was not true.

As it is the case, people find what they consider to be a weakness (in our case, our children) to make a point. Once, while still in the United States, somebody forcefully argued that it would be very difficult to raise children in Ethiopia in the early 1990s and beyond. He cited problems with education opportunities, healthcare and even basic commodities like diapers, tissue papers etc.

'It is true,' I responded, 'it is also true that there are over ten million children of my daughters' age living in Ethiopia. Why should our daughters be different from them? They will live and grow like them.' I have heard that kind argument from my father years ago!

---

5   When we returned to Ethiopia our children had a maternal female great grandparent who was alive.

My thinking was that children are a reflection of their parents. Usually, perhaps unknown to their parents, they watch and imitate what their parents do, and want to become exactly like them. If that is generally true, I felt I could be and have plenty of time to be a good role model to my kids only if I lived in Ethiopia. I recognize, at the same time, that they can make their own decisions in due course.

There was some pressure from our close family members to stay and raise our children in the United States. On one occasion my father sent one of his friends, who happened to be visiting the United States, to urge me to change my mind about returning home. I do not usually disobey my father, but I did this one time in my life.

On another occasion, my father-in-law sent me a letter to consider the fate of our children when I decided to return to Ethiopia. I wrote back stating politely that I appreciated his concerns, and that I did not believe anyone would be more concerned about my own children than me. I knew both my father and my father-in-law meant well. But they had very little idea what it meant for me and for my wife to live and raise our children in Ethiopia, like millions of Ethiopians do.

Fourth, on a more philosophical note, I believe that there was no value of leaving a place if one did not come back and experience what it meant to be away. I know this is a bit difficult to explain. But, at least in my case, unless I had not returned to my country, my going away would have become meaningless; life in my adopted country would have just been a given. It would have been a life that I had gotten used to and taken for granted without the benefit of knowing what it meant to have left in the first place.

In other words, how would I ever know the full impact of my spending time in the United States unless I came back to Ethiopia? I believe one would have to come back to where one left in order to know one has gone at all. I believe my stay in the United States would have become almost meaningless - to the point where I might as well have not gone at all - if I had not come back to Ethiopia. I argue, most people who left a place and did not return (I am not talking short visits), may never know the impact of 'leaving'; they may never know what it meant to have left.

In a way, it is like retirement. I believe that the fruits of one's hard work could only be amplified if he/she retired. Just like the impacts of 'leaving' can be fully understood only by 'returning.' What to do after retiring or returning home need not be known in advance; it will follow its own course. But that is the move that makes the circle, the experience of life complete!

Else, one stops at a semicircle; and sadly, an incomplete life!

*****

Those being the main reasons, in my view, there were additional arguments in favor of returning.

First, I believe there is something called 'overstaying'. This, in my view, should work both from the perspective of the 'guest' and from the perspective of the 'host.' If I had considered myself a guest in the United States, obviously I have to end that status. Similarly, a host cannot be expected to host indefinitely. This relationship has to end and amicably, within a given time frame; or else!

Second, I very strongly believe that all that matters at the end of the day is 'people'. In my view, there is no point in reaching the highest of the highs in one's career or education, no matter in what field; if it is not shared with people, it is useless. If that is generally true, where to begin but with the people closest to you? I leave the answer as to what constitutes 'closest people' to the reader; I think I know mine.

Third, a generation of able Ethiopians was lost to other countries between the 1970s and 2000s. Many I know were bright people with tremendous potentials to bring about positive changes for the country and for its people while, at the same time, taking care of themselves, families and relatives. Many have now reached the age of retirement and some have opted to spend the rest of their time in Ethiopia. It is never too late, something is better than nothing; and, they have a country to come back to.

Fourth, and finally, again in a more philosophical outlook, I believe that we are all destined to age and die, whether we live in the United States, Timbuktu or Ethiopia. By deciding where to live, one would not guarantee an eternal life, or even a happy life. Therefore, I would argue, we might as well age and die where we belonged which, in my case, would be Ethiopia without a doubt.

So, when all is said and done, I returned to Ethiopia mostly for my own selfish reasons; just like people who go to churches, mosques and synagogues etc. The difference may be in that the latter do it to facilitate a better life after death while I did it to facilitate a better life for the remaining of my years on earth.

Who knows what happens after that!

The battle of justifications, no winners

I am not sure if there is a difference between 'excuses', 'reasons', and 'justifications' when it comes to making a fundamental decision or a commitment to a course of action. But, for the purposes of the discussion below, I use the word 'justifications' since I believe it captures the concepts discussed more than the other two.

I believe it is only natural for people to justify their decisions. I justify my return to Ethiopia as much as those who justify their decision to stay in the United States. In a way, it is a draw; there are no winners or losers in the battle of justifications.

When I decide to return and stay in Ethiopia, then I become the wishful thinker whose family's well-being is at stake. So, obviously, I hope, sometimes against hope, the best for the country. On the other hand, those who choose to stay in the united Sates tend to amplify the negative aspects and shrug-off the positive aspects of Ethiopia. Since their immediate family members are not in danger, such people do not hesitate from stressing negatives about Ethiopia, which, in turn, justify their decisions to stay away.

So, the arguments to return or not, in a way, is a battle of justifications. I found most of my discussions with my friends who opted not to return evolving around this issue of justifications of decisions; they may not necessarily depict their true sentiments.

*****

Once I had an interesting discussion with a friend from my boyhood years in Gore who happened to 'visit' Ethiopia with his family after a long absence in the United States. I invited them to diner to our house and we started talking over glasses of Acacia wine, made in Ethiopia.

Friend: *One of the many things I cannot tolerate in this country is how people drive.*

Aklilu: *What do you find intolerable?*

Friend: *The drivers have no discipline; they cut you; do not give you the right of way…*

Aklilu: *You used to derive before you left Addis, right?*

Friend: *Yes, but things have gotten so much worse now. You do not have these kinds of driving problems in the United States; it is all disciplined.*

Aklilu: *I agree, but don't forget you are comparing the richest country with one of the poorest countries on earth. Ok, what else do you find intolerable in Addis?*

Friend: *So many things; like you cannot get quick services wherever you go; there are frequent power or water shortages; people stare at you as if you have come from a different planet; the streets are crowded and unclean; no public toilets or parks! Tell me where do you go to relax in Addis? It is hard to tolerate all these!*

Aklilu: *That may be true; but don't you have other kinds of problems, or even worse, in the United States that you somehow tolerate?*

Friend: *Like what?*

Aklilu: *Race relations, police brutality, for instance? Haven't you heard about the recent shootings of unarmed young black men on the streets?*

Friend: *So, what about them?*

Aklilu: *You have to tolerate all these to live there, right?*

Friend: *They did not happen to me.*

Aklilu: *Yes, but as a black person it could have been you or your children or relatives…*

Friend: *I do not like them; yes they bother me.*

Aklilu: *But, you do tolerate them; that is why you are not leaving the country; right?*

Friend: *So, what is your point?*

Aklilu: *My point is if you tolerate racism and police brutality in the United States why can't you tolerate power shortages or rude taxi drivers in Ethiopia?*

Friend: *I think you miss my point.*

Aklilu: *What is your point?*

Friend: *What I am saying is that I would rather be abused in a foreign land than in my own land.*

Aklilu: *Why is that?*

Friend: *Because, it hurts me more when my rights are violated in my own country.*

Aklilu: *What about in the United States?*

Friend: *That is different; it doesn't hurt as much and I can shrug it off because I could leave any time. Do you understand?*

Aklilu: *I am trying, but if it is harder for you to accept abuse in your own country than in the United States… I guess you have a point.*

I lost the argument. Interesting, I said to myself, I have never heard that kind of justification to stay in the United States before. But, it confirmed to me that my friend, despite his decision not to return and his American passport, still considered Ethiopia as 'my own'; he probably was not an exception.

It was also clear to me that he was listing his 'justifications' to stay, just like I was listing mine, to return. Interestingly, they were both not so difficult to do.

*****

In another occasion in Chicago, I was at my niece's home after attending the funeral of my sister in-law, when I heard a certain gentleman who was referred to as 'Dr.' and surrounded by a group of Ethiopians, loudly talking about Ethiopia. I usually deliberately avoid being dragged into discussions that involved the state of Ethiopia, especially with people I do not know very well. Besides, in a poorly concealed bravado, he was telling everybody that it has been over 30 years since he had last been to Ethiopia. And, I had already concluded that he knew very little, if any, about the realities in Ethiopia.

But one thing led to the other and one Ethiopian who I have know for a long time, asked me about my opinion. *'Aklilu'*, he asked *'you live in Ethiopia why don't you tell us what you think?'*

Before I answered the question, this Ethiopian 'Dr.' introduced himself as the expert in Ethiopian matters who also had written many articles on the subject and, with everybody in the house listening, intervened with a barrage of hostile questions at me.

Dr.: *Yes, why don't you tell us what is going on in Ethiopia?*
Aklilu: *Regarding what?*
Dr.: *The overall situation?*
Aklilu: *I would rather speak of a specific situation if you have one in mind.*
Dr.: *Ok, for instance, how do you live with the political conditions in the country?*
Aklilu: *Can you be more specific?*
Dr.: *I mean, for instance, the political joke that is going on in the country; that every seat in parliament, and every position in regional and local government is occupied by the ruling party. Where is the democracy or the multiparty system? What is your view about the 100% wining rate by the ruling party?*
Aklilu: *Well, I do not like it; in fact, I consider it an embarrassment. By the way, I think things are not much different here in the United States too; it may be a bit more subtle and complex though. In any case, there are other things that I like about what is being done in Ethiopia.*
Dr.: *Like what?*
Aklilu: *Like the infrastructure development of roads, housing, hydroelectric dams, schools, health facilities etc.*
Dr.: *But you said the election in the country is an embarrassment why don't you do something about it?*
Aklilu: *Like what?*
Dr.: *Like going out in protest; or even joining an opposition party?*
Aklilu: *I admit, I have not done any of those things; but that doesn't mean I support the government.*

Dr.: *Then, why are you there? You are not effective in bringing about any changes in the country; you are giving legitimacy to the government by living there.*

Aklilu: *I am living in my country.*

Dr.: *You are not achieving anything.*

Aklilu: *That may be true, but I do not think you can achieve much by staying away either.*

Dr.: *We can bring about changes by agitating for change from outside the country.*

Aklilu: *I am not sure about that.*

Dr.: *What do you mean? Do you question our effectiveness or sincerity?*

Aklilu: *Absolutely not; I do not question your sincerity at all. But, I do not believe you can hit anybody by throwing stones from nine thousand kilometers away.*

Dr.: *What are you trying to say?*

Aklilu: *If you really want to bring about changes, and if you dare, you would do it from there, and be ready to reap the fruits or pay for the consequences.*

Dr.: *I do not have to be there to bring about changes in the country; but I can agitate for change from a distance.*

Aklilu: *So you want to come to reap the fruits? I do not think you would like to come to pay for the consequences of your agitations if they go wrong; would you?*

Dr.: *I am not sure where you are getting at.*

Aklilu: *Since you started it, let me try and explain. You said you would like to agitate for change from a safe distance. It is like what my friend once described as 'to touch the fire with somebody else's finger.' In short, you agitate, somebody else pays the price. Right? Don't you think there is something wrong with that?*

Dr.: *Of course, I have the right to agitate for change in my country from wherever I am.*

Aklilu: *That may be true; but I am asking if you would be around to pay for the consequences if things went wrong?*

Dr.: *Are you suggesting that what I am agitating for is not valid or correct?*

Aklilu: *Absolutely not; I am not even talking about whether the agitation is correct or not. My question is simple and straightforward, and let me re-phrase it in a different way: regardless of the sincerity or correctness of your agitation, would you physically be there to face the consequences? A follow-up question is, if assuming that you would not be there, especially if things went*

> *wrong, and other people who have nothing to do with the agitation get harmed, do you have at least the moral authority to agitate in the first place?*
> Dr.: *So, what are you trying to get at? Are you denying me the right to agitate for change in my own country?*
> Aklilu: *No, I am not. I apologize if that is how it sounded.*
> Dr.: *You also talked about 'moral authority', what moral authority do you have to talk about Ethiopia that I do not?*
> Aklilu: *Well, if we are talking about the same country, by being there physically, at least I see, touch and smell the good and bad things in Ethiopia; I do not hear or read about them. I am there at a stone's throwing distance; not on the other side of the Atlantic, safe and void.*
> Dr: *I do not believe there is a difference.*

I have made my point, there was no use in discussing the issue any further; it was like my country's proverb, when loosely translated into English, goes: *'No amount of noise would wake someone who is pretending to be asleep.'*

I did not want the discussion to turn nasty because he was my guest at my niece's house where I was staying. I went back to my safe corner and started chatting with my niece. But, just before he left, however, the 'Dr.' came to me and said, *'Aklilu, nobody ever talked to me the way you did tonight. I do not necessarily agree with you, but I appreciate your honest opinion. Your points have given me some different perspectives, and I am thankful.'*

I told him I apologized if I had hurt his feelings in any way; and he walked out of the house shaking his head; I never saw him again.

*****

In yet another occasion, only a couple of years after we moved to Ethiopia, I was in the United Sates for some conference when my own cousin confronted me with an argument that I thought was a hit below the belt. He hit me where he thought it would hurt: the fate of our children's education in Ethiopia.

Cousin: *Aklilu, Ok, you decided to return but what about your children?*

Aklilu: *What about them?*

Cousin: *Their education, for instance?*

Aklilu: *They go to Cathedral Nativity Girls' School, where they are doing fine. Their mother went to the same school, and she is now a successful person by all standards.*

Cousin: *That was the good old days. Do you really believe that they are now getting good education there?*

Aklilu: *Maybe not; but I do not believe staying in the United States necessarily guarantees good education either. I might also add, if things go bad for our children in Ethiopia, they probably could go worse in the United States.*

Cousin: *Ok, didn't you say there were 85 students in one class at their elementary school?*

Aklilu: *Yes, I did; they are so tiny you wouldn't know there were 85 of them in one class! They look so cute!*

Cousin: *Doesn't that bother you about the kind of education or attention they are getting?*

Aklilu: *Not much. In fact, it is great; it is a great mix of backgrounds!*

Cousin: *What do you mean?*

Aklilu: *All 85 of them come from various backgrounds; there are Muslims and Christians; poor and rich; they come from liberal and conservative families; from well educated and poorly educated. It is a great mix of students.*

Cousin: *How is that great?*

Aklilu: *It is a great learning experience to have to deal with all kinds of backgrounds. Imagine, if you can handle such a large and diverse group at an early age, nothing in future life would be difficult.*

Cousin: *Ok, that is fine; but what about their future?*

Aklilu: *What do you mean?*

Cousin: *Once they finish elementary, where do they go?*

Aklilu: *They go to high school; still in Ethiopia if you want to know.*

Cousin: *Are there high schools that provide good education?*

Aklilu: *May be not, but I believe good education begins at high school even if the high school may not be that good.*

Cousin: *What do you mean?*

Aklilu: *That is when parents should invest their time and money on assisting their children in all ways possible.*

Cousin: *Not all parents have the capacity to do so.*

Aklilu: *I believe most parents, if they thought about it, could help their children in one way or another. If, for instance, they cannot support them academically, they can help them develop the discipline to study or to do their homework on time; they can teach them how to manage their time, including allowing some recreational activities.*

Cousin: *Do you really think that works if the school is not up to standard?*

Aklilu: *Yes; parents can play a major role to fill the gap. But, sadly, what I noticed in Ethiopia is that parents, fathers in particular, do not pay much attention to their children's education especially at the high school level. I see them wasting plenty of time socializing, time that could have been invested on their children; I see them spending plenty of money on drinks or food after work; money that could have been spent on paying for tutors for their children. By the way, this may be true in the United Sates too.*

The conversation went on for a while, and my cousin was not convinced. After all, the education of his children was one of the most important justifications for him not to return to Ethiopia. I respected that without having to necessarily agree with him.

Such arguments with my friends and cousins are just examples of each of us trying to justify our respective decisions and course of actions. As I accuse them of coming up with a list of justifications to stay in the United States, I, too, am 'guilty' of listing justifications to return home.

There are no winners in the battle of justifications.

*****

Although I do not have a blanket condemnation of the Ethiopian government like most people who chose not to return, I do have very different outlook from the government on many issues. For instance, I believe the government's all-out war against any varying views or parties, deliberately stifling the opposition, is wrong. So is the monopoly of political, not to speak of security and military powers. These might have been justified the first few years of the government's existence but, twenty-five years into the making, it is not only embarrassing but also dangerous.

On the other hand, I believe the government deserves credit where credit is due. For instance, the improvements in infrastructure, public health and education, although one might rightfully raise the issue of quality, have been encouraging since we set foot in the country over 24 years ago. That is *'calling a spade a spade!'*

At the same time, I do not believe in bad-mouthing one another either, especially the government or people in power, since it will not get us anywhere. In our culture, people have the tendency to dig-in, establish fighting positions or foxholes and defend their positions even more rigidly when they are criticized or attacked. This is true even if the criticism was well founded; even truer when one is dealing with people who fought their way to power.

I believe 'opposition' need not imply 'conflict', especially physical. Instead, it requires a wise and patient approach of dialogue, consensus and change - in that order. In the Ethiopian context, the opposition is well advised to start by thanking the government and people in power for what they have done for the country and for the people so far; give them credit where credit was due, and then try and impress upon them, in a civilized but firm way, that times have changed and we should move on with leadership that the times demanded.

Tragically, more often than not, governments and opposition groups ignore the importance of such an approach - at their own peril.

Landing on both feet, the mark of resolve

'So', many people would ask me, *'if you had to return, why didn't you return with a green card or, even better, an American Citizenship?'* Their arguments were, with a green card or a citizenship (i) I could pack up and go back to the United States if things did not work out in Ethiopia, and (ii) I could easily travel anywhere in the world without the hassle of getting visas.

It was true that in the 70s' and 80s, given the political persecution by the socialist government in Ethiopia, it was relatively easy for Ethiopians to get green card and, later, American citizenship. Every Ethiopian I knew in the United States in those days had one of the two. And, I had the opportunity to obtain one of the two, or both if I wanted to, after going through the process, of course. But this, in my view, defeated the whole purpose of returning.

Now, I do not discount the value of a green card or American or any other countries' citizenship at all. But, to change my citizenship as a matter of 'convenience' would have been a tough call for me to make; besides, there was no need to do so.

First, both my wife and I went to the United States with a student's visa and, as long as we maintained our grades and renewed our student's visas on time, there was no need to apply for a green card. As far as international tuition was concerned, I studied most of the time with a research assistantship which paid for my tuition along with a decent living allowance. Yes, we struggled but we managed to pay my wife's tuition.

Second, with a green card or a citizenship, it would have been a half-baked decision to return home. In other words, it would mean that I would have one foot in Ethiopia and another in the United States, just in case something went wrong with the former. I have known people who had come back to Ethiopia with a green card or American citizenship only to drag their Ethiopian foot back to the United States; sometimes for reasons that are too embarrassing to mention. Well, I do not blame them, it is their prerogative.

So, when push came to shove for us in Ethiopia, we improvised. For instance, in the absence of imported diapers for our children, we made home-made diapers - just like the ones many people of my generation used when babies; in the absence of powdered milk, we contracted organic milk from a neighbor who had a couple of cows; in the absence of imported pasta or tomato sauce, we made better ones ourselves at home.

If there is a will, there is a way! Besides, we had both feet in Ethiopia; where would we go?

Third, we (my wife and I) had maintained a valid student's visa while in the United States; and a two-year multiple entry visa to the United States after we came back to Ethiopia. As long as we maintained the visas without abuse, travel to the United States and to the rest of the world, for that matter, has never been a problem.

But I admit, when I applied for a United States visa in 1993, a year after I returned to Ethiopia, for a brief visit to my former university, I had to wake up early in the morning; line up at the gate of American embassy for hours; convince the consul why I should be given a visa, and patiently waited for the result -just like everybody else. I was given the visa and I have never been denied a two-year multiple entry visa since then; that was all I needed. The same is true for my wife.

*****

It is true, though, whenever we have a rare family trip outside Ethiopia, our children with American passports would breeze through the passport control within minutes while my wife and I would have to stand in line for hours before our visas would be cleared. But, that was a small price we chose to pay for whatever benefits there were of living in our own country, with our country's passports. And, yes, when we return to Ethiopia, we breeze through the passport control while our daughters, along with other foreigners, line up to get their visas. Such is life.

Hence, our decision was to land in Ethiopia on both feet; there were no safety nets even with two children in tow. It was just like twenty-five years earlier, when a true unconditional friendship was established between my twin friends and me: no calculation, no risk analysis, no safety net, no plan B!

That is not to say we did not have some serious problems; we did. For instance, one day, about two weeks after we returned to Ethiopia, we moved to a small town house that my sister and her husband, Hami and Tesfu, had left when they moved to Canada. It was not habited for a few weeks. So, we cleaned the house, put our furniture and settled. At night we all slept in one bedroom, as usual.

What we didn't see before we went to bed was a swarm of mosquitoes that had settled on the ceiling of the bedroom. Throughout the night they attacked us relentlessly like Japan's Kamikaze suicide bombers and caused considerable skin bites especially to our two-year old daughter, Hasabie. In the morning, her entire body was covered with painful mosquito bites, and she cried all the time. There were no private clinics or pharmacies in Addis Ababa at that time. We couldn't get the ointment to relieve her pain, and she toughed it out.

If we had a green card at the time, who knows?

Some life lessons

Over the years, one cannot help but learn about relevant expressions or meet people with wisdom who provide useful life lessons.

One of my favorite expressions, something that I stole from the Center for Communications Program (CCP) at Johns Hopkins University in the United States, reads:

Think big,
Start small,
Act now!

This expression was explained very well by an award winning journalist, Matt Pearl, as follows:

It is a simple and logical idea, really. With whatever you want to achieve in life, you should aim high and remove any false ceilings. But you should also acknowledge that any path to "big" involves starting "small" - taking a series of steps to move you gradually closer to your end goal. And even those steps begin with some kind of action, so why wait to begin?

I had this expression on the wall of my office for over fifteen years, and given copies to many. Our Center started small with only two people, including myself. We did not waste time to act, and a series of successfully completed small-scale research projects generated a chain of medium and relatively large-size research projects that were having an impact on the country's public health programs and projects.

*****

I was also lucky enough to meet people of wisdom. Back in 1988 when I realized that my initial dissertation topic was not getting me anywhere, I had to change my topic. This was easier said than done, since it first required coming up with an alternative topic, develop a proposal, get departmental approval, and a lot of preliminary literature search.

So one day, I told my immediate boss at the time, Don Berry, that I was having problems choosing a topic for my dissertation. I had actually spent a few months trying to develop a research proposal on a topic that was hard to research: *Integrating drought in development planning in sub-Saharan Africa.*

Don, always ready to help, suggested that we went and talked to the late Greg Alexander, Professor of Public Health at Johns Hopkins University, Baltimore, which was only an hour's drive from our campus in Newark, Delaware. So, one morning, Don and I went to Baltimore to talk to Greg; we hoped he might have a solution. He received us warmly, and asked how he could help us.

Greg: *How can I help you, gentlemen?*
Don: *Thank you for receiving us; Aklilu has come for your advice on identifying a topic for his dissertation.*
Greg: *How can I help you, Aklilu?*
Aklilu: *I am having problems finding a topic for my dissertation. So, I was wondering if you could suggest something.*
Greg: *What is your area of interest?*
Aklilu: *It would be great if it were related to my work which is looking at fertility and mortality trends in the state of Delaware, in comparison to the United States.*
Greg: *If you are interested, there was always something that had interested me for some time. Maybe you can take it over.*

Aklilu: *What is it?*

Greg: *I have always wanted to look at the public health aspect of homicide mortality as opposed to the criminal aspect; and I do not think it has been studied extensively.*

Aklilu: *That sounds like a very interesting topic.*

Greg: *It is also related to your work.*

Aklilu: *Yes, absolutely.*

Greg: *Then, if you like it, why don't you consider it as your dissertation topic?*

Aklilu: *No, I cannot do that; it is your idea, you should pursue it.*

Greg: *Yes, the idea may be mine but I haven't done much more than collecting the background literature. I can share those with you if you want.*

Aklilu: *No, it is your idea and I do not want to steal it from you.*

Greg: *Do not worry, you are not stealing it. Take the topic, I will try and come up with another idea when I get the chance.*

Aklilu: *I really cannot do that, it is yours.*

Greg insisted, and I could not argue against his suggestion; and the prospect of looking homicides from a public health point of view appealed to me. For too long homicide and the related violence was seen in the context of criminal justice; and I thought maybe something interesting might come out of my research.

In any case, what Greg was saying was that people who keep knowledge (or other material possessions, for that matter) to themselves were those who do not have the confidence and/or the ability to create new ones. In reverse, people who share are those who believe they have the capacity to produce more new ones.

I have noted later in life that, in general, people who do not 'share' are also those most likely to be lonelier and unhappier than those who do.

*****

Sometimes the words or actions of wisdom come from an unexpected source. In 2013, my niece Mistre who was about 18 at the time, and her mother, Haimanot who is my wife's

302 | COUNTRY ROADS
302 | COUNTRY ROADS

younger sister, lived with us for about six months before they moved to the United States; our children had already left by then. Mistre was finishing her last year of high school at Cathedral. Now, my wife and I were very similar with Mistre and her mother in everything else, but one: our 'religious' orientations.

Haimanot had converted from Coptic Christian to P'ent'ay (aka Pentecostal) several years earlier, and Mistre had been born into it. My wife is a non-practicing Coptic Christian, and I do not have any religion. So, religiously speaking, it was these three different groups of people living together in the same house; although for all intends and purposes, my wife and I belonged to the same category.

Here were some of the differences in our respective life styles.

Haimanot and Mistre would go to church every Sunday morning while my wife and I would be sitting at the verandah of our house watching birds or playing with our dogs, with cups of coffee in our hands. And, we all met for lunch.

Haimanot and Mistre would routinely pray before meals while my wife and I would be sitting quietly with our heads bent till they finished, and would join them with an 'Amen' at the end, mostly for solidarity's sake. And, we all ate the same food.

Haimanot and Mistre would be listening to church songs whenever they relaxed at home, while my wife and I would be listening to old Ethiopian songs or classical music, mixed with Motown songs. We equally entertained ourselves, but in different ways.

Haimanot and Mistre would be reading the Bible during their spare times while my wife and I would be reading novels or autobiographies; I would watch soccer once in a while. Again, it was entertainment for each according to his/her wish.

Haimanot and Mistre would be drinking water or tea while my wife and I would be drinking beer or wine to relax ourselves. We all quenched our thirsts in every which way we enjoyed.

But, we lived in the same house peacefully; in spite of all these differences in our choices of life style or beliefs. I do not remember a single incident when we argued, much less get at each other's throats. We lived in peace, and respect for each other. The secret was that we kept each other's boundaries - the imaginary lines between people.

In other words, we knew where our limits in influencing each other's beliefs and thoughts, decisions and choices were. Hence, we avoided arguments over our respective choices and decisions in life. Haimanot and Mistre did what they chose to do, and we did what we chose to do. No one side attempted to influence the other side; in short, we lived and let live.

But, one morning, as I was driving Mistre to school, we had a long and interesting discussion. I did not usually drive her to school since she was just too independent; she would tough it out with mini-bus taxis. But on that day she had mock exams, and I did not want her to be late. Since the road was under construction, it took over an hour to get to the school.

As we were driving to school, and while she still tried to keep her boundary, she wanted to know a few more things about my position on certain religious issues risking, *'curiosity killed the cat.'*

'So, uncle Aklilu, what is your religion?'
'I don't have one; don't you know?'
'Yes, I know, but don't you believe in anything or anybody?'
'Yes I do; I believe in doing good. If you want to know, I also believe in good music, good wine..good humor...'
'Ok, ok ...what is your religion then?'
'My religion is the same thing: doing good as much as I can, that is all.'
'So, how do you know what is good and what is bad? Somebody needs to tell you!'
'Not necessarily...something inside me tells me. At my age I have developed that skill. You are still too young for that. You can try it later in life.'
'But, what is that something inside you?'
'I am not exactly sure what it is called; maybe my gut feeling or my conscience..or..'

'Hmm, Ok, do you believe in hell and heaven?'

'I don't know; in my 63 years of life, I haven't seen anybody who has been either to hell or to heaven. Wouldn't that be like coming back from death?'

'No..but ...it is written in the Bible; and the prophets wrote the bible.'

'I don't know, I haven't read the bible; nor do I know who the prophets were. I suppose they had some interests to promote.'

'Hmm...still... it would not hurt to read the bible since it talks about the good things you want to do.'

'That may be true..but, you see, I do not want to do good things because somebody told me to do so or because I read about them in a book. Besides, I don't think you have to read the bible to be a good person; conversely, I don't think those who read the bible are necessarily good people either.'

'But the bible is not just a book...it is much more than that.'

'That may be true for you...but not necessarily for me too.'

'I do not understand you uncle Aklilu; in fact you are confusing me.'

'I am sorry, Mistre, I am not trying to change your religion or your beliefs. You started this and, since I respect you, I didn't want to lie to you. I hope I wasn't harsh on you; and please do not take me too seriously. But here is my advice to you: choose any faith you want and respect it. Let others choose their faiths and you show respect for their choices too. You run into a problem only when you want to impose your choice on others.'

'I know that, uncle Aklilu.'

'OK good...we are almost there...by the way Mistre, can I give you some pocket money for refreshment etc...'

'No thanks, uncle Aklilu, I am loaded!'

'Wow! Have a nice day! Best of luck with your mocks.....'

She disappeared into a multitude of young girls with identical attire that were very familiar to me. So, even if I had a different view from her, I was glad Mistre was firm and confident about her choice of religious beliefs.

And, at an early age, she has wisely learnt to stay within her boundary; and I hope she would stay that way!

One or two words about 'identity' and 'country'

Finally, let me say one or two words about what I think about my identity, something I talked about a lot in this book, in relation to my country.

What happened when I was abroad had nothing to do with forming my identity; I see it only as a learning experience that took place way after I had already developed an identity. Similarly, I do not believe I am responsible for what my ancestors may have done during their lifetimes, which may have influenced my identity, one way or another, as I was growing up.

So, the way I see it is simple: I was born in Asebe Teferi, and raised in Gore and Addis Ababa. As I was growing up, the languages I spoke; the games I played with my friends and classmates; the good times that I enjoyed and the bad times and frustrations I endured; the wisdom I was fortunate enough to receive from my teachers; the various celebrations and festivities that I enjoyed with my relatives, friends and neighbors; and the love I was showered by my parents created my 'identity' - again, for whatever it's worth.

The context within which all this happened is my country, Ethiopia, which provided the air, the water, the vegetation, the food, the social and religious norms, the people and the animals etc etc. I believe, for most of my friends and people I knew, things were not much different; they went through more or less the same experience in forming an identity.

Now this, for me, cannot change; just like one of my heroes, Yaseer Arafat, once said, *'One cannot jump out of his skin.'* I agree. My skin is and will remain the identity I formed when I was growing up; I cannot, in all sincerity, shed it and get another identity.

I believe, without my country, I do not have an identity. I can, of course, declare a new 'identity' on a piece of paper for reasons that have to do with convenient living; but, fundamentally, I cannot jump out of my skin.

If that is generally true, where is that I want to live, not necessarily with convenience, but with my identity? That was the fundamental question that I answered in June 1992 when I returned to my country. That decision had nothing to do with my 'host' country, the United States, while it had everything to do with my identity, which cannot exist outside my 'home' country, Ethiopia.

Also, whether I liked it or not, I grew up in an environment where I, and everybody I knew at the time, did not distinguish between poor and rich because we were all poor, even in relative terms. Nor did we divide ourselves by ethnic or religious groups to the extent that one group antagonized and became hostile to the other. On the contrary, at least at school, unconditional friendship and loyalty existed among us regardless of our ethnic or religious categorizations.

I understand some people may disagree but, as I was growing up in Gore, I am not sure I saw or felt the difference between a poor Amhara and a poor Oromo; or a poor Christian and a poor Muslim. Yes, different ethnic and religious groups existed but, for whatever it's worth and for all intents and purposes, I believe we were all Ethiopians, and basically equal.

Whatever economic differences there were, they did not necessarily determine the fate of a child. For most of us, future differences in socioeconomic status may have come as a result of differences in educational attainment; period. Access to education was equally available to most of us, at least in Gore, save those whose location made it difficult to go to school or those who did not know or believe education would make a difference in their lives. The latter may have taken a different approach altogether.

Hence, there is no doubt in my mind, for instance, that my poor Oromo or my poor Muslim friends in Gore would have had the same chance to be where I (so-called Amhara) am now - only if they had a little bit of luck, a little bit of hard work, and support from good wiling random individuals. In fact, for all I know, there may have been hundreds, if not thousands, of Muslim or Oromo Ethiopians, with an upbringing very much like mine, but who have succeeded even at a higher level than my modest one.[6]

But, in my classroom in Gore, we all started from the same line.

So, the most difficult and painful question for me is when I am asked about my ethnic group, as if it had made a difference. I never had to answer this question until I got to be in my 40s, and I am not sure why I have to answer it now. Neither would I like to answer what I believe to be irrelevant questions about my religious orientation since it really is not anybody's business.

I understand, as a social science researcher, that these may be relevant questions to collect data in order to plan economic development or health programs and, to that extent, I accept them. But, more often than not, questions on ethnicity and religion, in any country for that matter, are asked mainly to divide people and rule, and I regret that. If there were times when I was coerced to answer such questions, like if I wanted to get my driving license, I would do it unwillingly and with a lot of discomfort and hypocrisy. Why on earth, for instance, would one be interested to see my ethnicity on my ID card?

On the other hand, the easiest question for me is when I am asked about my nationality. I am Ethiopian, for all the flaws of the country. It is an answer that I would be happy to provide, even without being asked. This is not only because it is who I am but also who I want to remain to be; besides, I cannot have any other answer.

So, that is why if, at the end of the day, I am going to live and die anyway, I might as well live and die as an Ethiopian - in Ethiopia. Who knows what happens after that!

All I know now is *'Country Roads'* have brought me back home, and I am eternally grateful!

---

6   In fact, I do know individuals from Gore who started from very humble origins only to end up as board members and chairs of some of the major insurance companies and banks in the country.

One-to-one in-depth interview with a woman in her reproductive years. Miz-Hasab Research Center, 1996-2015

Celebratoing 10th anniversary, Miz-Hasab Research Center core staff. Addis Ababa Hilton, 2006

INDEX